MANAGING THE BIG PICTURE IN COLLEGES AND UNIVERSITIES

MANAGING THE BIG PICTURE IN COLLEGES AND UNIVERSITIES

From Tactics to Strategy

Richard L. Alfred

Associates
Christopher Shults
Mary Ramirez
Tara Sullivan
Eric Chambers
Danielle Knabjian-Molina

Foreword by Stanley O. Ikenberry

AMERICAN COUNCIL ON EDUCATION
PRAEGER
Series on Higher Education

Library of Congress Cataloging-in-Publication Data

Alfred, Richard L.
  Managing the big picture in colleges and universities : from tactics to strategy
  / Richard L. Alfred ; associates, Christopher Shults . . . [et al.] ; foreword by
  Stanley O. Ikenberry.
      p.   cm.—(ACE/Praeger series on higher education)
  Includes bibliographical references and index.
  ISBN 0–275–98528–8 (alk. paper)
    1. Universities and colleges—Administration.   2. Strategic planning.   I. Title.
  II. American Council on Education/Praeger series on higher education.
  LB2341.A49 2006
  378.1'01—dc22   2005019180

British Library Cataloguing in Publication Data is available.

Library of Congress Catalog Card Number: 2005019180
ISBN: 0–275–98528–8

First published in 2006

Praeger Publishers, 88 Post Road West, Westport, CT 06881
An imprint of Greenwood Publishing Group, Inc.
www.praeger.com

Printed in the United States of America

The paper used in this book complies with the
Permanent Paper Standard issued by the National
Information Standards Organization (Z39.48–1984).

10 9 8 7 6 5 4 3 2 1

For Pat
—the love of my life—

CONTENTS

FOREWORD

rank Rhodes, former president of Cornell, and by most accounts the most eloquent voice in contemporary higher education, is also capable of being a harsh but friendly critic of academic leadership. I asked him to write the lead article in the inaugural issue of the American Council on Education's magazine, *The Presidency*. He observed:

> [It] is not setting small goals; it is setting no goals that leads to presidential failure. Aimless, day-to-day management, busy inertia, preoccupied drift, and high-minded indecision mark too many presidencies, because incumbents set no goals. The first and greatest task of a president [or any leader] is to articulate the vision, champion the goals, and enunciate the objectives.[1]

Whether for presidents or chancellors, provosts, deans or department heads, governing bodies or faculties, thinking and acting for the long-term is fundamental. Mission needs to be seen in the context of a rapidly changing environment. Developing and sharing a strategic vision are among the essential building blocks of academic leadership.

Strategy, in whatever form, is a concept more common in the business world than in academe. In corporate America, strategic planning and execution are the most valued of leadership tools. Microsoft, Genentech, Dell, and Enron all grew out of powerful strategic judgments and visions. Three were hugely successful; one, an unforgettable disaster. None, however, could be accused of aimless, preoccupied, high-minded drift. Thinking and acting strategically is a crucial component of leadership, be it in the corporate sector or academe. Consider Johns Hopkins, Maricopa County Community College, Michigan State, Boston University, Phoenix, MIT, Berea College District, and Northeastern. Each grew, evolved, and prospered because of a distinctive strategic vision that differentiated it from other institutions and enabled it to prosper in the changed environment of the times.

Leadership and strategic planning might be largely irrelevant in a stable world. It is only in the real world of the twenty-first century, a world characterized by far-reaching and constant change, that thinking, planning, leading, and acting strategically becomes so crucial. Knowledge itself is changing. The bright lines defining disciplines have become blurred. The relative opportunities and demands in different professional fields of study are in flux. Technology has made it easier and cheaper to store and move information, to offer learning opportunities in new ways, with more convenience, without the normal constraints of time and space. In fact, the very definition of the "environment" has shifted from local to global. For-profit and not-for-profit distinctions, public and private governance and financing systems, secondary and postsecondary learning, these and countless other hallowed hallmarks of an earlier day are in flux. When added to demographic and cultural transformations, and students' changing career interests, ages, lifestyles and priorities, it should be easy to grasp the importance of strategy. The precise implications are wildly different from institution to institution. Not only is there no single cookie cutter, the whole challenge of strategic thinking is one of differentiation, not homogenization. And yet, if one looks back on the recent history of American higher education one sees more drift toward homogenization than bold strategic differentiation. Homogenization is easier, more comfortable, and may be in the short run less risky. Strategic differentiation, however, breaking from the pack, is precisely what will be required if American higher education is to survive and thrive in the century ahead.

One recurring theme found in the pages that follow is the distinction between strategy and tactics. To borrow from an analogy oft times used to distinguish between leadership and management, tactics have to do with doing things right, efficiently, at a high level of quality. Strategy is all about doing the right thing. In the end, successful execution of "the right thing," makes all the difference. We should ask ourselves why strategic thinking and planning are not a more common leadership tools for colleges and universities. Why is there so little evidence of successful strategic planning on college and university campuses? For one, we are much more likely to grapple with the serious tactical questions that threaten and frustrate us in the short term: the dysfunctional IT system, enrollment management, budget shortfalls, conflict resolution, accountability demands; the list is endless. These short-term pains often crowd out the longer term strategic questions, but the same is true of United Airlines, Ford, and GM, which find themselves struggling as well.

A second factor that explains much of higher education's failure to grapple with strategy is cultural. Colleges and universities tend to be "conservative" organizations, often resistant to change. The academic enterprise values academic freedom and a high degree of decentralization. As Clark Kerr put it, universities "are mostly still in the same locations, with some of the same buildings, with professors and students doing much the same things, with the governance carried on in much the same ways. . . . Universities have not been subject to any major technological changes, as have industry and agriculture and transportation. Faculty members continue to operate largely as individual craftspersons. . . . They have, on occasion, through what has gone on within them, helped change the world but have themselves been much less changed than most of the rest of the world."[2]

Universities and colleges are now feeling the winds of change as never before. Technology is transforming and redefining teaching, research, and public service. Changes in the very financial foundation of higher education are occurring in public universities and colleges as state support drifts downward and tuition and fees drift upward. As society spins ever faster in response to the forces of change, it is folly to suppose higher education can somehow remain insulated. Thinking and leading strategically will carry a higher and higher premium. Creating and executing strategy is a team sport. In the future, as in the past, a strategic vision for most academic institutions will not survive or thrive from the top down. Gaining and sharing a common vision is an iterative process, one of sharing and listening, challenging, acting, testing, and revising. Strategic leadership is about long-term positioning, the successful execution of a multiyear strategy. Such leadership, and the strategy that drives it, evolves from the environment in which institutions find themselves, from threats and opportunities, and from a clear sense of core purpose and mission. It seeks to reposition the institution in new and fresh ways with stakeholders, it seeks differentiation not homogenization, and it seeks to thrive, not just to survive.

The challenge of moving from tactical to strategic leadership is different in every setting. As the authors of this volume argue, context shapes strategy, and that context will be different for liberal arts colleges, for comprehensive state universities, for research-intensive campuses, and for community colleges. Whatever the context, however, academic programs and organizations of all stripes face challenges and opportunities that cry out for strong, creative, transformational leaders who are sustained by an inspired strategic vision. Grasping and executing such a vision is not easy. As these pages suggest, strategic thinking gives careful attention to the broader long-term trends and forces in the environment that touch the institution in one way or another. It analyzes the competition. It defines the stakeholders and the underlying values, expectations, and outcomes crucial to students and parents, teachers and researchers, governments and donors, communities and regions, business and the professions, and society at large. It means thinking boldly, but realistically. It means seeking comparative advantage, while placing a premium on sustainability.

For leaders, be they academic leaders at any level, or be they members of governing and policy-making bodies, managing the big picture is the one constant challenge. In the end, it is all that matters, since doing the right thing, even with great stress and difficulty, trumps the dangers of drift and complacency. In these pages the reader will capture the dimensions and dynamics of strategy; grasp the relationship between context and strategy, which is especially important given the uniqueness of academic organizations; and understand the hands-on world of strategy and how it works. Here is an invitation to take a journey, a timely journey, at a crucial point in the evolution of higher education in America.

Stanley O. Ikenberry
Regent Professor and Former President
University of Illinois

NOTES

1. H. T. Rhodes, "The Art of the Presidency," *The Presidency* 1, no. 1 (Spring 1998): 14.

2. Clark Kerr, *The Gold and the Blue: A Personal Memoir of the University of California, 1949–1967* (Berkeley: University of California Press, 2001), 289.

PREFACE

The future is today. Boundaries between profit and nonprofit organizations are eroding as corporations move aggressively into the business of education and sophisticated new technology is used to enhance learning. Growing numbers of students are looking into for-profit schools and taking classes electronically. The senior year of high school is being disaggregated and replaced by educational options provided through a host of organizations—business and industry, traditional colleges, electronic providers, community service organizations, and more—all tied directly to student goals and interests. Responsibility for postsecondary education is beginning to shift to the individual, and government funding is changing accordingly. An education is expected to be functional—that is, each individual should be educated to hold a job and educational providers should be held accountable for connecting learners to jobs. At the same time, there is increasing pressure on institutions to handle a new wave of immigration and to operate globally to provide trained specialists for businesses throughout the world. In this new market, a spate of challenges arise that institutions have never encountered before—all tied, in one way or another, to the increased use of technology. It is a market driven by hypercompetition, commercialization, commoditization, and, in a word, turbulence.

Although for many this market may seem several years away, it is already here when one considers how matter-of-fact Americans are about technology, social change, and product innovation. The boundaries of what has traditionally been viewed as postsecondary education are blurring and will become even fuzzier as institutions, driven by necessity and enlightened self-interest, reinvent the market—not once or twice, but over and over and over again. It is sheer folly for colleges and universities to live only in the present and react to, rather than anticipate, the next wave. The threat of competition can come from any direction. A narrow focus on instructional design and delivery will almost certainly miss the next generation of electronic users. A focus on traditional faculty selection and hiring practices could miss the impact of corporations entering the business of education and seeking to attract the same talent pool of professionals. A focus on price as a means to attract students could fail to factor in future trends in public policy and donor behavior that affect funding. To thrive in the new market, colleges and universities will need to live by a whole new set of rules. *Strategy* and *anticipation of change* will become part of every institution's agenda.

WHAT IS STRATEGY? WHY IS IT IMPORTANT? HOW IS IT DIFFERENT?

A brief introduction to strategy will help the reader understand why it is important and how it is different from the glossary of meanings and ideas we normally consider to be "strategic." In this book, we define strategy as a systematic way of positioning an institution with stakeholders in its environment to create value that differentiates it from competitors and leads to a sustainable advantage. In my position as an academic writing about organizational transformation and as a consultant helping colleges to develop plans for the future, I have spent a lot of time thinking about what really makes a difference in the development of an institution. Not the small picture of what a college is doing through plans, priorities, and resources, but the big picture of where it is going and why. Much to my amazement (and sometimes to my chagrin), I have found that leaders tend to confuse strategy with tactics. What they call *strategy* is in fact, *tactical*, a world of small-picture plans, operating goals, and actions—what a college must "have" or "do" to achieve its goals. Common examples would be a strategic plan, a vision statement, a statement of institutional goals and priorities, or a fund-raising campaign theme.

The big picture involving *strategy* is very different. In reach and scope, it extends considerably beyond small-picture tactics. Its focus is on the position of the institution in a continually changing world of constituencies, customers, and competitors. A leader conversant with strategy would be able to answer the following questions without hesitation: In one sentence, what is your institution's unique "signature," and how does it differ from competitors in the minds of key stakeholders? The world of strategy is one of leveraging and of creating advantage that one institution builds and maintains in relationship to others. It is not to be confused with the world of daily, operational tactics.

Some illustrations might help to distinguish *strategy* from *tactics* in college and university management. The University of Phoenix is a good example of an institution whose leaders have used strategy to build advantage through growth over a short period of time. Over the past five years, Phoenix has become the fastest growing and one of the largest post-secondary institutions in the nation. Many are aware of its basic formula for success—a focus on the market for working adults. This focus includes convenient access to courses and services which fit the lifestyles and work schedules of adult learners, course content and learning with direct application to the market through design and delivery by industry-based professionals, and constant assessment of value delivered to key stakeholders. Phoenix's success is not the result of guesswork or being in the right place at the right time. It is part of a strategy that can readily be discerned by examining its leaders' approach to business.

Phoenix administrators began by identifying the market they wanted to serve—adult learners—and by determining that this market was poorly served by traditional providers. Next, they determined that the university could establish a niche for itself through a strategy of *convenience*—developing a bachelors' and graduate curriculum and services keyed to the schedules and lifestyles of working adults. Making upper-level courses and services easily accessible to adult learners enabled Phoenix to enter a market that was relatively untapped by traditional providers. When Phoenix combined the use of advanced technology in educational delivery with the courses and curricula relevant to the career marketplace, the overall result was high learner satisfaction. Over time, Phoenix has been able to grow the initial strategy of convenience into one of *nonlinearity*. That is, it has redefined the market by providing progressively superior services to adult learners (online and hybrid courses, electronic services, virtual advisement, learner chat rooms, and so forth), which place the university beyond the reach of competitors and differentiate it in the minds of customers. The tactics underlying this strategy are its delivery arms—accessible courses and services, advanced use of technology, market relevance, and continuous assessment. These tactics are created and executed through planning and resource allocation. By itself, any one of them would be easy to duplicate and incapable of building an advantage. Woven together as part of a strategy, however, they resist duplication and lead to a sustainable advantage.

Turning to the venerable world of traditional colleges and universities, strategy is part of the arsenal that elite providers explicitly or implicitly use to build advantage in the quest for students and resources. Consider Harvard University and, in particular, the Harvard Business School. Its vast intellectual resources—nationally and internationally recognized professors, heavily resourced programs, executive education programs, the *Harvard Business Review* and Harvard Business School Press, Web sites, and other teaching resources—are all elements of a strategy of *traditional prestige* that it uses to build advantage. Its accumulated prestige, along with a capacity to use incremental resources to pursue important objectives, enables it to continually increase its visibility and, ultimately, to overwhelm competitors.

Northeastern University offers an illustration of strategy that a breakthrough provider could employ to build advantage in a changing market. Recognizing that work and classroom learning are separated by time and space and that the decreasing half-life of knowledge has made learning from experience an increasingly critical competency for undergraduate learners, Northeastern in the mid-1990s moved to revise its undergraduate curriculum. A practice-oriented education model was developed, fusing academics and paid professional experience in a five-year undergraduate program. This model differs from traditional approaches because it uses principles of action learning to integrate work experience with classroom study, theory with practice, and the liberal arts with professional education. In applying these principles, Northeastern has put in motion a strategy of providing *extraordinary experience* to students through experiential learning. It has extended itself beyond providing courses and delivering services to becoming an organization in the business of *changing* students. Learners are trained to continuously reflect on their experience and to integrate it with theory. In so doing, they take responsibility for their own learning and transform themselves into lifelong learners. By producing reflective professionals for profit and nonprofit organizations, Northeastern has become an educational provider of choice. It has also redefined the market for undergraduate education in New England.

Formulating strategy is not a science, it is an art. It is the art of asking intelligent questions and of thinking through issues in a creative way. It is the art of exploring possible answers, of experimenting with possible solutions, and of starting the thinking process all over again by questioning current practice. It requires thinking beyond the limits of traditional approaches to organizing and operating; and to do this, decision makers must understand the difference between strategy and tactics. If they are able to distinguish between these important concepts, they will be more likely to focus on the big picture and to bring success to the institutions they lead.

PURPOSE AND SCOPE OF THIS BOOK

The greatest challenge—and the purpose of this book—is to open the world of strategy to college and university administrators by defining what it is and how it differs from tactics. Our major purpose in writing this book is to describe the dimensions and dynamics of strategy in colleges and universities as organizations, and to provide a practical guide for its development and execution and for determining its impact. Our goal is to convincingly show why strategy is important and why it must be a part of every institution's management arsenal.

Leaders are beginning to rethink how to shape the future of their institutions. They have discovered that short-term plans and limited changes may not be sufficient to achieve success. More is needed. *Managing the Big Picture in Colleges and Universities: From Tactics to Strategy* is intended as a road map for college and university decision makers who want to use strategy to optimize the development of their institution, division, department, or service unit.

AUDIENCE

This book is the first comprehensive examination of strategy in the field of higher education. It will be particularly useful for

Campus Decision Makers

- Executive officers (presidents, vice presidents, and deans) making strategic decisions about institutional direction.
- Middle administrators (division chairs, department heads, and service unit coordinators) developing plans, budgets, and operating objectives for academic and service divisions.
- Informal but influential leaders within institutions who are positioned to shape decisions by virtue of their stature, longevity, and experience.
- Members of governing boards that create policy and empower administrators to carry it out.
- Members of collective bargaining units and other staff organizations who have an interest in, and are impacted by, decisions that direct the institution.

Higher Education Policy Makers and Advisory/Advocacy Organizations

- Members of state-level higher education boards that create and enforce policy, approve programs and budgets, and allocate resources.
- Members of accrediting agencies and advocacy organizations (e.g., American Council on Education, Education Commission of the States, National Association of Independent Colleges and Universities, American Association of Community Colleges) engaged in activities that monitor and support institutional development.

Regulatory Bodies

- Members of state and federal government agencies that impact educational policy, appropriations, and legislation affecting colleges and universities.

ORGANIZATION OF THIS BOOK

This book is divided into three parts designed to address fundamental questions regarding strategy: (1) What are the dimensions and dynamics of strategy? (2) How does context shape strategy? and (3) How does strategy work?

Part I, "Dimensions and Dynamics of Strategy," articulates the conceptual underpinnings of strategy and its application in contemporary organizations. Chapter 1 defines strategy and uses institution-specific illustrations to distinguish between strategy and tactics. Chapter 2 describes the evolution of strategy and details its application in contemporary organizations exemplifying different approaches or "schools" developed by theorists and practitioners. And chapter 3 outlines those components of strategy essential to its creation and implementation.

Part II, "Situating Strategy in Colleges and Universities," describes the relationship between context and strategy across the diverse spectrum of higher education in this nation. It discusses how critical factors related to the mission, control, and culture of institutions shape strategy, and notes that what is appropriate for a liberal arts college may be inappropriate for a teaching university or a community college. Factors shaping the relationship between strategy and context are identified and described in chapter 4. Chapters 5, 6, and 7 examine strategic approaches and applications that would likely unfold in different institutional settings, that is, colleges focused on the liberal arts, institutions with a comprehensive mission, and for-profit institutions. Each chapter provides case studies to illustrate how context shapes strategy.

Part III, "How Strategy Works," moves to the hands-on world of strategy formulation and implementation inside institutions. Chapter 8 describes the steps and protocols that are essential for the framing and articulation of strategy. Chapter 9 outlines key concepts for building an implementation plan. Chapter 10 provides a framework for evaluating the impact of strategy. The purpose of this section is to provide decision makers with the practical tools needed to create, implement, and evaluate strategy.

Richard Alfred
Ann Arbor, Michigan

ACKNOWLEDGMENTS

I have had the privilege and pleasure of working with five doctoral students in the Center for the Study of Higher and Postsecondary Education at the University of Michigan in the conceptualization and development of this book. They are described in earlier pages as associates, but in reality they are members of a remarkable team who worked together over the course of a year to forge a comprehensive understanding of strategy. There were no agendas for our meetings, no distinctions among players, and no rules guiding our discussions. This was the ultimate graduate seminar in which each of us learned about and leveraged our understanding of strategy through sharing with others. The associates—Chris Shults, Mary Ramirez, Tara Sullivan, Eric Chambers, and Dani Molina—are not merely graduate assistants and students, they are my colleagues. I owe an enormous debt to these colleagues from whom I have learned so much and to my faculty colleagues in the Center for the Study of Higher and Postsecondary Education, who, knowingly or unknowingly, enabled them to work with me.

Good fortune comes in many forms, and for me it arrived in the form of my partner in business and in life, Patricia Carter. Pat is an important part of the brain trust behind this book, and she is a brilliant content editor. She was with me every step of the way with ideas to shape and improve content. I owe a similar debt of gratitude to Susan Slesinger, executive editor with Greenwood Press and editor of the ACE/Praeger Series on Higher Education. Susan is the consummate professional one would hope to work with in creating and bringing a book to completion.

She was involved throughout the process—answering questions about protocol and procedure in the early going, providing guidance about form and content in the middle stages, and reading drafts and providing advice as the book neared completion.

My introduction to strategy, although I did not know it at the time, came in the mid-1970s with the closing of the City University of New York during the New York City budget crisis. The two-week hiatus from work and income became the equivalent of a 5 percent salary cut for all City University employees. More importantly, it marked the beginning of a two-year period in which institutional budgets were slashed to the bone. My institution—New York City Community College—lost roughly a third of its operating budget over eighteen months. To bring costs into line with revenue, we were forced to downsize enrollment and staff and to pursue new funding for operations. We succeeded in making the case with state legislators for special funding by differentiating the college from peer institutions on the basis of career and technical programs that were vital to the economic development of New York City. In retrospect, however, it was not the infusion of new money that was most important. It was the realization that something vastly beyond tactics was involved and that we were part of something special. To the members of the executive team who comprised the "we"—Ursula Schwerin, Luther Johnson, Augie Tuosto, Evelyn Whitaker, Tom Carroll, and Arnie Dimond—I am forever in your debt. I have not forgotten you and what I learned from you through the pain and exhilaration of the budget crisis.

As a writer, consultant, and analyst of organizational behavior, I have had the opportunity to interact with hundreds of leaders and managers over the last decade. For the most part this has occurred in the setting provided by community colleges as part of a consulting team working with Pat Carter. This book in large part is the product of that interaction. Through organizational and leader development programs carried out under the sponsorship of the Center for Community College Development and through management consulting assignments in some of the nation's leading colleges, I have learned much about strategy and what it means to manage the big picture. I am particularly grateful to college leaders and colleagues who are part of the Strategic Horizon Program and those who participated in its forerunner, the Strategic Leadership Forum. Our work in collaboration with the twenty-five colleges in these programs provided much of the early impetus for our thinking about strategy. In particular, I would like to thank three people—Roy Church, president of Lorain County Community College in Ohio; David Hartleb, president of Northern Essex Community College in Massachusetts; and John Erwin, president of Illinois Central College—for the benefit of their counsel in testing and giving birth to new ideas, many of them involving a degree of risk.

I also benefited greatly from the wide variety of writing and research which preceded this book. My intellectual debt to the early architects of strategy—Alfred Chandler, Kenneth Andrews, and Igor Ansoff—is substantial and it is more yet to the generation of thinkers who have followed them—Michael Porter, Gary Hamel and C. K. Prahalad, Henry Mintzberg, Kathleen Eisenhardt, and many more. I am particularly indebted to Gary Hamel and C. K. Prahalad, whose 1994 book *Competing for the Future* opened my mind to the full venue and potential of strategy, and to Michael Porter, whose 1987 article "The State of Strategic Thinking," in *The Economist*, introduced me to the discipline and protocol of strategic thinking. I would be remiss not to acknowledge the work of Ellen Chaffee, whose 1991 article "Three Models of Strategy" (published in *Organization and Governance in Higher Education*) was the first effort toward the introduction of corporate strategy to colleges and universities. The framework Ellen used to examine and describe strategy was helpful to my exploration of strategy and was eventually adopted for use in this book. Gratitude is expressed as well to the writers and thinkers who served as benchmarks for the creation and expression of ideas in specific sections of the book—Richard Oliver and Susan Segal-Horn in the historical overview of strategy; Joseph and Jimmie Boyett in the examination of strategy perspectives; John Bryson in the framing and articulation of strategy; Charles Noble in strategy implementation; and Seymour Tilles in evaluating strategy. The framework used to conceptualize, formulate, and execute strategy owes much to their work.

Most of all I want to thank my wife and family, whose love, patience, and support made this book possible. The demands of creating and producing this book pushed family and personal responsibilities backstage. To Pat, our sons and daughters, and our high-energy grandchildren (how quickly one forgets), I give a heartfelt thanks.

PART I

Dimensions and Dynamics of Strategy

CHAPTER 1

Distinguishing Strategy from Tactics

Put aside your beliefs and perceptions and take a long, hard look at your college. Look at changes in the market it is serving, both real and anticipated. Read your college's vision and marketing statements and consider its competitive position. What criteria are used to measure your college's success? What issues and challenges are preoccupying faculty and staff? Look toward the future and ponder your college's ability to shape its destiny in years to come.

Ask yourself: Do faculty and staff have a clear and broadly shared understanding of how the market may be different in the future? Do they have a keen sense of market forces, student needs and expectations, and customer satisfaction? Are they alert to challenges posed by new, unconventional competitors? Are they aware of innovations that could change the way education is designed and delivered? Do they have a clear sense of the value that your college offers and how it compares with competitors? Do they possess a sense of urgency about what the college must do to thrive in the future?

Put your college's vision and marketing statements on a table with similar materials from other colleges. How are they positioned in relationship to competitors? Are they unique or do they look the same as those from other colleges? Is your college continually defining new ways of delivering education, building new capabilities, and offering more value to students? Is your college a change leader or does it follow other institutions? Is it more interested in challenging current practice or adhering to convention?

Ask yourself: What drives how we lead and manage—our view of future opportunities, the actions of competitors, or our need to adhere to current practice? What is most important—keeping today's operations moving or being an architect of the future? Do we devote more energy to tackling small problems or to creating big picture strategy? What is our primary focus—tactics or strategy? These are not rhetorical questions. Get a pencil and rate your college.

AWARENESS

Do faculty and staff have a clear and broadly shared understanding of how the market will be different in the future?

Unclear   Don't know   Clear and broadly shared

Do faculty and staff have a keen sense of market forces, student needs and expectations, and customer satisfaction?

No   Not sure   Yes

Do faculty and staff have a clear sense of the value your college offers and how it compares with competitors?

No   Not sure   Yes

DISTINCTIVENESS

Is your college competitively unique or does it look the same as other colleges?

Looks the same   Don't know   Competitively unique

Is your college an innovative leader or does it follow other institutions?

Mostly a follower   Depends on circumstances   Mostly a leader

Are staff more interested in challenging current practice or in adhering to convention?

Adhering to convention   Varies among staff   Challenging current practice

FOCUS

What is the primary driver of how we do business?

Tradition   Competitors   Our vision of the future

To what extent are you a manager keeping operations moving or an architect of big picture strategy?

Mostly a manager   Some of each   Mostly an architect

What is your primary focus?

Tactics   Not sure   Strategy

Adapted from the work of Hamel and Prahalad (1994), these questions provide a simple but effective barometer of leaders' and institutions' involvement strategy.[1] Their premise is simple: If your marks fall somewhere in the middle or off to the left of the chart, you may be devoting too much energy to tactics and not enough to creating strategy for the future.

In the process of our work with colleges and universities, we frequently ask campus leaders about their strategy for the future through a set of interrelated questions. First, where are you taking this college and why? Second, what does this college stand for—what does it represent—in the minds of those who work here and those it serves? Third, what "value" does this college deliver and is it different from that of your competitors? We ask that each question be answered in a paragraph or less.

The answers we get reveal a startling lack of understanding of strategy and big picture thinking in colleges and universities. Leaders typically focus on tactics—the plans, actions, and resources needed to address current operating problems. By experience and training, they are pragmatic problem solvers rather than systematic long-range thinkers. Experience has taught them that it is best to narrow down complicated matters so as to isolate the practical problem at hand, and then to get on with finding a solution. Strategy, by contrast, is a pursuit that requires a contrary method: to connect diverse ideas and information into a systematic pattern, then to craft an approach—often long-range—to dealing with the whole.

It takes substantial energy and a willingness to look at things in a different way to develop robust answers to questions such as what direction a college should take, what value it should create, and what it must do to become distinctive in the minds of stakeholders. We believe such questions have received too little attention in colleges and universities. Moreover, the analytical framework needed to answer them—a comprehensive understanding of strategy—is not part of the skill set of contemporary campus leaders, managers, and decision makers.

FROM TACTICS TO STRATEGY

If it is not the future, what is occupying the attention of leaders and staff? In a word, tactics. As a concept, tactics has many meanings, but in this book it refers to the means or actions carried out by a college to achieve a specific end. These take many forms including statements describing institutional purpose and offerings, strategic and operational plans, goals and objectives, budgets, systems and processes, compliance reports, and more. These are important in the life of any institution, but they have more to do with implementing current plans and carrying out today's business than creating a position in tomorrow's market. Tactics are not a substitute for strategy, which is more concerned with imagining and creating the future. A college that employs sound tactics, but fails to envision a position for itself in the future, will find itself on a treadmill a step ahead of institutions committed to convention.

What Is Strategy?

In theory, strategy and tactics have generally been considered as related but different concepts and used in conceptually distinct ways. Strategy has been described as dealing with wide spaces, long periods of time, and large movements of resources while tactics have been described as dealing with the opposite.[2] Strategy is usually considered to be the prelude to action and tactics as the action itself. As a result, much of the literature and theory of strategy has focused on identifying the most favorable position an organization can occupy in a market of fast-moving competitors and changing customers. In practice, however, strategy and tactics cannot be easily separated. Movement begets action and action results in new movement. The one merges into the other. Strategy gives tactics its mission and wherewithal and seeks to reap the results of action. But tactics are an important conditioning factor of strategy, and as they change, so does strategy.

Recognizing the symbiotic nature of these concepts, but knowing the importance of drawing a distinction between them in college and university management, we define strategy as "a systematic way of positioning an institution with stakeholders in its environment to create value that differentiates it from competitors and leads to a sustainable advantage." Underlying this definition are four important questions about the future of the institution and its position in the market: (1) Who are the stakeholders? (2) What kind of value is created for these stakeholders? (3) Does the value created lead to advantage by differentiating the institution from its competitors? and (4) Is the advantage sustainable?

Value is the very essence of strategy. It is every institution's business, but it does not turn into advantage until it contributes, or is perceived as contributing, to the needs and expectations of stakeholders in ways unmatched by competitors. For example, colleges and universities routinely describe themselves as committed to quality in the delivery of education. But what is *quality*, and when and how does one institution deliver more quality than others? A tactician falls short by limiting the focus to the resources required to deliver services in relationship to an internally defined standard of quality. What financial and educational resources are required to deliver quality service? What are the requirements for faculty and technology? What approach to delivery yields the best results? A strategist, on the other hand, attempts to answer the question by seeking a deep understanding of what quality is about, what it means to students and stakeholders, and when and how it distinguishes one institution from another. A series of questions are asked: What do students want from postsecondary education? What are they looking for when they enroll in college? What choices are available to them? If the objective is to offer a quality education, then perhaps it is important to understand why students become involved with college in the first place.

An answer to the questions posed by the strategist comes back: "students expect to achieve a higher standard of living through postsecondary education and to enjoy the experience while doing it." The strategist presses on with more questions: What is the institution doing to propel students to a higher standard of living through its programs, courses, and services? How does this compare with what competitors are doing? What unseen forces are likely to impact the definition of quality in the future? Where does advantage lie in the conceptualization and delivery of quality? What quality conceptualization would enable the institution to gain an advantage by differentiating it from competitors? What is its capability for delivering quality along the lines of this new conceptualization?

To forge strategy, leaders and managers need to ask the right questions and set the right kinds of goals. Tacticians ask necessary and important questions, but they lack the depth required to create the building blocks of strategy: value and advantage. Moving from tactics to strategy means resisting easy answers in search of distinctive ways of delivering value. An illustration using information routinely published by colleges and universities will help make the point. At the beginning of the chapter we asked whether or not your college is competitively unique. Gather enrollment and marketing materials, mission and vision statements, and planning priorities for your college and for regional and national competitors of the same genre. Remove all identifying characteristics from the materials and put them on a table. Challenge your colleagues to determine which material belongs to your college. If the literature for your college does not readily stand out from the others, the point regarding the distinction between tactics and strategy will have been made.[3]

The most important and commonly used statements of colleges and universities do little to differentiate them. So little, in fact, that it is almost impossible to distinguish one institution from another using internally developed literature. The four elements of strategy—(1) Who are the stakeholders? (2) What kind of value is created? (3) Does this value lead to advantage? and (4) Is the advantage sustainable?—are not addressed in and through published statements. Replace these statements, however, with a clear statement of value that a college delivers to its students—some form of personal or economic gain, convenience, cost savings, or great experience—and suddenly it is possible to differentiate one institution from another. Institutions that are able to move to this level of performance establish a distinctiveness for themselves because they are doing (or, at least, portraying themselves as doing) something that other institutions have not done or thought about doing. They are using strategy to build an advantage by creating and identifying value that distinguishes them from competitors. Everything else that institutions do to advance themselves—marketing, goal setting, planning, and budgeting—is tactics because it has little to do with establishing a distinctive place through the creation of value.

Implicit here is a view of management quite different from that prevailing in many institutions. It is a view that emphasizes working with the big picture—the position of a college and its distinctiveness—in contrast to the small picture of operations and resources. It is a view that recognizes it is not enough to position an institution among competitors adhering to convention in today's market; the challenge is to develop foresight into tomorrow's market.[4] It is a view of management that acknowledges the need for more than incremental action—tweaking a mission or vision statement, building a strategic plan, reallocating resources in the budget—to achieve a unique position; what is needed is strategy to guide the institution to the future. In management, as in art, what distinguishes strategy from tactics is the ability to uniquely imagine what could be.

An Old and New Perspective

Although, to date, strategy has played a small role in the management arsenal of colleges and universities, it has been central to people and organizations for a long time. It is ancient, in fact, dating back to the importance of strategic thinking in military warfare discussed by Sun Tzu Wu (500 B.C.E.), Karl von Clausewitz (nineteenth century), and the political ideology of Machiavelli, who wrote *The Prince* in 1513.[5] In modern history, strategy's roots are most apparent in the world of business, exemplified by the corporate barons of the mid-1800s and early 1900s. Cornelius Vanderbilt, J. P. Morgan, and John D. Rockefeller amassed considerable power and wealth by establishing large-scale, far-flung business operations. While not referred to as such, strategy for these barons focused on price wars, consolidation, and the drive to monopoly, which vanquished competitors using a more conventional regional approach.

The advent of logistically complex and globally oriented systems in World War II advanced the development of strategy in ways that earlier command-and-control techniques used in national organizations did not. Vast amounts of competitive intelligence, large-scale operations, sophisticated technology, and intricate decision making and coordination were required to wage war. Capabilities for planning, organizing, and coordination developed by the military in this period were embraced by a corporate world undergoing rapid expansion in the 1960s. Alfred Chandler's book *Strategy and Structure* (1962), which declared "structure follows strategy," opened up a new venue for management by framing strategy as a distinctive business function that is deliberate and iterative. Andrews' *Concept of Corporate Strategy* (1971) added the need to focus on a firm's strengths and weaknesses as an important ingredient in decisions, and Ansoff argued in *Corporate Strategy* (1965) that a leader faces distinct strategic choices.[6]

These new concepts called for "deliberate and focused action" to propel an organization toward its goals and moved the concept of strategy into a future-oriented function focused on more than planning and budgeting. Although strategy relies on information gathered through tactical activities, such as planning for its formulation and management for its implementation, it transcends tactics because it requires more from people and organizations. It requires broad thinking, an analytical approach, and iterative development—capabilities identified by Michael Porter in *Competitive Advantage* (1985) as essential for coping with competition. Porter's approach opened a floodgate and a host of strategists poured in with new conceptions of strategy. Among them were Mintzberg (1990), who argues that markets are moving too fast for old-style analysis and that strategy needs to be action oriented; Hamel and Prahalad (1994), who emphasize the importance of core competencies as the critical strategic dimension of an organization and the need to reinvent markets through enhanced competencies; and Hammer (1990), who introduces the concept of reengineering as a way to increase speed and flexibility through the redesign of organizational systems, structures, and processes.[7] Today, technology plays an increasingly important role in strategy. Business information systems such as enterprise resource planning and customer-relationship management have emerged, and the focus of strategy has expanded to include competencies to support such systems.

STRATEGIC DISTINCTIONS

Evidence of the growing importance of strategy to leaders can be seen everywhere. One encounters marketing strategies, legal strategies, team strategies in sports, campaign strategies in domestic politics, player strategies in card games, curriculum strategies in universities, and so on. Even more prominent is the outpouring of books describing strategies that can be used to improve organizational performance through enhanced vision (Collins), continuous innovation (Christensen), powerful customer experience (Pine and Gilmore), and many more.[8] In conceptual or applied form, strategic thinking permeates modern society.

But what does this have to do with managing colleges and universities? Part of the answer lies with technology, which obliterates boundaries between organizations, and part with the increasing sophistication of customers and competition, which drives the ongoing search for differentiation. These forces are at the leading edge of change facing every institution. They are well documented in the literature and are pieces of the answer, but they are not the answer itself. The real answer resides in the increasingly turbulent market that colleges and universities are operating in as well as the effectiveness of conventional management techniques. Turbulence encourages the emergence of new competitors and new forms of delivery. It also increases the bargaining power of students by providing them with more choices. As the array of choices increase, institutions naturally seek new ways to differentiate themselves from competitors by offering something they think students will want or value—for example, more convenience (24/7/365 service on the Internet), better experience (a focus on learning in contrast to teaching), or unparalleled outcomes (better market connections and higher earnings). Each innovation or enhancement raises the bar of expectation and renders current practice obsolete.

As summarized in Table 1.1, a strategic approach to management in colleges and universities (*strategy*) differs in important ways from conventional approaches (*declarations and tactics*) to management. These distinctions demonstrate how each successive category of behavior creates greater benefit for the institution by differentiating it from alternative providers. All too often some institution will claim that it occupies a distinctive niche because it is doing something that other colleges are not doing, when, in fact, its actions can be, or have been, duplicated. This perception results, in part, from a self-fulfilling behavior that occurs when an institution and its leaders fail to fully comprehend the distinction between tactics and strategy.

Table 1.1
Strategic Distinctions

	Declarations	Tactics	Strategy
Form of Expression	Philosophy, mission, goals, vision, and marketing statements	Goals, plans, objectives, priorities, budgets	Position, distinctiveness, advantage
Purpose	Communicate intentions	Take action	Establish an advantage
Value Created	Low	Moderate	High
Competitive Position	Undifferentiated	Transitional	Differentiated
Stakeholder Interest	Low	Moderate	High

The simple descriptions given below for declarations, tactics, and strategy will help the reader understand the role and place of each in a progression from declarations to strategy in college and university management.

Declarations

In their simplest form, declarations are statements that make a college's intentions known regarding its purpose and the nature of its business. The most fundamental of these is the *mission statement*—a comprehensive assertion disclosing the concept of the organization, the nature of its business, the reason the organization exists, the people it serves, and the principles and values under which it intends to operate.[9] Closely related, but more focused is a *vision statement*—a representation of a desired future state that a college wants to achieve and how it wants to be seen by students, staff, and important stakeholders.

In theory, the mission statement is supposed to serve as a foundation, or internal guide, for all major decisions that an administrative team will make. In practice, however, it is often a shelf document that is rarely consulted or considered in decision making. *Marketing and promotional statements* that communicate the attributes and capabilities of a college that make it attractive to stakeholders are routinely used in place of the mission statement to motivate and engage those with a vested interest in the institution.

By definition, declarations are static—they evolve slowly over time, they are developed using language and protocols widely shared among institutions, and only rarely do they have the capacity to differentiate institutions. Look, for example, at a cross section of college and university mission statements taken from the Internet. A striking sameness among institutions is apparent.

Liberal Arts Colleges

The mission of [a northeastern liberal arts college] is to "educate students in the tradition of the liberal arts. Our academic program, co-curricular activities, and support services exist primarily to serve this purpose." Almost without exception, the mission statements and admissions materials of liberal arts colleges portray the same things—excellence, liberal education, small classes, individual attention, a menu of highly attractive majors, a full battery of co-curricular services and activities, sports, diversity and internationalism, and a highly prepared faculty, many with terminal degrees. Students graduating from these colleges, the statements claim, will join an elite group of alumni and leave with an education propelling them to success in whatever they do. They are prepared not only for a career, but also for life.

Community Colleges

The mission of [a West Coast community college] is to "promote the success of students and the well-being of our community by providing the best possible education which leads to intellectual growth, social and economic mobility, economic development, and an understanding of diverse ideas and people." Community colleges almost universally portray themselves as open-access institutions that extend opportunity by offering a convenient low-cost education to a diverse citizenry. Teaching is central to their mission and their goal is to help students achieve important academic, career, and life goals. They are responsive to student and community needs, offer a comprehensive curriculum, are committed to lifelong learning, and emphasize preparation for the workforce.

Teaching Universities

The mission of [a midwestern teaching university] is to "provide a broad range of undergraduate and graduate programs and services to prepare its students for varied roles as responsible citizens and leaders in a democratic and diverse society. Our programs encourage intellectual and moral growth, prepare students for meaningful careers and professions, instill the values of lifelong learning, and encourage civic responsibility, public service, and understanding among social groups in a global society. Reflected in the marketing materials of teaching universities are a broad range of undergraduate programs leading to the bachelor's degree. Most emphasize breadth in curricula and service offerings, intellectual and personal growth, preparation for meaningful careers and professions, a commitment to public service, responsible citizenship, excellent teaching, and student-focused learning.

Declarations like the above communicate intent, but they do little to advance the institution because they are not tied to the real world of operations and resources. In the absence of statements that bind people to the broad purposes of the institution, interest wanes and units begin to operate independently, sometimes at cross purposes. Ask a director or department chair, Where are you trying to get to as a college? and few will be able to articulate anything more than vague ideals ("provide excellent instruction" or "deliver quality service") or short-term operational goals ("respond more quickly to student needs" or "increase operating resources"). In many colleges, faculty and staff do not have a clear sense of purpose beyond that of short-term unit performance. In other words, because of their ethereal nature, declarations do not have the capacity to galvanize an institution to achieve a desired future state. They lack the urgency and dynamism required to command ongoing attention and allegiance from staff.

Tactics

Tactics are broadly defined as the means a college will employ to achieve its mission and purpose. As such, the ends (mission, purpose, and goals) and means (plans, actions, and budgets) are interrelated and inseparable components of institutional behavior. Neither one alone is sufficient to carry out the institution's mission. Plans and budgets without goals are meaningless. Goals without resources are empty. They give meaning to actions, but without a description of how they are to be achieved, they are merely statements of desire and hope.

Tactics serve two primary roles in the strategic life of an institution. At the macro level, they are the driving force behind an institution's behavior. They provide a rationale for the allocation of resources, they impel staff to action, and they serve as a unifying and integrating force within the institution.[10] At the micro level, tactics provide context and meaning for individual behavior. This is especially important in relationship to the ability of a college to change direction. The launch of a new program or redesign of a system to meet changing student needs can be a traumatic or fluid experience depending on how clearly goals and objectives are specified. The commitment and effort of leaders to change a system may appear to be irrational or misguided until it is understood in the context of a goal to improve service to students as a means of elevating satisfaction and retaining them until graduation.

Just as declarations do little to create value or to distinguish colleges from one another, the same could be said of tactics. In the act of formulating a goal or a priority, leaders and staff invariably restrict their focus to actions that will achieve results over a short period of time. For example, the way in which a strategic planning priority, such as "enhancing student success through improved services," is framed will narrow the focus of staff, in this case to actions that must be taken to improve services. Short-term action steps such as assessing student needs and preferences, measuring student satisfaction, and expanding professional development opportunities for staff will be carried out. Lip service will be given to the need to relate these actions to the larger context in which the institution operates, but the way in which a priority is written will limit the effort of staff to what they can see, to what they are told, or to the boundaries of their experience. Little, if any, attention will be given to ideas that lie beyond the visual horizon—for example, the position of the institution in future markets and what it must do in service delivery to differentiate itself from competitors.

Leaders often confuse tactics with strategy. In the process of developing plans, identifying priorities, and allocating resources, they earnestly believe that they are positioning the institution for the future. Tactics fall short of tackling big-picture issues, however, because their focus is on the present, not the future; on short-term action, not long-term advantage; and on achieving goals, not differentiating the institution from competitors. For these and other reasons, tactics are not to be confused with strategy.

Strategy

Institutions move from tactics to strategy when the focus shifts from the achievement of short-term goals to long-term differentiation. While declarations communicate intentions and tactics prescribe action, strategy seeks to establish advantage. Leaders interested in strategy try to create value for stakeholders in ways that cannot easily be duplicated by competitors—delivering higher quality at lower cost, offering more convenience to students, delivering one-of-a-kind programs and services, responding more quickly to changing needs, building memorable experiences into curricula and courses. The concept of advantage is easy to talk about, but not easy to build. It is rooted in information about the market, the capacity of competitors, and the competencies of the home institution, which must be mined and scrutinized to identify a superior position.

In colleges that use strategy, the focus is on finding a position in the market where tactics can be used to shape the competition. Corinthian Colleges, Inc., one of the largest for-profit, postsecondary education companies in the United States, uses a strategy of growth to distinguish itself in the rapidly expanding market of adult learners seeking career-oriented educations.[11] Corinthian carries out this strategy using tactics of speed, operational efficiency, and decentralized delivery to develop and implement new programs oriented toward adult learners. In fiscal 2003, it opened six new branch campuses, enlarged twenty existing facilities, developed fifty new programs in existing schools, and purchased three technology colleges. Its rapid growth is testimony to the effectiveness of these tactics in a market characterized by a growing demand for skilled labor, positive demographic trends, the increasing value of postsecondary education to learners, and budgetary constraints at public colleges and universities. Corinthian's strategy has put it in a position of advantage in a market in which stakeholders see growth as a sign of a successful enterprise—an enterprise that is well capitalized and worthy of affiliation. This strategy of growth begets more growth, and increasing size enables Corinthian to offer more programs thereby enhancing its status as an engine of economic gain for adult learners.

Alverno College in Milwaukee has used a different, but equally successful, strategy to establish a unique position for itself. Its strategy is one of redefining education to emphasize "ability-based education," that is, learning the abilities needed to put knowledge to use in the worlds of work, family, and civic community.[12] Eight abilities are learned by students: communication, analysis, problem-solving, valuing in decision-making, social interaction, developing a global perspective, effective citizenship, and aesthetic engagement. To evaluate whether students have mastered these abilities, faculty have developed a multidimensional approach to assessment. Course-based and integrative assessments that focus on student learning in several courses are used to elicit samples of performance. Faculty and trained assessors observe and judge a student's performance using explicit criteria. Their feedback, as well as the reflective practice of self-assessment by each student, helps to create a continuous process that improves learning by integrating it with assessment. The goal is to make explicit the expectation that students should be able to do something with what they know. Consistently ranked as one of the best regional liberal arts colleges in the Midwest, Alverno has established a reputation among students and experts alike as the purveyor of a unique design for postsecondary education.

The success of these institutions is easily recognized, but it is attributed more to opportunity and leadership than to strategy. Strip away the language related to accomplishment, however, and in each can be found a distinctive position based on clear answers to four questions:

1. Who are the stakeholders?

    Corinthian Colleges: Adult learners seeking career-oriented education.

    Alverno College: Students, staff, and instructors committed to a new design for learning.

2. What kind of value is created for stakeholders?

    Corinthian Colleges: Rapid job and income enhancement through programs that connect learners directly to the workforce.

    Alverno College: Mastery of specific abilities that enable students to succeed in work, family, and community.

3. Does the value created lead to advantage by differentiating the institution from competitors?

    Corinthian Colleges: A reputation for speed in developing programs that provide economic gain for learners distinguishes it from competitors moving at a slower pace.

    Alverno College: Recognition as one of a small number of colleges that experts expect to be at the cutting edge brings added value to stakeholders and distinguishes it from competitors.

4. Is the advantage sustainable?

    Corinthian Colleges: High capitalization and unmatched speed make it difficult for colleges with conventional systems and limited resources to keep pace.

    Alverno College: Competitors find duplication difficult because they cannot obtain broad commitment from staff to a different design for learning.

These examples show how institutions can use strategy to wrap value around their programs and services to differentiate themselves from competitors. Colleges that move quickly or have the freedom to innovate have an advantage in this regard because they are not wedded to convention. They can enhance the value they create for stakeholders by allocating resources differently and otherwise engage stakeholders in ways that make them distinctive in the minds of those they serve.

THE STRATEGY PROGRESSION

The samples of mission statements earlier in the chapter showed that value delivered by colleges and universities is not evident in and through their declarations. Let's extend this analysis a step further by using findings that could turn up in focus-group meetings conducted with leaders of external organizations (business and industry executives, K–12 superintendents, elected officials, influential citizens, hospital and health industry leaders, etc.) as part of strategic planning. With the advent of externally focused strategic planning, meetings of this type have become more commonplace as a requisite step in planning. The results they yield, however, can become decidedly uncommon, depending on the nature of the questions asked and the way in which answers are given.

Most administrators are familiar with the questions asked in such meetings: What are the key trends and forces facing your organization? What are your organization's needs now and in the future? What can College X do to help you address these needs? Is College X a visible and active player in relationship to your organization? What is it not doing that it should be doing? What can it do better? These questions mean different things to different people, and that is exactly the way in which they are answered. Under the belief that they are helping the institution, some meeting participants will try to deflect criticism by indicating that it is "well known and valued." Others will identify problems that can readily be solved through tactics—more marketing, more money, more attention to constituency needs, and so forth. And, every so often, a lightning bolt will come from a meeting participant in the form of a question or challenge that cuts to the very heart of the college: What do you stand for? Tell me in one sentence what makes your college different from competitors in the eyes of those you serve.

The experience of the focus-group meeting illustrates the strategy progression depicted in Figure 1.1.[13] Each step upward in participant verbalization—praise and support (declarations), identifying problems and practical solutions (tactics), and a challenge regarding the overall position of the college (strategy)—makes the college more interesting to stakeholders because it tells them more about the *value* they will receive through affiliation. And, because colleges and universities depend so heavily on declarations to communicate their intentions and offerings, efforts undertaken by any one institution to establish the value it delivers through strategy will *differentiate* it from others.

One college that well illustrates the concept of the strategy progression is Rio Salado College in Phoenix. Established in 1978 as a "college

Figure 1.1
The Strategy Progression

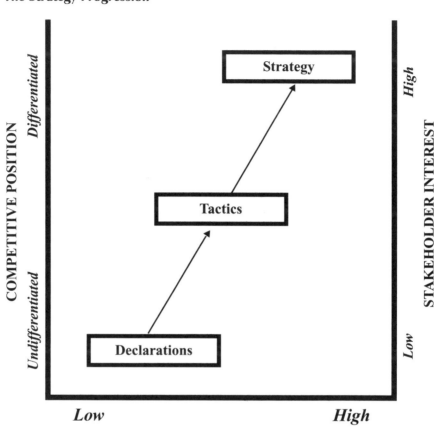

without walls" in the ten-campus Maricopa County Community College District, Rio's objective was and still is to provide working adults with flexible, convenient educational opportunities. It does not maintain a traditional campus. Instead, courses are delivered for diverse populations using customized programs and partnerships, accelerated formats, and distance learning. Learning opportunities are delivered on-site at corporations and government agencies and at community centers. From its beginning, Rio has been recognized as the innovative or "experimental college" in the Maricopa system; it is often the first college to offer a new program or service.[14]

After a promising beginning, Rio's enrollment began to fall in the 1980s—a reflection of problems that a "college without walls" would encounter in trying to meet the needs of unique populations without a consistent service philosophy. In order to serve diverse constituencies in distinctly different geographic regions that were part of a 9,000-square-mile service region, Rio operated as five distinct entities, each with a specific regional focus. Students in each region were provided with a broad selection of courses, but in so doing, the college inadvertently gained a reputation for canceling courses due to insufficient enrollment. Although many courses were offered in each regional market, they were not organized into curricula that could become "home" programs for students. Also, as a "college without walls," Rio relied on rental facilities, which students perceived as second rate compared to those of traditional college campuses.

With the entry of a new president in 1994, Rio decided to embark on a different path. It devised a strategy to create more value for students through convenience and relevance, bringing education directly to students through multiple delivery systems and ensuring that learning is connected to desired outcomes through external partnerships. A major investment was made in distance learning, and the time required to earn a degree was reduced by developing a system that allowed students to enroll in online courses every two weeks. This system enabled the college to develop a policy of never canceling a course due to limited enrollment.

Rio moved to establish unique programs and to forge customized partnerships with employers, thereby connecting education and work. The staffing model of the college was changed to differentiate professional roles in the design and delivery of education. Faculty roles were expanded to include responsibility for curriculum design and development; full-time marketing specialists were added to identify the instructional and service needs of organizations and learners in the external community; and advisors who serve as testing and assessment specialists were hired to determine student needs and capabilities for the purpose of channeling them into appropriate delivery systems. A course development and production unit was established to develop high quality online courses, which are supported by Rio's system of online services.

Through its new staffing model, Rio Salado College has entered the business of delivering convenience-based customized education that challenges the limits of tradition. In so doing, it has moved up the strategy progression from a focus on declarations and tactics a decade ago to a focus on strategy today.

WHAT'S AHEAD?

As new and aggressive competitors enter the increasingly turbulent world of postsecondary education, more than a few institutions will find they need to learn how to develop and implement strategy in order to survive. It is hard to imagine how a nondescript, less-selective liberal arts college living in the past or a poorly capitalized proprietary college strapped for resources in the present will survive in competition with a growing number of institutions involved with strategy.

Deepening interest and involvement with strategy among college and university leaders will bring about a proliferation of change in management, which has been long overdue. Leaders who seek a distinctive place for their institutions will become navigators on a highway to the future. Those who don't will become motorists looking for a rest stop or for a way to exit the highway. To avoid this fate, leaders will need to embrace strategy and learn how it works from conceptualization to implementation.

NOTES

1. The framework for these questions is derived from the work of Gary Hamel and C. K. Prahalad in *Competing for the Future* (Boston: Harvard Business School Press, 1994).

2. George L. Morrisey, *A Guide to Strategic Thinking: Building Your Planning Foundation* (San Francisco: Jossey-Bass, 1996).

3. See, for example, William J. Carroll, "A Discordant Melody of Sameness," *Trusteeship* 11, no. 2 (2003): 13–17.

4. For an industry foresight view of the market, see Hamel and Prahalad, *Competing*.

5. Susan Segal-Horn, *The Strategy Reader* (Oxford: Blackwell, 1998), 10.

6. This overview of the formative roots of business strategy is derived from Richard Oliver, "The Future of Strategy: Historic Prologue," *Journal of Business Strategy* July/August 2002: 6–9.

7. See, for example, Henry Mintzberg, "Strategy Formulation: Schools of Thought," in *Perspectives on Strategic Management* (New York: Harper Business Books, 1990); C. K. Prahalad and Gary Hamel, "The Core Competence of the Corporation," *Harvard Business Review*, May/June 1990, 79–91; and Michael Hammer, "Reengineering Work: Don't Automate, Obliterate," *Harvard Business Review*, July/August 1990, 104–112.

8. See, for example, Jim Collins, *Good to Great* (New York: HarperCollins Books, 2001); Clayton Christensen, *The Innovator's Dilemma: When New Technologies Cause Great Firms to Fail* (Boston: Harvard Business School Press, 1997); and B. Joseph Pine and James Gilmore, *The Experience Economy* (Boston: Harvard Business School Press, 1999).

9. See, for example, working definitions provided by Morrisey, *A Guide to Strategic Thinking*.

10. George Morrisey, *A Guide to Tactical Planning: Producing Your Short-Term Results* (San Francisco: Jossey-Bass, 1996).

11. Information derived from the Web site of Corinthian Colleges, Inc., www.corinthian.com (accessed 2004).

12. Information derived from the Web site of Alverno College, www.alverno. edu (accessed 2004).

13. The framework for Figure 1.1 and portions of the approach to analysis are derived from Pine and Gilmore, *Experience Economy*, 20–24.

14. Information derived through campus visitations and conversations with executive officers in 1997 and 2002 and Web site exploration (www.riosalado. edu) and executive conversations in 2004.

CHAPTER

Conceptualization and Application in Contemporary Organizations

The idea of strategy has been around for millennia as a way of thinking about survival and success in war or politics. Leaders have always had to make choices about direction and policy, the resources at their disposal, and how best to distribute those resources in pursuit of objectives. So, although the term *strategy* initially achieved popularity in the 1960s in business schools, activities which most modern managers would now think of as strategic have been understood and acted upon for centuries. Classic texts such as Sun Tzu's *The Art of War*, written in China 2,500 years ago; the political strategy of Machiavelli, who wrote *The Prince* in 1513; and German military strategists such as Clausewitz in the nineteenth century, are still well known and influential.[1] In the wisdom and words of these architects can be found the roots of strategy in contemporary organizations. Through their ideas we observe that strategy entails internal competencies, external conditions, and careful thought toward achieving ends.

EVOLUTION OF STRATEGIC THOUGHT

The transition of strategy into fields and disciplines other than the military began with the introduction of nuclear firepower in World War II. At this point, because of the possibility of mutual annihilation, the ultimate goal of strategy shifted from victory to capitulation. Strategy became more than a means of obtaining an advantage over an enemy. It evolved into a thought process involving psychological factors and became a distinctly human phenomenon—the intersection of contesting wills each seeking to produce in the other a condition of capitulation or compromise. This condition constitutes the prime objective of strategy today, supplanting the old idea of victory.

The shifting conceptualization of strategy from classical to contemporary times after World War II enabled different disciplines to experiment with the concept. A natural transition was made to the world of business as the market moved from a relatively stable environment into a more rapidly changing and competitive environment after World War II. In 1962 a business historian named Alfred Chandler introduced a book that would eventually bring strategy into the mainstream of business and industry. *Strategy and Structure* was the study of four corporations using different business approaches and the relationship of their organizational structure to growth. Chandler's definition of strategy was "the determination of the long-term goals and objectives of an enterprise, the adoption of a course of action, and the allocation of resources necessary for carrying out these goals."[2]

The four decades since Chandler's book have been filled with theories and ideas about the role of strategy in successful business practice. A number of writers have emerged as visionary thinkers, and key events have given rise to an increasing reliance on strategy in for-profit organizations. Among the writers and theorists, Michael Porter is widely recognized as having developed the necessary analytic tools for forging strategy through his landmark book *Competitive Strategy*.[3] Key developments that have accelerated interest in strategy include military strategic studies converted to civilian use following World War II; business policy teaching at the Harvard Business School; the steady shift of management education from an internal to an external orientation, best exemplified by the arrival of the marketing concept in the early 1950s; and the growing influence of systems thinking in the 1960s and beyond.

MODELING STRATEGY IN CONTEMPORARY ORGANIZATIONS

Organizations can survive, and indeed do well, over extended periods of time in conditions of relative stability, low environmental turbulence, and limited competition for resources. However, virtually none of these conditions prevail today for organizations in any sector—public or private, profit or nonprofit. Hence, strategy is needed to help organizations choose effectively between alternatives and deploy resources for maximum effect. Strategy, however, is not a commodity that can easily be created or acquired. It must be grounded in the reality of an organization:

it cannot be purchased in boilerplate, taken off a shelf, or borrowed from another organization. More importantly, it is a complex subject with almost as many ways of thinking about it as there are people interested in it.

Those who think about the strategy construct agree on several dimensions as summarized by Chaffee.[4] They implicitly agree that the study of strategy includes both the conceptual basis for actions taken—the content of strategy—and the processes by which actions are decided and implemented. They agree that *intended* (planned), *emergent* (occurring, but unplanned), and *realized* (occurring, planned or not) strategies exist and may differ from one another. They also agree that firms may have both a corporate strategy (what business are we in?) and business strategy (how should we compete in the business?). Finally, they concur that the creation of strategy involves conceptual as well as analytical skills. Beyond this, agreement breaks down, and theorists and practitioners pursue the concept in different ways depending on their approach to strategic thought.

Although strategy is a complex subject with many forms and faces, the view taken in this book is that it is a more integrated construct than its treatment in the literature would indicate. It can be viewed in a holistic perspective by analyzing the literature, clustering the ideas of like-minded thinkers into discernible perspectives, and then integrating these perspectives using a conceptual model. A word of caution is important at this point. Although individual thinkers can be grouped together or clustered to form a perspective, it is unlikely that any particular view of strategy can be confined entirely within that perspective, or that the writings of a theorist can be limited to that perspective. It is even more unlikely that any theorist deliberately sets out to establish or become part of a particular perspective. So, the strategy perspectives described below are artificial and arbitrary. They are useful primarily as a heuristic device, a way of clarifying or organizing a complex field of information.

Using the clustering technique, six perspectives covering forty years of strategy evolution are described in this chapter. First, a model integrating the different perspectives is presented. Then, the operating precepts of each perspective are described, along with their contribution to management practice in contemporary organizations.[5] The chapter closes with an analysis of the extent to which different perspectives are at work and their implications for leadership and management in colleges and universities.

Perspectives on Strategy

Beginning with the work of Chandler in the early 1960s and extending to contemporary thinkers, different perspectives on strategy can be depicted on three axes as shown in Figure 2.1. The first axis (A-B) depicts strategy in terms of the *scale* or extent of change an organization will undergo as part of strategy creation and execution. At one end of the spectrum lies the rational or *deliberate* perspective, which involves minimal change because the activity involved in strategy formulation and execution is planned, logical, and within the boundaries of the organization. In this perspective, strategy is a way of explicitly shaping the long-term goals and objectives of the organization, defining the major actions needed to achieve these objectives, and deploying the necessary resources. At the other end of the spectrum lies the nonlinear or *dynamic* perspective, which involves rapid and large-scale change inside and outside of the organization. Predictable relationships between the organization, its competitors and the market become unpredictable as new rules for engagement are written that change the basis for competition. In its most extreme form, this perspective may amount to revolution with everything else becoming tactics.

The second axis (C-D) depicts strategy in terms of the *locus* or connection of an organization to its external environment. At one end of the spectrum lies the resource-based or *competency-driven* perspective: developing core competencies of the organization. At the other end, is the adaptive or *market-driven* perspective: developing a viable match between opportunities and risks present in the external environment and the organization's resources. In other words, if the focus of strategy is on building the organization from within by developing superior competencies, the organization-environment relationship can be said to be resource-based. If, on the other hand, the focus of strategy involves matching the resources of the organization with opportunities in the environment, then the organization-environment relationship is market-driven; advantage is achieved by allocating resources to the pursuit of opportunities.

The third axis (E-F) corresponds to the *basis* for creation of strategy. At one end of the spectrum lies the processual or *process-based* perspective in which strategy is shaped through an evolutionary process representing a set of pragmatic compromises between stakeholders in the organization. Strategy is evolutionary rather than planned, emergent rather than deliberate. At the other end of the spectrum lies the systemic or *context-based* perspective in which strategy is contingent on context—social, economic, political, and so on—rather than the actions of stake-

Figure 2.1
Conceptualizations of Strategy in Contemporary Organizations

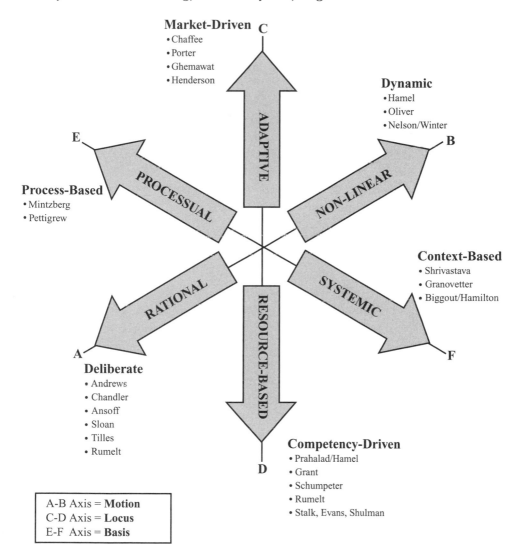

holders. The conditions that contribute to context change rapidly in a turbulent market, so strategic thinking under one set of conditions can be markedly different from the approach to thought under another. Although process and context may appear to be closely related as a basis for strategy—it is difficult to detach process from context—they are, in fact, quite different. Stakeholders holding a relationship with an organization shape strategy as part of process, whereas forces and influences inside and outside of the organization shape strategy as part of context.

The intersection of these axes defines six broad realms of strategy that are at work in contemporary organizations. The perspectives that make up these realms are inclusive rather than exclusive and may operate singly or in combination. Any one perspective could serve as a basis for development of organizational strategy. For example, a decision made by an organization to pursue a nonlinear or dynamic strategy by bringing a product or service to market, changes the basis for competition. Likewise, some or all of these perspectives could function simultaneously in the same organization as part of its business strategy. An executive team shaping long-range goals through strategic planning would favor a deliberate approach while research and development professionals engaged in new product development would be more likely to favor a dynamic approach. In the same organization, a marketing department looking for top talent to increase product visibility would subscribe to a competency-driven approach, while a planning division scanning the horizon for new opportunities would favor a market-driven approach. Finally, infighting among stakeholders representing key interests in the organization could lead to a process-based strategy, and strategy emerging in response to changes in the context surrounding the organization would be context-based. Each of these approaches to strategy is viable in today's market, and leaders would be well advised to understand and use all of them.

Strategy as *Scale*

As depicted in the A-B axis, *scale* concerns the extent of change an organization will undergo as part of strategy creation and execution. Organizations are inclined toward varying levels of risk in different types of environments. In periods of low environmental turbulence and limited competition for resources they do not have to entertain risk. It is fitting, then, that the first strategy perspective to be considered—the rational perspective—developed in the period of relative market stability and low risk that marked the 1960s and 1970s.

Rational Perspective

The rational perspective is linear and focuses on planning. The term *rational* is used because it connotes the deliberate, methodical, sequential action involved in planning.[6] The concepts that define this perspective came into being in the 1920s, when Alfred Sloan at General Motors and a few of his contemporaries were engineering a new concept: diversification. They discovered that diversification benefited from a divisional structure and that tightly designed planning and control systems in turn supported this structure.[7] Divisions grouped according to activity and placed under the coordination of a senior executive made it possible to establish decentralization which in turn led to profit maximization. To this day, the strategy-structure-systems link is an article of faith in corporate management as reflected in the design of industry production systems, reinforced in consultants' reports, and confirmed in the actions and mind-sets of managers.[8] Top managers view themselves as the designers of strategy, the architects of structure, and the managers of systems that direct and drive their companies.

Major characteristics of the rational perspective and the names of theorists whose definitions of strategy are consistent with this perspective are listed in Table 2.1.[9] As the dates in the citations suggest, interest in the rational approach developed early under the leadership of pioneering thinkers. One was Alfred Chandler, a business historian, whose research marked the beginning of interest in strategy from a teaching and research perspective. Chandler viewed strategy in terms of a relationship between the long-term goals of an enterprise, the action to achieve these goals, and the allocation of resources necessary for carrying out that action.[10] This view emphasized both the formation of goals and objectives (ends) and resource commitments (means) to achieve objectives. In addition to Chandler, early proponents of the rational perspective included Seymour Tilles, Igor Ansoff, Kenneth Andrews, Roland Christensen, and Peter Drucker. Tilles (1963) drew parallels to military science by defining strategy as a set of major goals and policies that outline what an organization is trying to achieve and become.[11] For Ansoff (1965), strategy was comprised of four components: (1) product/market scope, (2) growth vector, (3) competitive advantage, and (4) synergy.[12] And Andrews (1971) defined strategy as "the pattern of objectives, purposes, or goals and major policies and plans for achieving these goals, stated in such a way as to define what business the company is in or is to be in and the kind of company it is, or is to be."[13]

Although these early thinkers differed on the relative emphasis they

Table 2.1
Summary of Rational Perspective on Strategy

Descriptor	Rational Perspective
Definition	Determination of the basic long-term goals of an enterprise, and the adoption of courses of action and the allocation of resources necessary for carrying out these goals (Chandler, 1962)
Works best in	Stable, predictable environments in which long-range forecasts achieve some degree of accuracy, pressure for change is low, and competition is limited
Aim of strategy	Goal achievement
Key elements	Goals, actions, and resource allocation
Means	Strategic planning
Key thinkers	Sloan (1920s) Chandler (1962) Tilles (1963) Ansoff (1965) Andrews (1971) Drucker (1974)

placed on goals and forces in the environment, collectively they viewed strategy as consisting of integrated decisions, actions, and plans that frame and drive the achievement of organizational goals. Both goals and the means of achieving them are the results of strategic decisions. To reach these goals, organizations create products and services or perform entrepreneurial activities to increase market share. The structure of the organization is the conduit through which top managers allocate resources to achieve strategic objectives. Managers go through a prototypical rational decision-making process: they identify goals, generate methods of achieving them, weigh the likelihood that alternative methods will succeed, and then decide which ones to implement.[14] In the course of this process, they capitalize on future trends that are favorable, while avoiding or counteracting those that are not. For planning to succeed, the organization needs to be tightly coupled, so that all ramifications of decisions made at the top can be implemented throughout the organization.

The major flaw in the rational perspective lies in its objective of minimizing the idiosyncrasies of human behavior through a strategy-structure-systems framework. Over time as organizational size and diversity have expanded, strategies, structures, and reporting and planning systems have become more and more complex and employee activities increasingly fragmented. Increasing turbulence in the economic environment, combined with challenges of overcapacity and intense competition in a global economy, have rendered linear approaches to strategy ineffective. The planning framework in the rational perspective is time-consuming and forward-looking. Decisions made today are based on beliefs about future conditions that may never come to pass. In order to believe that making such decisions is not a waste of time, one must assume either that the environment is relatively predictable or that the organization is well insulated from the environment.[15]

The concept of path dependency is also a serious problem for organizations pursuing a rational approach to strategy.[16] In many industries, once a certain path is taken, the magnitude of the commitment locks the organization into its chosen strategy. For example, airlines must periodically make massive capital investments in aircraft and associated infrastructure. They tend to operate with a homogeneous fleet composed of a small number of aircraft types, usually purchased from the same manufacturer. There are sound economic reasons for maintaining this type of homogeneity. If a plane becomes unserviceable, a spare aircraft of the same type can be more easily substituted. In addition, pilots and mechanics must be rated on each aircraft type. The use of multiple aircraft types increases training costs and spare-parts inventories. It also builds inflexibility into flight schedules as planes must be shifted to accommodate pilots who cannot fly certain types of aircraft. As the average service life is fifteen to twenty years, airlines tend to become locked into their choice of aircraft type. This can have serious performance-related implications if the chosen aircraft type does not match emerging market requirements. Consider the case where an airline buys a small number of large jet aircraft and the combination of soaring fuel costs and changing market demand favors a higher frequency of smaller flights. The nature of path-dependent future commitments made through rational planning is that organizations cannot easily switch from one position to another. The cost of changing paths is significant, and organizations must maintain flexibility in committing resources through strategy or face the prospect of diminished capacity.

Nevertheless, the work of Chandler, Andrews, Ansoff, and other rational theorists propelled the notion of strategy into the forefront of management. It is a tribute to the soundness of their early work that it can comfortably encompass fifty years of management practice. The rational approach to strategy, under the rubric of strategic planning, is still at work in many organizations today, particularly those engaged in slower cycles of change such as colleges and universities.

Nonlinear Perspective

In contrast to the emphasis on planning in the rational perspective, the nonlinear approach to strategy runs at the pace of an action-packed video game. Managers dodge and fire reflexively, pouncing on opportunities the instant they arise. The market is moving faster than organizations are becoming resilient as informationally empowered customers place exacting demands for quality, variety, service, price, and convenience. Organizations seeking success must be fast and flexible to meet the daunting challenges of the twenty-first-century business environment, which include rapid and disruptive change, globalization, technological change, fleeting opportunities, and an overall sense of uncertainty.[17]

Market volatility encourages a nonlinear perspective in which strategy is synonymous with dynamic change. This requires shifting resources to endeavors with uncertain, or nonlinear, outcomes. The results of nonlinear thinking are all around us. Perennially successful companies like General Motors and IBM are finding it more difficult to deliver consistently superior returns. In their 1994 bestseller *Built to Last*, Collins and Porras singled out eighteen "visionary" companies that had consistently outperformed their peers between 1950 and 1990.[18] Twelve of these companies—a group which includes Disney, Motorola, Ford, Nordstrom, Sony, and Hewlett-Packard—failed to outperform the Dow Jones Industrial Average between 1990 and 2000. Success has never been more fragile. What theory can explain how Canon put such a huge dent in Xerox's market share? How can Toyota outrun General Motors? And what about Sony versus RCA? It isn't simply that resource-hungry challengers have some kind of advantage in operating efficiency or labor costs—there is something more.[19]

The "more," according to Hamel and Prahalad in *Competing for the Future* (1994), is that challengers using a nonlinear approach to business have succeeded in creating entirely new forms of competitive advantage and rewritten the rules of engagement.[20] Managers of upstart challengers are more creative than traditional managers. They have a capacity to imagine products, services, and even entire industries that do not exist and then create them. The quest for advantage begins not with a battle over market share, but with a battle for intellectual leadership of the market.[21] The task for organizations using nonlinear strategy is to develop foresight even if it means a revolution in the way products and services are conceived and delivered to the market. Savvy leaders reverse the basis of the rational approach. Rather than building organizations that develop around a predetermined strategy, they create flexible organizations and

Table 2.2
Summary of Nonlinear Perspective on Strategy

Descriptor	Nonlinear Perspective
Definition	Strategy is revolution because of permanent turbulence in the market and rapid changes in the context in which organizations work. Revolution in the form of frame-breaking innovations that depart from past practice is the only method that will create sustainable advantage
Works best in	Turbulent, unpredictable environments in which pressure for change is high, competition is intense, technology reduces barriers to market entry, and customers wield significant bargaining power
Aim of strategy	Revolutionize the market
Key elements	Ideas, innovation, disruption, radical change, and revolution
Means	Nonlinear thinking and continuous innovation
Key thinkers	Nelson and Winter (1982) Henderson (1989) Romanelli and Tushman (1994) Kim and Mauborgne (1999) Sastry (1997) Oliver (1999) Alfred, Carter and Terwilliger (2000) Hamel (2002) Clemons and Santamaria (2002) Hamel and Valikangas (2004)

let strategy evolve through interaction with customers. Success is achieved by the most nimble. Usually that means those who are new to the industry and not married to old rules or those who are established players who can break free of their dependence on the past methods that made them successful.

Major characteristics of the nonlinear perspective and the names of theorists whose views of strategy are consistent with this perspective are listed in Table 2.2. The recent dates of the citations indicate that this approach has evolved as a function of increasing market turbulence and organizational thinking that seeks to move beyond rather than regress toward competition. One of its leading advocates is Gary Hamel who equates strategy with revolution.[22] Hamel believes that the ideology of optimization embraced by rational theorists—do more better, faster, and cheaper—is not sufficient in a market undergoing fundamental change.

Organizations which focus on matching or beating the competition, leveraging and extending current capabilities, or retaining and extending their existing customers are off the mark. A record company seeking a profitable online business model, an airline seeking to outmaneuver Southwest, a college trying to deliver quality education despite deep budget cuts, a large department store getting pummeled by discount retailers, an impoverished school district intent on curbing its dropout rate, or any organization where more of the same is not enough have one thing in common: optimization will not lead them to organizational success.

Revolution, in stark contrast to optimization, requires organizations and leaders to engage in high-risk, unpredictable behavior that disrupts established rules and changes the basis of competition. Rather than striving to match or outperform the competition, organizations must establish a capacity for continuous value innovation. Value innovation is quite different from outperforming competitors and is not about building an advantage. Nor is it about segmenting the market and accommodating customers' individual needs and differences. Value innovation makes competition irrelevant by offering fundamentally new and superior value to customers in existing markets and by enabling a quantum leap in customer value to create new markets.

An example provided by Kim and Mauborgne will illustrate how value innovation works.[23] Callaway Golf, the U.S. golf-club manufacturer, launched the "Big Bertha" golf club in 1991 to open up the game of golf to new customers. The product rose rapidly to dominate the market, wresting market share from rivals and expanding the total golf-club market. How did Callaway do this? Despite intense competition, it did not focus on competitors. Rival golf clubs looked alike and featured sophisticated enhancements, a result of intensive benchmarking of competitors' products. Callaway focused on the "country club" markets of golf and tennis and found that many people play tennis because they find the task of hitting a small ball with a small club to be daunting. Recognizing a business opportunity, Callaway made a golf club with a larger head that made playing golf less difficult and more fun. The result: not only were new players drawn into the market, but Callaway captured an overwhelming share of existing players as well. By using a nonlinear approach and thinking in terms of alternative industries—golf versus tennis—as opposed to thinking rationally about competitors and how to outperform them, Callaway redefined the problem and revolutionized the market.

Similar examples of nonlinear thinking can be found in diverse industries. Consider CNN in news broadcasting, Wal-Mart in discount retailing, IKEA in home products retail, Amazon in book retailing, Southwest in air travel, and many others. Their steady growth and high profits are not a consequence of daring young entrepreneurs, of being a small start-up, of being in attractive industries, or of making big commitments to the latest technology. Instead, these high-performing companies are united in their pursuit of innovation outside of a conventional context. They ask: How can we offer customers greater value that will result in profitable growth, irrespective of industry or competitive conditions? Because they question everything about a particular industry, they explore a wider range of strategic options than other companies. This broadens their creative scope, allowing them to find opportunities where other companies can only see constraints.

Strategy as *Locus*

As depicted in the C-D axis in Figure 2.1, *locus* concerns the realm in to which strategy is created—the organization itself or the environment in which the organization is situated. Organizations can choose to concentrate on building internal competencies and resources (a resource-based approach to strategy) or anticipate and capitalize on opportunities in the environment (an adaptive approach to strategy). Both perspectives are popular and offer advantages to organizations in periods of turbulence. They are described below.

Adaptive Perspective

The adaptive perspective assumes that a primary aim of any organization is its own survival and, by extension, for the resources that will ensure its survival. The organization faces an uncertain environment and, like a living organism, must adapt to changing circumstances to elicit sufficient resources. The realm in which strategy is created is the external environment and the strategic tasks are to anticipate the future, monitor key factors in the environment, recognize opportunities and threats, and maintain enough flexibility and resources to enable the organization to capitalize on opportunities and evade threats.[24] Critically important in this perspective is the development of a match between opportunities in the external environment, including the behavior of competitors, and the organization's resources.

Among the early theorists working with this perspective was Charles Hofer (1973), who defined strategy as the "development of a viable match between the opportunities and risks present in the external environment and the organization's capabilities and resources for exploiting these opportunities."[25] Rumelt (1984) elaborated on the idea of an organization-environment match, stating, "the normative use of strategy has no counterpoint in biology, but might be thought of as the problem of designing a living creature . . . to exist in some environment."[26] This perspective assumes less predictability in the external environment than the rational perspective, as well as a highly permeable boundary between the organization and its environment. To survive and thrive, an organization must continually assess external conditions, the behavior of competitors, and its internal capabilities and resources. Assessment then leads to adjustments within the organization or its environment to create satisfactory alignments of environmental opportunities and risks, on the one hand, and organizational capabilities and resources, on the other.

Interest in the adaptive perspective escalated in 1980 through the work of Michael Porter—one of the foremost architects of corporate strategy. Porter examined state-of-the-art approaches to competitive strategy, found them wanting, and distilled three decades of research on corporate performance into a set of prescriptions for managers. In *Competitive Strategy* (1980), Porter argued the essence of strategy formulation is coping with outside forces like competition, and competition in an industry comes not simply from direct competitors, but from the underlying economics of the industry.[27] He identified five forces that determine the nature of competition in an industry—all of them outside of the organization. They are

- the threat of new entrants to the industry
- the threat of substitute products or services
- the bargaining power of customers
- the bargaining power of suppliers
- the extent of rivalry among existing competitors in the industry

Porter's first competitive force, *threat of entry*, deals with the ease or difficulty a new competitor may experience when beginning to do business in an industry. The more difficult entry is, the less the competition and the greater the likelihood of success over the long term. Key factors that make market entry difficult are (1) economies of scale achieved by organizations with the capability to decrease unit costs as volume of production increases, (2) product differentiation implicit in brand reputation built up by established firms over time, (3) capital resources required to start a business, (4) cost disadvantages independent of scale, (5) access to distribution channels, and (6) government policy.

The second competitive force, *pressure from substitute products*, relates to the ease with which customers can substitute one type of product or service for another. For example, high-fructose corn syrup is a substitute for sugar with discernible impact on the sugar cane industry. Porter notes that substitutes become a threat when they provide not only an alternative source for the customer, but also a significant improvement in price and performance. For example, distance delivery education has an impact on enrollment in direct contact courses because it provides a similar or equivalent value to students at an increased level of convenience.

The remaining three forces—the *bargaining power of customers*, the *bargaining power of suppliers*, and *rivalry among existing competitors*—determine the nature of competition by facilitating or constraining access to operating resources. The bargaining power of customers can significantly impact organizations when customers do one or more of the following: purchase in large volume, have a significant interest in savings, purchase standard or commodity products, provide the service or the product themselves, are highly concerned about the quality of the product or service they are buying, have full information, and many choices. The bargaining power of suppliers can change the basis of competition when supplier groups are dominated by a few companies, organizations seeking a product or service have a small number of choices, and the supplier's product or service is unique in some way or would be costly or troublesome for an organization to find a substitute product. Rivalry among competitors shapes competition in an industry when the following conditions prevail: numerous organizations are competing that are equivalent in size and/or resources, the industry is growing slowly, organizations have high fixed costs, organizations are under time restraints within which the product or service must be sold (colleges can never recover the revenue on classroom seats that are unfilled or dormitory rooms that are empty), or the service is perceived as a commodity for which the customer has many options and the cost to the customer of switching from one supplier to another is small.

Porter believes that organizations can, by the way they choose to compete, influence each of the five forces.[28] What they must do is search for a sustainable competitive advantage, which comes from developing a distinctive way of competing. Simply speaking, an advantage can be achieved either by having consistently lower costs than rivals or by differentiating a product or service from that provided by competitors. But choosing one or another is not enough and choosing both may lead to problems. The best competitors, therefore, are those that have more than one key strength and integrate a number of business activities in a way that is consistent and mutually reinforcing.

Major characteristics of the adaptive perspective and the names of theorists whose views of strategy are consistent with this perspective are listed in Table 2.3.[29] The adaptive perspective differs from other per-

Table 2.3
Summary of Adaptive Perspective on Strategy

Descriptor	Adaptive Perspective
Definition	Concerned with the development of a viable match between opportunities and risks present in the external environment and the organization's capabilities and resources for exploiting those opportunities (Hofer, 1973)
Works best in	Environments in which opportunities for change are numerous and continuous
Aim of strategy	Achieving a match
Key elements	Environmental forces, organizational capabilities and resources, permeability, flexibility
Means	Scanning and assessment
Key thinkers	Hofer (1973) Hofer and Schendel (1978) Rumelt (1979) Hambrick (1980) Porter (1980) Quinn (1980) Kotler and Murphy (1981) Chakravarthy (1982) Miles and Cameron (1982)

spectives in several ways. As described by Chaffee, monitoring the environment and making changes are simultaneous and continuous functions in the adaptive approach.[30] The time lag for planning implicit in the rational approach is not present, and the drive to revolutionize the market characteristic of the nonlinear approach exceeds the boundaries of organizational risk. Advance planning is relatively unimportant in the adaptive approach, so strategy is less centralized in top management. Second, the adaptive approach does not deal as emphatically as the rational model with decisions about goals; it is more concerned about the means for alignment with the environment. Finally, in the adaptive approach the environment is considered to be a complex organizational life-support system, consisting of trends, events, competitors, and stakeholders. The boundary between the organization and the environment is permeable and, contrary to the rational and nonlinear approaches, the environment is a major focus in determining organizational action.

The adaptive perspective on strategy has been seriously challenged by theorists who believe that core competencies within the organization, in contrast to market forces, are the most important determinant of strategy in turbulent markets. Where Porter and adaptive theorists emphasized the need for an organization to build strategy in context with external and competitive forces shaping its industry, a new breed of theorists emphasized instead the need for an organization to identify its core competencies and build strategy around them. This is the resource-based perspective on strategy and it is profiled in the next section.

Resource-Based Perspective

The objective of Porter's approach to strategy—and the underlying rationale of the adaptive perspective—is to take the guesswork out of the future and bring order to the world of business. The basic premise is simple: If every organization plans diligently, then competition will be predictable, with every cost leader, differentiator, and focused organization achieving a position in the competitive market. The problem, as pointed out by Mintzberg in *The Rise and Fall of Strategic Planning* (1994), is that markets cannot be counted on to remain stable and companies to follow predictable rules governing how they compete.[31] Throughout the 1980s, for example, Japanese companies like Toyota and Honda and American upstarts like Wal-Mart did what Porter had defined as impossible. They shifted the approach to strategy away from the environment and into the organization and became low-cost and differentiated at the same time. Not only did they survive and prosper, they ushered in a new approach to strategy focused on developing core competencies of the organization. This view of strategy assumes that the roots of competitive advantage are inside the organization and that the adoption of new strategy is constrained by the current level of the organization's resources.

Fundamental to the resource-based approach is the notion that differences in organizational performance evolve because successful organizations possess resources and capabilities not possessed by other organizations, thus enabling them to gain an advantage.[32] *Resources* are viewed as inputs into the organization's operations rather than products or services. Examples include personnel, capital equipment, technology, and so on. A *capability* is defined as a capacity to perform a task or activity that involves complex patterns of coordination and cooperation between people and resources.[33] Capabilities include research and development, excellent customer service, and high-quality manufacturing.

Leading theorists like Grant and Hamel and Prahalad believe that instead of thinking of an organization as a collection of business units, managers must begin to think of it as a bundle of resources that have to be developed to provide benefits to customers. These resources constitute basic inputs into "core competencies" that are built up within each organization.[34] How effectively these competencies are developed and managed is determined by managerial capabilities. Since managerial capabilities will vary, two organizations with the same resources but different managerial talent will generate different levels and types of performance. In the same industry therefore, organizations may pursue different strategies and achieve different results using similar resources. This places a premium on the role of management in creating critical processes for competence building within the organization.

Further, Hamel and Prahalad (1994) suggest that if organizations are to achieve an advantage, managers must begin to think about the underlying functionality of products and services, not simply about the products and services themselves.[35] Instead of asking, What is our product or service? they should ask, What benefits do existing products and services deliver to customers? Managers would then discover whole new possibilities for their business. For example, if academic administrators ask themselves, "What is the functionality of teaching?" they could answer, "To impart knowledge and skills to students in real time within a small group." This answer might lead them to realize that in the act of shaping the curriculum and course content, the instructor is the primary customer of teaching. In turn, this realization might prompt them to reconceive of teaching as a medium for transformation of learners by providing compelling experience through active learning. By thinking in terms of teaching's functionality, rather than just in terms of teaching itself, academic administrators could revolutionize the act of teaching for an entire generation of learners.

Stalk, Evans, and Schulman (1992) pursue a similar line of reasoning in their conception of strategy as capabilities-based competition.[36] In turbulent environments the essence of strategy is not the structure of an organization's products, services, and markets, but the dynamics of its behavior. The goal is to identify and develop hard-to-imitate organizational capabilities that distinguish an organization from its competitors in the eyes of customers. The principles of capabilities-based competition are the following:

- The building blocks of organizational strategy are not products and markets, but business processes.
- Competitive success depends on transforming an organization's key processes into strategic capabilities that consistently provide superior value to the customer.
- A capability is strategic only when it begins and ends with the customer.

- Organizations create strategic capabilities by investing resources in a capability and making sure that personnel have the necessary skills and resources to achieve it.

- Capabilities are often mutually exclusive; developing the right ones is the essence of strategy.

The kind of breakthrough thinking required to develop "core competencies" and compete on the basis of "capabilities" will not come easily to tradition-bound managers. Organizations interested in innovative thinking will need to engage people outside of industry dogma—current and potential customers and newcomers to the organization—to gain access to fresh perspectives and new ideas. Effective information gathering with these groups should culminate in an organizational development plan or "strategic architecture" that provides a blueprint of the competencies and capabilities that need to be developed by an organization to deliver superior value to customers. Hamel and Prahalad (1994) describe a strategic architecture as

> the essential link between today and tomorrow, between short term and long term. It shows the organization what competencies it must begin building *right now*, what new customer groups it must begin to understand *right now*, what new channels it should be exploring *right now*, and what new development opportunities it should be pursuing *right now* to intercept the future. Strategic architecture is a broad opportunity plan. The question addressed by a strategic architecture is not what we must do to maximize our revenues or share in an existing product market, but what must we do today, in terms of competence acquisition, to prepare ourselves to capture a significant share of the future revenues in an emerging opportunity area.[37]

Table 2.4 summarizes the major characteristics of the resource-based perspective and the names of theorists whose views are consistent with this perspective. Received with accolades in the early- and mid-1990s as a necessary counterbalance to the lockstep views of the rational theorists, the resource-based perspective is the subject of continuing interest and inquiry. Rumelt's (1974) definition of strategy as the "balanced consideration of a firm's skills and resources, the opportunities extant in the economic environment, and the personal desires of management," has resurfaced.[38] And offshoot theories have emerged like that of Amit and Schoemaker (1993), who propose an approach to strategy that specifically seeks to integrate the adaptive and resource-based paradigms by

Table 2.4
Summary of Resource-Based Perspective on Strategy

Descriptor	Resource-Based Perspective
Definition	Seeks to develop competencies that are fundamental to an organization's performance and strategy by: (1) making a disproportionate contribution to the value received by customers, (2) increasing the efficiency by which that value is delivered, and (3) providing a basis for entering new markets (Hamel and Prahalad, 1994)
Works best in	Turbulent and unpredictable environments
Aim of strategy	Achieving a sustainable competitive advantage
Key elements	Competition, core competencies, capabilities, strategic architecture, competitive advantage
Means	Building core competencies
Key thinkers	Barney (1986) Prahalad and Hamel (1990) Grant (1991) Hambrick (1991) Stalk, Evans, and Schulman (1992) Amit and Schoemaker (1993) Hamel and Prahalad (1994)

viewing them as two sides of the same coin and fundamentally interrelated.[39]

Amit and Schoemaker present two constructs, "strategic industry factors" (SIFs) and "strategic assets" (SAs), that merge the environment and organizational capabilities into a unified conception of strategy.[40] Strategic industry factors are key determinants of an organization's success in an industry and are determined at the market level through complex interactions involving the organization's customers, competitors, regulators, innovators, and other stakeholders. This construct clearly draws on terminology from Porter's five-forces model, thereby making the model more palatable to adherents of the adaptive approach. Likewise, the definition of strategic assets draws heavily on the resource-based language of competitive advantage. Strategic assets are the "set of difficult to trade and imitate, scarce, and specialized resources and capabilities that bestow the firm's competitive advantage."[41] Beyond its obvious value of integrating important concepts in strategy, the combination of SIFs and SAs creates a new frame of reference for strategy that opens dialogue among theorists holding different views.

Strategy as *Basis*

Basis describes the ground or foundation for the creation of strategy. As depicted in the E-F axis in Figure 2.1, strategy can be viewed as evolving on a continuum with "process" on one end and "context" on the other. As a process, strategy is created through interaction between and pragmatic compromises among stakeholders in an organization. As "context" it is contingent on the setting or environment—social, economic, political, and the like—rather than the actions of stakeholders.

Processual Perspective

The processual approach to strategy, like the nonlinear and resource-based approaches, holds that long-range planning is of less relevance than the *process* by which strategy emerges from a combination of influences within the organization. In this perspective, whose best-known proponent is Henry Mintzberg (1987), a strategy is emergent rather than deliberate and evolutionary rather than planned.[42] It is a process that not only reflects the views of top management, but represents a set of pragmatic compromises between various stakeholders in the organization. The implication of this view of strategy is that those strategies which are imposed top-down without incorporating other organizational constituencies, are unlikely in practice to be effective.

The interest of Mintzberg and others oriented to the processual perspective was triggered in 1971 by an unusual definition of strategy as a "pattern in a stream of actions."[43] Working with this definition, Mintzberg and a team of researchers tracked the strategic behavior of eleven organizations over several decades of their history. They (1) developed chronological lists and graphs of the most important actions taken by each organization such as store openings and closings, new flight destinations, new product introductions, and the like, (2) inferred patterns in these actions and labeled them as strategies, (3) represented graphically all the strategies inferred for an organization in order to determine distinct periods in their development, (4) used interviews and in-depth reports to analyze what appeared to be key points of change in each organization's history, and (5) studied the full set of findings for each organization to develop conclusions about the process of strategy formation. The data pointed to an inescapable conclusion: Although in common parlance *strategy* is defined as a consciously intended course of action to achieve a goal, strategy creation is not an orderly, definable process.[44] It is crafted over time from an ongoing stream of small and large decisions and a wealth of experience.

A painter sitting before an empty canvas wants to create something entirely new, whole, and special. But each brush stroke, and the pattern of color, is derived from all of the painter's past failures and successes. The same kind of relationship exists with business strategy. When executives are asked about their company's strategies, they talk about the future (their plans), the present (what they are doing), and the past (what they have done). Every organization has plans, but the actual act of strategy creation may have nothing to do with the plan. The artist, for example, once engaged in the act of painting, may end up junking every idea he started with. The subject of the painting could change, or a choice could be made to work with a different medium (watercolors instead of oil) and different colors. When the painting is done, the strategy is clear, but during the process things may have been untidy, unstable, and incomprehensible. The same is true of life in complex organizations. Staff work with customers, receiving a wide range of opinions about a product or service, from praise to criticism. Managers receive and analyze this information and respond by making adjustments to improve the situation. Over time, the accumulated decisions and actions of the organization add up to a strategy.[45]

Strategies can be consciously formulated as well as formed through a process of evolution. Mintzberg, a taxonomist par excellence, acknowledges this with a typology of five contexts in which strategy can take shape:[46]

Strategy as . . .	Description
Plan	A consciously intended course of action, made in advance of the action to which it applies, stated in an explicitly formal document known as a plan
Ploy	A specific maneuver intended to outwit an opponent or competitor
Position	Any viable position adopted by an organization, whether or not directly competitive (i.e., occupying a niche in the market)
Pattern	A pattern in a stream of actions—consistency in behavior whether or not intended
Perspective	A commitment to a way of acting and responding

A strategy is *intended* when it is part of a plan, ploy, or position deliberately created to achieve a specific end. Often, however, what is intended does not reach fruition in its originally planned form. That which is neither planned nor intended, but is actually realized, is called *emergent* strategy. Together, intended and emergent strategies yield the full range of *realized* strategy. There need not be a formal separation between in-

Table 2.5
Summary of Processual Perspective on Strategy

Descriptor	Processual Perspective
Definition	A pattern in a stream of actions; a consistency in behavior whether or not intended evolving over time in an organization (Mintzberg, 1987)
Works best in	Independent of market conditions
Aim of strategy	Create a niche or position for the organization that leads to success
Key elements	Pattern of actions over time, emergent or deliberate, consistency, organizational experience, and learning
Means	Organizational experience, views of top management, and compromises made by stakeholders
Key thinkers	Pettigrew (1985) Brunet, Mintzberg, and Waters (1986) Mintzberg (1987, 1994) Weick (1990)

tended and emergent strategy. According to Mintzberg (1987), the value of viewing strategy as evolving through process is that it avoids the limiting assumption that thought must precede action.[47] If a strategic plan is followed blindly, then an organization cannot learn from short-term experience. Religious adherence to a plan also severely limits the opportunity for taking advantage of discovery, unusual ideas, or just plain luck. Success often develops in unusual places, and organizations need to be willing to follow the path reality sets before them.

Table 2.5 summarizes the major characteristics of the processual perspective and the names of theorists whose views are consistent with this perspective. The value of this perspective may not be in the perspective itself, but in the brilliance of Mintzberg's thinking underlying the perspective. Strategy is multidimensional; it walks on two feet: one deliberate, the other emergent. Management requires a deft touch—to direct to realize intentions while simultaneously responding to an unfolding pattern of action. The relative emphasis may shift from time to time, but not the need to attend to both sides of the equation.

Systemic Perspective

Systemic theorists stress the importance, and to some extent the uniqueness, of the social systems in which diverse attitudes toward, and conceptualizations about, strategic issues occur. Strategy thus is the child of context, be it social, geographic, political, cultural, or organizational. It reflects attributes of both the macro (external environment) and micro (organization) social systems in which it is created. It follows then that strategy is not absolute; it is contingent on context. Asian strategic thinking may differ from Western or Eastern European strategic thinking; the culture and approach to strategy in one organization may be different from that of another; and people working in different parts of the same organization may experience the organization in different ways. Viable strategies will, therefore, be context-specific.

The effect of context is variable. Some theorists presume leaders can make choices that influence outcomes, while others see leaders as having a limited influence in organizations operating in a turbulent, fast-changing environment. It follows, therefore, that strategy is contingent rather than absolute. Strategic thinking in periods of market stability and predictability may vary considerably from strategic thinking in periods of market turbulence. For example, traditional approaches to strategic planning do not work very well in periods of uncertainty because they do not fully capture the array of options or opportunities organizations can pursue during periods of rapid change. For this reason, viable strategies are context-specific and capable of continuous revision to fit changes in context.

One of the early theorists embracing the systemic perspective was Edward Wilson. In a landmark 1975 study, *Sociobiology*, Wilson tried to synthesize all that is known about population, biology, zoology, genetics, and animal behavior.[48] What emerged was a framework for understanding the success of species in terms of their social behavior or competition for resources. This synthesis provided a foundation for the systemic approach by integrating information from different disciplines—or contextual fields—into a unified framework with abundant parallels for organizational behavior (Henderson, 1989).

In a 1989 article entitled *The Origin of Strategy*, Henderson articulated the fundamental precepts of the systemic perspective.[49] For any organization, strategy is an iterative process that begins with where the organization is and what it has now. It involves a deliberate search for a plan that will develop a competitive advantage and compound it. Understanding competitors and the entire competitive environment, therefore, is essential to creating strategy. This can be accomplished through understanding the systematic interaction of competitors with one another in a defined environment.

According to Henderson, competition can assume two forms: natural competition, which is evolutionary, cautious, and expedient in its moment-to-moment evolution, and strategic competition, which compresses time in a deliberate, carefully considered approach to action. To succeed, leaders must understand both forms of competition. The basic elements of competition are (1) the ability to understand competitive behavior as a system in which competitors, customers, resources, people, and external forces continually interact, (2) the ability to use this understanding to predict how a given strategic move will rebalance the competitive equilibrium, (3) the availability of resources that can be permanently committed to new uses even though the benefits will be deferred, (4) the ability to predict risk and return with enough accuracy and confidence to justify the commitment of resources, and (5) the willingness to act.[50] Natural competition works by a process of low-risk, incremental trial and error. Small changes are tried and tested, and those that are beneficial are gradually adopted and maintained. There is no need for foresight or commitment, what matters is adaptation to context—the way things are now. That is why in geopolitics and military affairs as well as in business, periods of equilibrium are punctuated by sharp shifts in competitive relationships. Natural competition continues during periods of equilibrium and strategic competition intensifies in turbulent times. In business, however, turbulent times are the norm, therefore strategic competition prevails.

Porter (1990) furthers our understanding of the systemic perspective by using it to describe the impact of context on the competitive capacity of nations.[51] In a world of increasingly global competition, nations have become more, not less, important. Competitive advantage is created and sustained through a highly localized process. Differences in national values, culture, economic structures, institutions, and histories all contribute to competitive success. There are striking differences in the patterns of competitiveness in every nation. The contextual conditions in some nations, however, enable companies to compete effectively in the global market whereas conditions in other nations do not have the same effect. Attributes that account for these differences demonstrate the importance of context for strategy. They are as follows:[52]

1. *Factor Conditions.* The nation's position in factors of production, such as skilled labor or infrastructure, necessary to compete in a given industry.
2. *Demand Conditions.* The nature of the home market demand for the industry's product or service.
3. *Related and Supporting Industries.* The presence or absence in the nation of supplier industries and other related industries that are internationally competitive.

4. *Firm Strategy, Structure, and Rivalry.* The conditions in the nation governing how companies are created, organized, and managed, as well as the nature of domestic rivalry.

These contextual determinants create the national environment in which companies are born and learn how to compete. Each attribute affects essential ingredients for achieving global competitive success. When a national environment, or context, permits and supports the rapid accumulation of specialized skills and resources, companies gain a competitive advantage. When a national environment affords better ongoing information and insight into product and process needs, companies gain a competitive advantage. And, when a national environment pressures companies to innovate and invest, companies both obtain a competitive advantage and compound that advantage over time. The impact of the attributes increases, however, when they coalesce to form a self-reinforcing system.[53] The role of domestic rivalry illustrates how the combination of attributes works as a self-reinforcing system. Vigorous domestic rivalry stimulates the development of unique pools of expertise and resources, particularly if the rivals are located in one region. The University of California at Davis, for example, has become one of the world's leading centers for winemaking research, working closely with the California wine industry. Active rivals also upgrade demand for quality in the industry. California consumers have learned to expect more and better wine because of the rapid pace of change in winemaking techniques, driven by intense rivalry.[54]

Table 2.6 summarizes the major characteristics of the systemic perspective and the names of theorists whose views are consistent with this perspective. Although it is the most complex of the strategy perspectives, the systemic approach offers considerable promise in understanding the role of strategy in dualistic organizations such as colleges and universities. When the environment that colleges and universities operate within is viewed as a macrosystem and the institution itself as a microsystem, it is possible to conceive of strategy as the child of context. That is, the strategy adopted by a particular type of institution is determined, in large part, by the specific features of the context in which it operates.

Synthesis. From its inception in business organizations in the 1960s, there has been a gradual evolution in strategic thought away from rational planning toward an emergent, nonlinear, and context-specific view of strategy. In this more recent way of thinking, context and op-

Table 2.6
Summary of Systemic Perspective on Strategy

Descriptor	Systemic Perspective
Definition	Strategy is a child of context. It reflects macro and micro aspects of the social system in which it is created
Works best in	Independent of market conditions
Aim of strategy	To create an advantage over competitors
Key elements	Contextual conditions, macro and micro aspects of context, systems
Means	Understanding of contextual conditions and system attributes
Key thinkers	Wilson (1975) Granovetter (1985) Shivrastava (1986) Henderson (1989) Porter (1990)

portunity shape strategic possibilities. However, organizations in slow-change industries continue to embrace a rational approach to organizational development. This suggests that strategic decision-making takes place in variable contexts, that it is complex and multifaceted, and that one size does not fit all. The complexity of the strategy concept makes it a vibrant subject for leaders and managers in contemporary organizations. It is at once *compelling*—leaders must understand it to guide their organizations through turbulent waters—and *elusive*. It is the subject of continuing interpretation and reinterpretation, rendering it almost impossible for leaders to fully comprehend. This aspect of strategy will be examined in greater depth in the following section on current and emerging perspectives.

CURRENT AND EMERGING PERSPECTIVES

In the fast-moving world that organizations operate in today, there have been many challenges to formalized perspectives on strategy. On one front, the very idea of strategy has come under attack. Work ranging from Mintzberg's critique of strategic planning to the burgeoning literature on hypercompetition suggests that formulaic strategic thinking is impractical in an ever-changing business environment. Studies of the intensely disruptive and turbulent environment of hypercompetition have shown that strategic paradigms that work well in stable environments may be a liability in unstable ones. During stable periods, for example, organizations are able to use Porter's five forces to formulate strategy with predictable results. In periods of turbulence, however, different approaches to strategy may yield better results. Numerous strategy perspectives are emerging to bridge organizations from the old to the new economy and from a market that was stable to one that is turbulent. Eight are presented here to provide a sense of the direction in which strategy is moving. This so-called direction can be likened to multiple streams feeding a river. One stream involves leveraging core competencies to accelerate growth. Another involves guerilla warfare—moving quickly, taking advantage of opportunity, and rapidly cutting losses. And a third stream involves the reinterpretation of competition to create a new paradigm for organizational success.

Leveraging Core Competencies

Operational Effectiveness. This approach to strategic thought moves away from formalized strategy to concepts like time-based competition, TQM, and reengineering as part of a belief that incremental changes in execution and quality are the most meaningful sources of competitive strength. A distinction is made between operational effectiveness and strategic positioning to yield a short-term advantage. Operational effectiveness means performing the same activities competitors perform, only better. Practices like benchmarking, co-creation with customers and suppliers, and TQM, therefore, are used to gain an advantage over competitors by providing a service more efficiently or effectively. The problem is that the advantage will probably be only temporary. The rapid diffusion of best practices means that organizations can duplicate products and services quickly with copiers often becoming more successful than originators.

Pursuing a Value Discipline. In *The Discipline of Market Leaders* (1995), Treacy and Wiersema presented three *value disciplines*, or ways of delivering customer value—operational excellence, product leadership, and customer intimacy—that could be mastered by organizations to build a competitive advantage.[55] Organizations seeking to dominate markets were advised to choose one, and only one, of these disciplines or risk ending up in the middle with a hybrid model leading to confusion, tension, and a loss of energy.

Value Discipline	Value Proposition	Leading Organizations
Operational excellence	Guaranteed low price/great service	Dell Computer, GE, Wal-Mart
Product leadership	Best product	Microsoft, 3M, Disney, Intel
Customer intimacy	Tailoring products to customers	Nordstrom, Home Depot, IBM

Choosing a value discipline is critical because in so doing an organization is not only choosing a path to greatness, but also purposefully deemphasizing other possible paths. Leadership is about making the hard choices of value discipline: what the organization will stand for in its market and how it will operate to back up its promises. The decision to select a value discipline commits an organization to a path that it will remain on for years, if not decades.

Accelerating Growth. Growth is an important value proposition for strategy in a turbulent market. While operational excellence is an important driver of profitability, it does not necessarily drive growth. Competition has intensified so much in fast-moving markets that exceeding customers' expectations, continuously improving, and adapting to the changing market no longer ensure accelerated growth. Something more is needed and that *more* is strategy. In *How to Grow When Markets Don't* (2003), Slywotzky, Wise, and Weber argue that hidden liabilities prevent organizations from identifying and seizing attractive growth opportunities.[56] In any large organization, there are twelve hidden liabilities: organizational mind-set, culture and history, leadership and commitment, organizational structure, skills and capabilities, measurement and incentive systems, budgeting and resource-allocation processes, information systems, brand authority, customer readiness, investor resistance, and alliances. Two or three liabilities acting together are fatal to a growth initiative. Therefore, forward-looking organizations will seek to identify, quantify, and map liabilities so that middle managers can navigate around them and leaders can create an organizational system conducive to growth.

Guerilla Warfare

In *Strategy as Simple Rules*, Eisenhardt and Sull (2001) liken strategy to simple rules which enable organizations to move quickly and efficiently in a turbulent market.[57] In conventional strategy, advantage comes from exploiting resources or stable market positions. In the new economy, organizations must capture unanticipated, fleeting opportunities to succeed. The greatest opportunities for competitive advantage lie in market confusion. Successful organizations probe for openings, jump on opportunities, build on successful forays, and shift flexibly among opportunities as circumstances dictate. They recognize the need for a few key strategic processes and a few simple rules to guide them through the chaos. Key processes should place the organization where the flow of opportunities is swiftest and deepest. These processes might include product and service innovation, partnering, or new market entry. The simple rules provide guidelines within which managers can pursue opportunities. For example, Yahoo's simple rules keep managers just organized enough to seize market opportunities. By pursuing opportunity after opportunity, Yahoo has migrated from a catalog of Web sites, to a content aggregator, to a community of users. Lately it has become a broad network of media, commerce, and communication services. Using traditional, textbook notions of strategy, Yahoo would appear to lack a strategy. Underneath, however, its strategy is very simple: keep moving, seize opportunities, and finish strong. No one can predict how long an advantage will last in a fast-moving market. Leaders should manage, therefore, as if it all could end tomorrow. This is best done with a handful of rules and key processes.

In *Strategy as Improvisational Theater*, Kanter (2002) espouses a view of strategy similar to Eisenhardt.[58] New competitors and technologies pose uncertainties for organizations, including the possibility of radical change. Some organizations seize the opportunity to outpace competitors while others fall behind. Those that succeed use an improvisational model of strategy in contrast to the traditional scripted model. In the latter, the organization seeks to craft the best possible plan so that it can be handed off for a predetermined course of execution involving a predictable set of events and a specific goal. The scripted model resembles traditional theater: the play is carefully written, parts are cast, and actors practice roles until they meet expectations for quality and predictability. The play's action comes to an unvarying conclusion in each performance and, after a good run, a new play takes its place. The improvisational model throws out the script, brings in the audience, and trusts the actors to be unpredictable—that is, to innovate. Mistakes, wrong moves, and false starts are tolerated as long as the organization is moving ahead with new ideas. The goal of improvisation is to move fast and make corrections as necessary. Organizations that employ this approach often attempt to establish a "no penalty" culture in which people can admit that they had a poor idea and move on to the next one. Strategy evolves spontaneously through the interaction of people in an organization that is an arena for the pursuit of ideas and the staging of experiments.

In *The Living Company*, deGeus (2001) likens strategy to an organic metaphor.[59] As speed and global scale become the order of the day in most industries, the organization needs to become a functioning dynamic entity that can quickly read environmental cues, communicate these cues to the right people, and react with reflexive speed—just as living organisms do. Strategic insight can be exercised at the top, but the nerve endings and ability to act must exist throughout the organization. Only then can an organization move at the speed of its instinct. Strategic instinct, in biological terms, is the balancing of constancy and change. There are four processes of strategic instinct inherent in every organization that parallel the survival instincts of living organisms. They are (1) the selection of the best previous strategic initiative for replication, (2) management analyses comparing the selected initiative to current environmental conditions, (3) constant evaluation of the current level of success in strategy execution through instantaneous feedback loops, and (4) rapid surgery to excise mutants—people, processes, programs, or policies that are inhibiting the success of the strategy.[60] A number of strategic tools—SWOT (strengths, weaknesses, opportunities, threats) analysis, core competencies, the value chain—remain useful concepts to provide data for analysis, but they are not to be confused with strategy itself. Strategy in the context of organic metaphor is understanding the evolution of current successful initiatives while developing ever more sophisticated initiatives for change.

Reinterpretation of Competition

Competition between organizations has been a primary focus in the creation of strategy. What if conditions, such as intense competition, which encourage the adoption of strategy, expire and another set of conditions takes their place? Theorists, such as James Moore in *The Death of Competition* (1996), argue that in today's economy, innovation wins.[61] Virtually all organizations can achieve financial rewards and success if they create innovative products, services, and processes more efficiently and effectively than competitors. But this does not happen easily. Innovation requires support for implementation. And the more radical an innovation, the more deeply and broadly must other players, especially customers, become involved. This places a premium on learning how to manage a wide community or network of organizations, in which the players share a vision about how to make an innovation happen. Cooperation is more important than competition, and organizations that succeed will understand that the network is as important as the organization itself.

IMPLICATIONS FOR COLLEGES AND UNIVERSITIES

The evolution of strategy in contemporary organizations has involved a search for a single theory to explain success and failure. Theorists have developed discernible perspectives and leaders have moved to adopt models to guide their strategic thinking—whether it is Porter's five forces model, Prahalad and Hamel's focus on leveraging core competencies, Hamel's strategy as periodic revolution, or the strategy du jour served up by a constant stream of new and insightful theories. In recent years, strategy has followed a more practical path. Leaders seeking tangible and timely results have migrated to value propositions like "operational excellence" or "simple rules" to fit their organizations to changing circumstances. On the surface, these approaches to strategy appear to diverge. Upon closer inspection however, they can be seen to converge around the concept of "advantage." Each of the major strategy perspectives and the emerging paradigms is really a different way of achieving a market advantage.

This leads to the first observation concerning implications of the strategy literature for colleges and universities. To succeed, an *organization must know where it stands in relationship to alternative providers in the same industry*, whether the organization is in a position of market advantage, disadvantage, or equilibrium. This is especially true of colleges and universities facing aggressive competitors in the knowledge industry. Strategy is essential to market advantage in this industry. As such, it involves a pattern of thinking that encourages leaders to address the questions that are essential to every organization's success. These questions, raised in the introductory chapter, are repeated here to underscore the importance of strategy in seeking market advantage: (1) Who are the stakeholders and what do they want? (2) What kind of value is being created for these stakeholders? (3) Does the value created lead to market advantage by differentiating the organization from its competitors? and (4) Is the advantage sustainable? As purveyors of education in the highly competitive knowledge industry, colleges and universities are not exempt from these questions. Answering them should be a part of every institution's business.

A second observation concerns the *array of strategy perspectives available to organizations in the form of systemic models or specific paradigms*. The American postsecondary education system is remarkably diverse. One size does not fit all, and the availability of multiple strategy perspectives that can be adopted by institutions with different histories, purposes, and goals presents a rich opportunity for leaders to blend context and strategic perspective in making a decision about the most effective use of strategy. Any and all of the major strategic paradigms have a utility on college and university campuses. The challenge is to recognize the differences among the paradigms and the circumstances in which they are appropriate.

Finally, all of the strategy perspectives described in this chapter *focus on the big picture involving the relationship between an institution and its external environment.* The overarching position of the institution in time, place, and cultural context is the focus. After strategy is created, it must be supported by appropriate actions to help an institution achieve its goals. However, these actions are not strategies, they are tactics and their larger purpose and practical use needs to be clearly understood. Strategy is most easily distinguished from tactics by asking and answering a series of questions. These questions and how they are used to create strategy are the subject of the next chapter.

NOTES

1. Susan Segal-Horn, ed., *The Strategy Reader* (Oxford: Blackwell, 1998), 10.

2. Alfred D. Chandler, *Strategy and Structure: Chapters in the History of the Industrial Enterprise* (Cambridge, MA: MIT Press, 1962), 16.

3. Michael E. Porter, *Competitive Strategy: Techniques for Examining Industries and Competitors* (New York: Free Press, 1980).

4. Ellen E. Chaffee, "Three Models of Strategy," in *Organization and Governance in Higher Education*, ed. M. W. Peterson (Needham Heights, MA: Simon and Schuster, 1991), 225–226.

5. The work of Ellen E. Chaffee was of considerable value in identifying and modeling different perspectives on strategy. The framework used to chart unique strategy perspectives was derived from Chaffee's approach to analysis in "Three Models of Strategy."

6. Ibid., 226–227.

7. Alfred Sloan, *My Years with General Motors* (London: Sedgewick and Jackson, 1963).

8. See, for example, Christopher Bartlett and Sumantra Ghosal, "Changing the Role of Top Management: Beyond Strategy to Purpose," *Harvard Business Review*, November/December 1994.

9. The framework and concepts descriptive of the Rational perspective were adapted from Chaffee, "Three Models of Strategy," 226–228.

10. Chandler, *Strategy and Structure*, 13.

11. Seymour Tilles, "How to Evaluate Corporate Strategy," *Harvard Business Review*, July/August 1963, 111–121.

12. Igor Ansoff, *Corporate Strategy: An Analytic Approach to Business Policy for Growth and Expansion* (New York: McGraw-Hill, 1965).

13. Kenneth Andrews, *The Concept of Corporate Strategy* (Homewood, IL: Dow Jones-Irwin, 1971).

14. Chaffee, "Three Models of Strategy," 227–230.

15. Ibid., 232.

16. For a discussion of path dependency, see Pankaj Ghemawat, *Commitment: The Dynamic of Strategy* (New York: Free Press, 1991). The illustration from the aviation industry is adapted from the Academy of Management, "A Review and Synthesis of the Theory of Strategy," in AOMonline, www.aom.pace.edu/bps/Papers/Thesis/2/2.html, 11.

17. Richard W. Oliver, "The Red Queen Rules," *Journal of Business Strategy* (May/June 1999): 8–10.

18. James C. Collins and Jerry I. Porras, *Built to Last: Successful Habits of Visionary Companies* (New York: Harper Business, 1994).

19. The work of Joseph H. Boyett and Jimmie T. Boyett, *The Guru Guide: The Best Ideas of the Top Management Thinkers* (New York: John Wiley and Sons, 1998), 175–232, provided helpful insights into differentiation in strategy perspectives and approaches to thought among strategy architects. The distinctions drawn by Boyett and Boyett were used to guide the approach to analysis in portions of this chapter.

20. Gary Hamel and C. K. Prahalad, *Competing for the Future* (Boston: Harvard Business School Press, 1994).

21. Ibid., 15–24.

22. Gary Hamel, "Strategy as Revolution," *Harvard Business Review*, July/August 1996, 69–82.

23. W. Chan Kim and Renee Mauborgne, "Strategy, Value Innovation, and the Knowledge Economy," *Sloan Management Review* (Spring 1999): 41–54.

24. Chaffee, "Three Models of Strategy," 228–230.

25. Charles W. Hofer, "Some Preliminary Research on Patterns of Strategic Behavior," *Academic Management Processes* 33 (1973): 46–59.

26. R. P. Rumelt, "Evaluation of Strategy: Theory and Models," in *Strategic Management: A New View of Business Policy and Planning*, eds. D. E. Schendel and C. W. Hofer (Boston: Little, Brown, 1979), 196–212.

27. Porter, *Competitive Strategy*.

28. Ibid.

29. The framework and concepts descriptive of the adaptive perspective were adapted from Chaffee, "Three Models of Strategy," 228–230.

30. Ibid., 228.

31. Henry Mintzberg, *The Rise and Fall of Strategic Planning* (New York: Free Press, 1994).

32. See, for example, C. K. Prahalad and Gary Hamel, "The Core Competence of the Corporation," *Harvard Business Review*, May/June 1990, 71–91.

33. Ibid.

34. Ibid.

35. Hamel and Prahalad, *Competing for the Future*, 85.

36. George Stalk, Philip Evans, and Lawrence Shulman, "Competing on Capabilities: The New Rules of Corporate Strategy," *Harvard Business Review* March/April 1992, 27–39.

37. Hamel and Prahalad, *Competing for the Future*, 110–111.

38. See, for example, Richard Rumelt, *Strategy, Structure and Economic Performance* (Cambridge, MA: Harvard University Press, 1974).

39. Raphael Amit and Paul Schoemaker, "Strategic Assets and Organizational Rent," in *The Strategy Reader*, ed. Susan Segal-Horn (Oxford: Blackwell, 1998), 201–219.

40. Ibid.

41. Ibid.

42. Henry Mintzberg, "Crafting Strategy," *Harvard Business Review*, July/August 1987, 53–63.

43. See, for example, Mintzberg, *The Rise and Fall*, 23–27.

44. Mintzberg, "Crafting Strategy," 63.

45. Ibid., 53–63.

46. Mintzberg, *The Rise and Fall*, 23–29.

47. Mintzberg, "Crafting Strategy," 53–63.

48. Edward O. Wilson, *Sociobiology: The New Synthesis* (Cambridge, MA: Belknap Press of Harvard University Press, 1975).

49. Bruce D. Henderson, "The Origin of Strategy," *Harvard Business Review*, November/December 1989, 139–143.

50. Ibid.

51. Michael E. Porter, "The Competitive Advantage of Nations," in *Strategy: Seeking and Securing Competitive Advantage*, eds. Michael E. Porter and Cynthia A. Montgomery (Boston: Harvard Business Press, 1991), 135–169.

52. Ibid.

53. Ibid.

54. Ibid.

55. Michael Treacy and Frederick Wiersema, *The Discipline of Market Leaders: Choose Your Customers, Narrow Your Focus, Dominate Your Market* (Reading, MA: Addison-Wesley, 1995).

56. Adrian Slywotzky, Richard Wise, and Karl Weber, *How to Grow When Markets Don't* (New York: Warner Books, 2003).

57. Kathleen M. Eisenhardt and Donald N. Sull, "Strategy as Simple Rules," *Harvard Business Review*, January 2001, 107–116.

58. Rosabeth Moss Kanter, "Strategy as Improvisational Theater," *Sloan Management Review* (Winter 2002): 76–81.

59. The organic metaphor is best described in the work of Arie deGeus, *The Living Company* (Boston: Harvard Business School Press, 1997).

60. Ibid.

61. James Moore, *The Death of Competition: Leadership and Strategy in the Age of Ecosystems* (New York: HarperCollins, 1996).

CHAPTER

Breaking Strategy into Manageable Parts

Behind every successful organization, there is a strategy—a path chosen by its leaders and stakeholders to deliver value in a way that differentiates the organization from competitors. The organization may have developed this strategy through systematic analysis, trial and error, intuition, or pure luck. No matter how it was developed, however, it is strategy that underlies the success of the organization. Even "lucky" strategies have a logic to them—a set of underlying principles. When leaders acknowledge that they have arrived at a successful strategy through intuition, it is possible to unearth—in retrospect—a logic behind the strategy.

Designing a successful strategy is never ending. Organizations which today have achieved success and have effective strategies may not be successful tomorrow. To maintain success, they must understand the underlying logic of strategy, a logic that operates in two realms: the present and the future. We are all familiar with the story of the frog who, when put in a pot of boiling water, jumps out. When the same frog is put in a pot of cold water and the water is slowly brought to a boil, it stays in the pot and dies. In the same manner, if an organization does not react to the constant changes taking place in its environment, it will find itself in a hazardous situation. An organization needs to create a fit with its current environment while remaining flexible enough to respond to, or create, changes in this environment. The trouble is that leaders often do not know what questions to ask. Strategic thinking is not a core managerial competency in many organizations, just as it is not in colleges and universities. Leaders hone their management capabilities by tackling short-term problems over and over again. Developing strategy and becoming familiar with its underlying logic is not a task that they face repeatedly. Consequently, they do not develop their capacity to think strategically. In fact, they often are unable to see beyond tactics, even when the environment demands more.

In this chapter, the logic underlying strategy and strategic thinking is examined.[1] The first section revisits the working definition of strategy presented earlier and describes its underlying logic. Next, a model is presented that breaks strategy into manageable parts. This model is comprised of both a progression of questions and a gathering of information to answer them. Different frames for strategy are described, and tactics for implementation are examined. Leaders can use this model to guide the process of strategy formulation and implementation on their campus. More importantly, they can use it to continually assess their institution's direction, thereby cultivating both their own competence in strategic thinking and their understanding of the interplay between strategic decisions and the market. In the closing section, an example of a fully articulated strategy, which follows the progression of the model, is provided.

THINKING STRATEGICALLY

College and university leaders routinely experience the sense of being left behind. Their institutions are being pushed to become more efficient, to adopt the latest technology, to embrace change, to get ahead of the competition, to move faster. "Do more with less" and "work smarter" they are told and, while you're at it, develop a clear and compelling map of where your institution is headed.

Building a map of the future is important for any organization. A map, however, is only as good as the information on which it is based and the thought process underlying its construction. Strategic thinking about the institution and the environment is the basis for such a map. Strategic thinking is also the basis for strategy. Improving quality is meaningless without knowing what type of quality is relevant in competitive terms. Redesigning institutional systems is useless unless those systems and processes are aligned with the needs of stakeholders. Organizational change that is unguided by a strategic perspective is much more likely to fail than to succeed. And, contrary to common belief, a strategic plan is not a substitute for strategy. Plans developed by colleges and universities often lack critical information for developing a full picture of the competitive landscape.

To be effective, strategy must be created through a systematic process, because it cannot be separated from the approach to thought underlying its formulation. This process can be illustrated by using the definition of strategy provided in chapter 1. Strategy is a "systematic way of positioning the institution with stakeholders in its environment to create value that differentiates it from competitors and leads to a sustainable advantage." Important concepts in this definition are "positioning," "stakeholders," "environment," "value," "competitors," and "advantage." These concepts are not a random collection of building blocks, but a carefully considered system of interdependent parts. Any one of them alone is insufficient to formulate of strategy. When viewed in relation to one another as interdependent parts, however, these concepts lead to a series of questions the answers to which form strategy: (1) What forces are at work in the external environment? (2) Who are the stakeholders and what do they want from the institution? (3) What kind of value is the institution creating for these stakeholders? (4) Does the value created lead to advantage by differentiating the institution from its competitors? and (5) Is the advantage sustainable? These questions can be broken down into key categories of information that goes into strategy.

Strategy requires systematically assembled information about

- *trends, forces, and conditions* in the external environment that impact the institution
- *competitors*, both known and unknown, seeking market share
- *stakeholders* served by the institution, both current and potential
- *value* created by the institution for its stakeholders
- *differentiation* in value created for stakeholders that distinguishes the institution from its competitors
- *advantage* over competitors that is created through differentiation
- *sustainability*, or the longevity of advantage

These constructs involve big-picture thinking about the institution, its relationship to its external environment and competitors, and potential or actual sources of advantage. Several categories are missing from this list that are important to strategy as well. They include information about the condition of the industry or enterprise the institution is part of, internal capabilities and resources the institution can use to meet competitive challenges, and alternative strategies, or frames, that it can pursue to create an advantage. These items are combined with those above to create a path for strategy as presented in Figure 3.1.

Figure 3.1
The Strategy Pathway

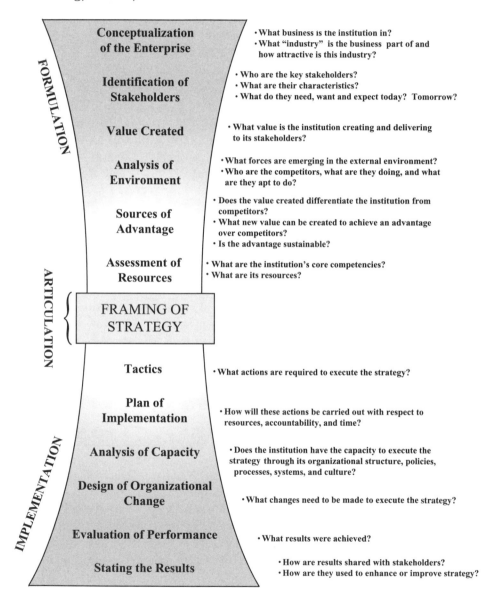

FORMULATION

Conceptualization
of the Enterprise

- What business is the institution in?
- What "industry" is the business part of and
  how attractive is this industry?

Identification of
Stakeholders

- Who are the key stakeholders?
- What are their characteristics?
- What do they need, want and expect today? Tomorrow?

Value Created

- What value is the institution creating and delivering
  to its stakeholders?

Analysis of
Environment

- What forces are emerging in the external environment?
- Who are the competitors, what are they doing, and what
  are they apt to do?

Sources of
Advantage

- Does the value created differentiate the institution from
  competitors?
- What new value can be created to achieve an advantage
  over competitors?
- Is the advantage sustainable?

Assessment of
Resources

- What are the institution's core competencies?
- What are its resources?

ARTICULATION

FRAMING OF
STRATEGY

Tactics

- What actions are required to execute the strategy?

Plan of
Implementation

- How will these actions be carried out with respect to
  resources, accountability, and time?

Analysis of Capacity

- Does the institution have the capacity to execute the
  strategy through its organizational structure, policies,
  processes, systems, and culture?

Design of Organizational
Change

- What changes need to be made to execute the strategy?

Evaluation of Performance

- What results were achieved?

Stating the Results

- How are results shared with stakeholders?
- How are they used to enhance or improve strategy?

IMPLEMENTATION

THE STRATEGY PATHWAY

Our organizational-development experience with colleges and universities supports a long-held belief in the importance of working with a simple and logical approach to any kind of new endeavor. Err on the side of simplicity and provide support through reinforcement, as opposed to miring staff in excessive detail and complexity. We have chosen to adhere to the lessons of experience and present a formula for strategy development comprised of three components: formulation, articulation, and implementation. These components are illustrated in Figure 3.1 with a step-by-step sequence that can drive the creation of strategy in any college or university.

Formulation

The formulation component is comprised of six steps in a progressive sequence leading to the articulation or framing of strategy. The first step is to identify the *business* the institution is in and the *industry* it is part of. A conventional description would be the business of "postsecondary education" in a "knowledge" industry, whereas a more ambitious description would be the business of "transformation" in an "experience" industry. Once the institution's business and industry have been determined, move to the next step: the identification of *stakeholders* served by the institution, both actual and potential. Who are the target audiences for institutional programs, services, and offerings today and who are they apt to be tomorrow? Clearly, students will figure prominently in the answer to this question, but so will entities such as business and industry employers, elected officials, schools and colleges, government agencies, and the like.

Knowing who the stakeholders are is only part of the equation. Equally important is knowing what they want and expect from the institution and what they receive from it. Benefits received in any form are known as *value*—a concept that is critically important in the strategy deliberations of an institution. Benefit (i.e., value) received can advantage or disadvantage an institution by distinguishing or failing to distinguish it from competitors in the quest for market share. For this reason *value* is the third step in the strategy sequence. It can best be understood in the form of the question: What value is this institution creating and delivering to its stakeholders?

But information about stakeholders and value means little without information about the institution's context. An important next step, therefore is to assess *forces and trends in the external environment* and the *nature of competition*: What forces are at work in the external environment? What effect will they have on the institution? Who are the competitors? and What are they doing or apt to do? In the process of scanning the environment and studying competitors, tough questions need to be asked about the position of the institution in the market: Is the value created and delivered by the institution different from that delivered by competitors? What new form(s) of value does the institution need to create to achieve an advantage? This information will provide a framework within which an institution's *capabilities and resources* can be assessed. The final step in the sequence is the determination of institutional capability. Does it have the capacity to create value that will lead to a sustainable advantage?

Articulation

Once the information, or the "ingredients" of strategy, has been gathered, the next stage in the strategy pathway is *articulation*, that is, to determine the approach to strategy or the "frame" that can most appropriately be used to achieve an advantage. An institution could attempt to establish an advantage by moving more quickly than competitors in the design and implementation of new programs. Its frame for strategy, or articulated strategy, would be *speed*. Another institution could choose to distance itself from competitors by opening up an array of new delivery options through continuous assessment of student needs. Its strategy-frame would be *convenience*. The possibilities are infinite, depending on circumstances inside and outside of the institution. And, as we shall explore in the next chapter, context is the foundation for strategy—it determines the frames that will work or will not work for an institution.

Implementation

The third and final component of strategy is *implementation*: the logistical component of strategic thinking. Formulation and implementation are obviously interdependent activities in strategy making. To come alive within an institution, strategy must be part of an orchestrated plan or a way of doing. Conversely, a plan of implementation without an articulated strategy to guide it is essentially meaningless. Strategy fails when thinking is disassociated from doing. For example, leaders talk about the importance of quality, but fail to provide operational definitions that enable it to be measured. Therefore, successful strategy depends as much on the tactics used to enact it as it does on the process used to formulate it. This means that the mundane activities commonly associated with implementation, such as the formulation of action steps, a timetable for action, accountability, achievement criteria, and assessment of performance, are not to be given short shrift. They are an essential part of strategy.

These components, and the sequence, or staging, of activities within them, are not new. They are rooted in strategic planning, where scanning and assessment are used to develop priorities for resource allocation. Illustrating them in the next section as part of a sequenced progression of activity leading to the creation and execution of strategy will help the reader to understand the "whole" as well as the various "parts" of strategy.

FORMULATING STRATEGY

Conceptualize the Enterprise

Defining an institution's business accurately is the first and most important action to take in strategy formulation. Colleges and universities traditionally have defined themselves as in the business of "higher or postsecondary education," which is part of a *credentialing* industry made up of degrees and certificates. As institutions have moved to more sharply define their business, the industry in which they are engaged has likewise shifted focus. Some institutions, for example, have chosen to define their primary business as knowledge production and dissemination, which is part of a *research and development* industry, or as human capital development, which is part of a *training* industry. Others have sought to broaden their base by indicating that they are in the business of learning, which is part of a *transformation* industry in which people are engaged, and their lives change. Colleges and universities engaged in learning depict themselves as connected with students in a personal, memorable way having less to do with credits awarded and progression toward a degree or award than with the merging of information, ideas, technology, values, and entertainment.

The way in which business is conceptualized has a lot to do with the industry the institution is part of and, ultimately, the selection and formulation of strategy. The credentialing and transformation industries have very different meanings for institutions and involve different approaches to competition and strategy. Technology and changing learner preferences have removed barriers to entry in the credentialing industry and made it more attractive to a wave of new competitors. The transformation industry has its roots in the worlds of health, business, and entertainment and is less well understood. The point is that the nature of the industry in which an institution is engaged is as important to its success as its position in the industry—a fact which leaders often overlook. A sound approach to analysis at this stage in strategy formulation should take into account how the industry might change in the future through the assessment of factors such as technological change, new competitors, government policy, and more. Key questions include

- What business is the institution in?
- What business could it be in?
- What business should it be in?
- What industry is this business part of?
- How attractive is this industry?
- What factors or conditions would make the industry more or less attractive?
- Could substitute providers, services, or processes enter and change the industry?
- What opportunities are present in this industry today?
- What opportunities will emerge tomorrow?

The starting point should be to articulate where the institution's efforts are currently focused. For example, a college can view its business too narrowly and concentrate on only a portion of an industry. At the same time, a college competing for market share can fall into the trap of viewing its business too broadly and squander its resources in an industry that is ill-defined. In a soundly conceptualized enterprise, the business of the institution is clear and the industry it is part of has scrutable boundaries that define the nature of competition.

Beyond the currently defined business of any institution is the business it *could, should, or should not* be in given available resources and opportunities. A liberal arts college, for example, could broaden its business to include workforce development by exploring a curriculum in the "applied liberal arts" developed specifically to meet the soft-skill training needs of employers. A community college might consider a "skilled trades academy" developed jointly with K–12 schools, local government agencies, and regional employers to get youth interested and engaged in trade careers at an early age. Reality takes over when an institution considers the business it should or should not be in. Broadening the conception of business may make the most sense for an institution with opportunities for substantial growth in a new market. Conversely, some opportunities involve risks that could adversely affect the core business of the institution. All of these factors are important in defining the business of the institution and, ultimately, the industry it is part of.

Identify the Key Stakeholders

Every institution has a series of stakeholders—also known as customers, constituents, users, clients, or beneficiaries—whose needs have to be satisfied. Stakeholders can be the initiators of transactions such as the faculty members delivering instruction or the staff providing a service, the primary beneficiaries of transactions such as the students receiving service, or the secondary beneficiaries of transactions such as employers hiring graduates. From a conventional standpoint, stakeholders are those who receive some form of benefit or value through service delivered by the institution. A partial list includes current and prospective students, parents, K–12 administrators and teachers, business and industry employers, local and regional elected officials, civic organizations, legislative/regulatory bodies, strategic alliance partners, communities in which colleges function, suppliers, and the general public. All are stakeholders and all receive some form of value from the institution.

Keeping the concept of the stakeholder squarely in front of the institution and determining the relative importance of each is fundamental to properly defining the business of an institution. A key stakeholder is someone—an individual, a group, or an organization—whose needs and wants the institution is in business to satisfy. In making this determination, it is important to work with the concept of stakeholders rather than markets in order to identify the tangible recipients of an institution's services. Getting a clear picture of who the stakeholders are, and the order in which their needs and wants must be satisfied, is a critical step in determining what strategy will or will not work. Key questions to be asked and answered in this regard are

- Who are the key stakeholders?
- What are their characteristics and needs—today? Tomorrow?
- In what order should their needs be satisfied?

Determining when and how stakeholder needs should be served requires that an institution learn about the precise dimensions of stakeholder wants, needs, expectations, and required performance. To do this, a college must gauge the expressed and unexpressed needs of its stakeholders through timely research. Think of a lost hiker trying to locate friends on an unfamiliar mountain at night. The hiker has two choices: wait until daylight (i.e., until stakeholders have provided conclusive evidence of their needs and expectations) or strike out in one direction in search of the main party calling out periodically in the hope of receiving a response. As each call goes out, a response or lack of response signals the accuracy of the direction to the hiker until the main party is found. Although waiting until daylight may guarantee that the main party is found, the hiker may run the risk of falling prey to a predator or experiencing inclement weather as the party moves further away. What counts most with stakeholders is not determining their needs on a one-time or first-time basis, but how quickly and accurately changing needs can be determined through continuous assessment. Little is learned about stakeholders in conversations with colleagues or in administrative meetings. True learning only occurs when a service is delivered to stakeholders and they are continually asked questions about their use of the service, their satisfaction with it, the value they assign to it, and their recommendations to make it better.

No one would disagree that stakeholder assessment is valuable and that every institution should engage in it. There is a problem with it, however. Stakeholder assessment is an intensive process the results of which may take months or years to realize in the form of gain for the institution. Thus, the practical problem of stakeholder assessment is how to reduce the time and expense associated with this lag between information and action—what could be called "service iteration." Speed of iteration refers to the time it takes an institution to design or redesign a program or service, launch it with stakeholders, accumulate insights from stakeholders about use and satisfaction, and adjust the program or service in accord with stakeholder feedback.[2] Other things being equal, a college with a twelve-month iteration cycle will be much more adept at meeting stakeholder needs than a college with a thirty-six-month iteration time.

Determine the Value Created for Stakeholders

A key element in strategy is the concept of value (outcomes, benefits, rewards, returns, etc.) created for stakeholders and whether or not this value is different from that delivered by competitors. Stakeholders are the ultimate judge of whether an institution's offerings satisfy needs. In formulating strategy, an institution should continually ask itself if a particular program or service makes a significant contribution to value as perceived by its stakeholders. Although most colleges and universities possess detailed cost breakdowns of their programs and services, few possess breakdowns of value received by different stakeholders. Questions to ask and answer include the following:

- What elements of value does the institution intend to deliver to its stakeholders through specific programs, services, and activities?
- What value are stakeholders paying for and expecting?
- Which elements of value are most important to stakeholders and make the largest contribution to their satisfaction?
- What value are stakeholders actually receiving?

In our experience, colleges and universities seldom penetrate the minds of stakeholders to uncover their unarticulated needs with respect to value. They almost always start with "what is" in terms of easily documented outcomes (e.g., GPA, program completion, graduation, withdrawal) in contrast to "what could be" in the minds of stakeholders. An incremental approach to assessment focused on easily measured outcomes in a world of profound change is unlikely to uncover new or hidden forms of value. This approach works well when the elements of value—verifiable assumptions about what stakeholders need and want, what they will pay for, and what will satisfy them—remain stable. But in postsecondary education, as in all industries, these elements are no longer stable. They are being altered by new competitors who have no stake in the past, and seismic shifts in technology, demographics, and the regulatory environment. Incremental assessment is well suited to the challenge of extending existing forms of value: improving convenience for students by making services available 24/7/365 on the Internet, for example. It is not well suited to the challenge of developing new forms of value: fundamentally changing the design of a program or service to deliver new value to students, for example.

The distinction between a traditional approach to assessment and one that would be designed to uncover new forms of value stands out starkly when one compares the elements of the two models:

	Incremental Assessment	Value-Based Assessment
Goal:	Improvement in current value provided by programs and services	Discovering entirely new forms of value desired by stakeholders
Process:	Formulaic: starts with What is?	Exploratory and open-ended: starts with What could be?
	Existing conceptions of value are the baseline	An understanding that hidden forms and new sources of value are the baseline
	Seeks fit between existing conceptions of value and current resources	Puts resources aside and seeks to enlarge horizons
Resources:	Selected administrators and assessment personnel	Faculty and staff throughout the institution
	Few experts	The collective wisdom of the institution

A value-based approach to assessment will enable colleges and universities to more fully understand the value they deliver to stakeholders. It will help them distinguish between an "academic conception of value"—the value intended through programs and services, and a "stakeholder conception of value"—the value of programs and services as perceived by stakeholders. There is a big difference in these conceptions, and understanding the latter is a critical to formulating a successful strategy.

Analyze the Environment

Understanding the nature and intensity of driving forces in the external environment, both current and emerging, is also a necessary precursor to formulating strategy. Without an understanding of these forces, leaders frequently end up formulating a strategy based on internal and operational needs rather than external and strategic perspectives. To quote Tregoe and Zimmerman in *Top Management Strategy* (1980):

> The operations palliative, if taken alone, is dangerous medicine for treating a crisis or change which could threaten the survival of the business. If an organization is headed in the wrong direction, the last thing it needs is to get there more efficiently. And if an organization is headed in the right direction, it surely does not need to have that direction unwittingly changed by operational action taken in a strategic void.[3]

Driving forces include trends in the external environment and the actions of competitors that are likely to have a major impact on the institution.[4] Analysis of these forces should move beyond standard examination and dialogue about market trends and the information gathered from competitors' Web pages, to understanding the basics of strategy. What kind of forces are, and will be, at work in the market? What will their impact be on the institution? What are competitors thinking and what are their likely future moves? What competitive challenges can the institution anticipate in the long term?

The makeup of the environment depends on the forces outlined in Figure 3.1. The strongest environmental force or forces, in combination with the mission, competencies, and resources of a given institution, will shape the approach to strategy that will ultimately be successful.

Rapidly Changing External Forces

Colleges and universities are surrounded by change and upheaval. Consider the array of change forces facing institutions and leaders at any point in time: demographic transition, shifts in values, globalization, volatility in economic markets, labor-force transitions, advancing technology, shifts in federal and state responsibilities and funding priorities, changing roles and relationships among educational providers, the privatization of public services, new funding mandates associated with safety and security, the changing regulatory environment, and many more. These change-forces are interwoven and are accelerated by the blurring of boundaries between domestic and international spheres in an interconnected world; policy arenas; and public, private, and nonprofit sectors.[5] The result is a world in which no organization or institution has a monopoly on anything, and yet many are involved or affected or have a responsibility to act. Porous boundaries and increased ambiguity are part of this world. The combination of fast change and ambiguity in a world in which boundaries have little meaning requires institutions to monitor forces of change in the environment as never before.

There are a number of questions about the external environment that colleges and universities need to ask in strategy formulation. These questions are big and small, global and regional, and quantitative and qualitative in nature. Ultimately, however, everything in the external environment that institutions must understand boils down to four basic questions: (1) What are the key forces in the external environment that will impact the institution now and in the future? (2) What changes are happening, or can be anticipated to happen, in student and stakeholder needs? (3) Who are the actual and emerging competitors? and (4) Who are the key resource providers now and in the future? In this section, the focus is on environmental forces—those external factors other than stakeholders and competitors that the institution cannot control. The remaining questions will be picked up in the sections to follow.

Key indicators describing forces of change in the external environment can be classified into five categories as presented in Table 3.1. It is important to note that this list does not include every category of information that is salient in environmental scanning. Short by design, it focuses on indicators with the most pervasive impact on institutions, most of which are within easy reach of researchers and planners on the Internet. Other sources of published information, in addition to the Internet, include government agency reports, regional and national forecast data, news media accounts, and research reports and statistical summaries developed by for-profit organizations. Sources of unpublished information include summaries of focus-group meetings and interviews, syntheses of large group meetings, and the results of specially prepared surveys.

Members of a college or university governing board are often better at identifying and assessing external forces (particularly those that are insidious or based on insider information) than are faculty and staff.[6] This is partly due to a governing board's responsibility for relating an institution to its external environment and vice versa. Unfortunately, neither governing boards nor college staff usually do a systematic or effective job of external scanning. As a result, many institutions are like ships trying to navigate turbulent waters without benefit of navigating tools.

Jockeying Among Current Competitors

Competition among traditional providers takes the form of jockeying for position, using tactics like convenience, cost competition through discounting, program and service innovation, disruptive practices in educational delivery, and marketing. Competition is intensifying because the number of institutions offering more and different options for postsecondary education is increasing. Further, the balance of power among institutions is more evenly distributed, and the programs and services they offer are more alike than they are different. As a result, colleges and universities offering equivalent services are trying to separate themselves from one another in the hunt for students and resources, but in a manner that involves minimal risk. Competing on traditional criteria can become costly for a college lacking unique attributes or a distinctive place in the market. As institutions leapfrog one another through serial inno-

Table 3.1
Key Indicators Describing the External Environment

Categories of Information	Form of Information	
	Published	Unpublished
Service Area Population		
Growth or decline	X	
Change in composition	X	
Economy/Labor Market		
Trends in key economic indicators	X	
Job projections by occupational category	X	
In-migration and out-migration of business and industry	X	X
Trends in regional employer needs	X	X
Technology		
New product development	X	X
Partnerships and networks for cost sharing	X	X
Systems for training and internal capacity building	X	X
Education		
Enrollment projections in K–12 schools	X	
K–12 graduation rates and trends in college attendance	X	
K–12 student perceptions of college, academic skills, and needs for assistance	X	X
Technology skills and usage patterns of K–12 students		X
Trends in adult learner needs for postsecondary education	X	X
Opportunities for partnering in educational delivery		X
Public Policy/Regulation		
Change in government spending priorities (e.g., national security)	X	X
Patterns and projections for public support of education	X	X
New and proposed legislation for education	X	X
Changing policies for state coordination	X	X
Trends in accreditation practices and standards	X	X

vation, the cost of creating an advantage exceeds the gain and the advantage is lost.

The state of competition among current providers can be sized up and understood through the analysis of multiple factors

- *Cost* (what students actually pay, factoring in the value of discounts)
- *Convenience* (ease of access to courses, programs, and services through flexible scheduling, fluid policies and systems)
- *Delivery* (the range of options available to students for educational delivery, e.g., distance learning, online classes, etc.)
- *Quality* (positively perceived features or attributes of an institution that distinguish it from competitors)
- *Innovation* (the capacity for new ways of doing things that alter existing rules of competition)
- *Systems, processes, and technology* (the flexibility and efficiency in systems and processes created through advanced technology)
- *Networks* (the synergy created by and for an institution through partnering with other organizations)
- *Administrative structure and governance* (the constraining or facilitating effect of organizational structure on institutional ability to respond to change in the environment)
- *Culture* (the extent to which culture enables or retards change within an institution)
- *Reputation* (the public esteem or regard distinguishing an institution from others in the industry)
- *Resources* (the assets available to an institution to improve capacity and performance)
- *Uniqueness* (the areas in which an institution is one of a kind or distinctively different from other providers in the industry)

While by no means exhaustive, these factors—individually or in combination—distinguish competing institutions from one another. Vying with rival institutions for students and resources through the attributes and resources listed above can be used to create advantage. This means asking questions about rivals: What are they currently doing with pricing, programs, and delivery systems to attract more and better students? What are they apt to do in the future? What will be the impact of disruptive practices in these and other areas in the market? What will we need to do to match or exceed the performance of rivals?

Where and how do institutions acquire information about rivals? There are multiple sources of information ranging from routinely available published reports to participating in competitors' systems. Institutional marketing publications, Web sites, institutional research reports, state-agency statistical reports and federal data can be used to gauge enrollment strength and market share. Newspaper clipping services and information generated by media in competitors' home locations can be used to gauge current and future capacity and the nature and direction of long-term plans. The customers served by competitors and competitors' vendors and suppliers are excellent sources of information about their current and future strategies, as are their marketing consultants. Former employees are also prime sources of information. Finally "shopping the competition" by participating in their internal systems, enrolling in courses, or using a rival's services and technology can provide useful information.

New Players

New players such as online providers, corporate universities, and for-profit colleges bring new capacity and a desire to gain market share to the competitive arena. Companies diversifying through acquisition into postsecondary education from other markets often leverage their own resources to achieve early success and are particularly adept at altering the rules of competition.

Like the proverbial new kid on the block, the potential for the entry of new players depends on barriers which encourage or discourage entry. If barriers to entry are high and a newcomer can expect stiff competition from established players, careful consideration will go into a decision on market entry.[7] Barriers that in previous years have discouraged entry into the postsecondary education market include the start-up cost of doing business, capital requirements, access to enrollment markets, economies of scale, accreditation and regulatory requirements, and student identification with traditional postsecondary institutions. Some of these barriers have been removed through technology, which reduces the need for investment of large-scale resources in fixed facilities and unrecoverable expenditures such as staffing and equipment. Others have been removed through partnering and collaboration, which have opened enrollment markets to new providers and the changing value of convenience for students, who increasingly view time as a critical resource. Online courses and the availability of 24/7 service on the Internet have expanded the array of options for students and opened the door to new patterns of course taking, packaging of credits and degrees, and relationships with institutions. As convenience has become more and more important, brand identification with institutions offering less convenience has begun to change and new patterns of student loyalty to emerge.

The perceived ease with which a new player can enter and achieve early success in a specific market will also have a lot to do with their decision to enter. Conditions for entry are favorable if the program, service, or delivery mode offered by a new player is uniquely different from that of established providers and/or it is believed to be attractive to students. Conditions are unfavorable if incumbents have previously overcome competitive threats or if they have substantial resources to fight back including extensive human and financial resources, partnering organizations, technology, political clout, a risk-embracing culture, and marketing channels to students and stakeholders that sustain deep loyalty.

From a strategic standpoint, barriers to entry are always changing in a turbulent market. Increasing interest on the part of adult learners and companies in the credential or certification for certain types of work, for instance, has opened up a new venue for career access and reduced the impact of the degree in specific fields. It is not surprising, therefore, that new players offering credentials in Web and software design, project management, physical therapy, and the like have entered the market. Conversely, timely strategic decisions involving a large segment of traditional providers can discourage new players. For example, the actions taken by a number of colleges and universities to offer a growing volume of courses and entire degree programs online as well as to make self-accessing services available on the Internet has undoubtedly discouraged or confined the competitive efforts of some newcomers. Similarly, efforts made by a growing number of institutions to streamline internal processes and systems, which has led to faster cycle times on course and curriculum development, have neutralized a key marketing ploy of new players: the time lag between information and action in traditional institutions.

Bargaining Power of Students and Stakeholders

Students and powerful stakeholders, such as business and industry employers and lawmakers, can exert bargaining power on colleges and universities by demanding higher quality or more and better service, and playing these institutions against each other—often at the expense of their operating revenues.[8] Students can become a potent force when the program and service offerings of institutions located in proximity to one another are undifferentiated. Faced with multiple options, students can squeeze resources from an institution in the form of courses and credits taken elsewhere and applied toward a degree at another institution, or in services provided at low or no cost before and after enrollment, or through new initiatives that a college must undertake to keep pace with the market before it can do so with efficiency. Legislators and policy makers similarly can exert power in a buyer's market loaded with competitors and options. More players and more opportunity often lead to inefficiency—a formidable trump card for lawmakers in periods of economic decline.

Diminishing support from traditional revenue sources also can enhance the bargaining position of students and stakeholders. Student buying power increases as institutional dependence on tuition rises in periods of economic downturn. When students can pay full cost, institutions may not adhere as rigorously to high standards in admissions and intake as they would be when operating with more resources. This is true in liberal arts colleges, when increasing tuition cannot be offset by proportional increases in discounting and in public colleges and universities when significant increases in tuition are required to offset rising expenditures.

Finally, students can exert power if they are part of an interest group requiring special attention or they can provide exceptional value to an institution in the form of academic credentials or unique accomplishments. When students are targeted for special consideration in admissions and retention for reasons such as historic underrepresentation, changing demographics, legislative mandate, or exceptional skills or accomplishments, institutions will more readily tailor academic and nonacademic services to meet special needs. Savvy players in favored groups can seek information from institutions about special services and benefits and use them to their advantage in the process of college selection.

A choice about which student markets to pursue and which stakeholders to satisfy should be viewed as a critical strategic decision. A college can improve its strategic position by concentrating on those students and stakeholders who possess the least power to influence it adversely. Questions that should be asked and answered about student markets include

- What student markets, interest groups, and stakeholders are currently most important to the institution?
- What kinds of bargaining power can these groups actually and potentially use?
- Are these groups different in the bargaining power they can use?
- Are important attributes of the institution—programs, services, delivery systems, etc.—distinctive enough to negate or neutralize student bargaining power?
- Under what conditions does bargaining power become excessive and require intervention?

- What student and stakeholder groups provide the greatest value to the institution because they possess the least power to influence it adversely?

Potential for Disruption and Discontinuity

By changing the way business is conducted or the rules of competition, discontinuities such as disruptive technology and the actions of a maverick competitor can alter the direction and tempo of an industry.[9] A competitor using sophisticated technology and a revolutionary design for service delivery could launch an entirely new approach to marketing and student recruiting. A new force in instructional delivery could emerge in the form of an individual or "teaching cartel" with content expertise in a high-demand field working outside of traditional organizational boundaries with direct support from a receiving organization. What institution or group of institutions, for example, could prevent a knowledge expert from establishing an independent business for the delivery of world-class instruction in business strategy in cooperation with ten global corporations? Research and teaching universities would need to upgrade the quality of their graduate programs in business or differentiate them somehow to avoid facing the prospect of a decline in competitive capacity and possibly prestige.

Generally, the more significant the advantage created by a discontinuity, the more passionately it will be pursued by a provider. Discontinuities that command attention from providers are those that are (a) easily and efficiently implemented and (b) capable of yielding immediate benefits. They are most effective in high-demand markets served by slow-moving institutions, which are vulnerable to competitors playing by a different set of rules.

Determine Sources of Advantage

An essential step in strategy is the leveraging of information into ideas or themes that can be used to create a niche or advantage for an institution. The terms *niche* and *advantage* are used interchangeably because they have roughly the same meaning for institutions in a turbulent market. They refer to the reality of competition and the importance for any institution of establishing a clear presence for itself in the minds of stakeholders. This can be accomplished by using information gathered about stakeholders and forces in the environment to identify areas in which the institution can differentiate itself from competitors. In other words, areas in which the institution can create an *advantage* over competitors.

To understand the concept of advantage and how it can be sought and achieved, it is first necessary to deconstruct the concept. A competitive advantage can be divided into two basic types: greater operational efficiency and lower cost than competitors, or the ability of an institution to differentiate itself from competitors in such a way as to justify higher cost.[10] A high-performing college has established one type of advantage or the other, or both, over competitors. To say it another way, superior performance is realized by doing something better than competitors or doing it as well at a lower cost or with greater efficiency. "Doing better"—differentiating an institution from its rivals—can take many forms: offering higher quality programs and services (depending on the operational definition of quality), offering more convenience to students, responding more quickly to student and stakeholder needs, generating better outcomes for students in work and further education, exceeding the performance of competitors in meeting business and industry needs for skilled workers, and so forth.

The important point is that advantage cannot be determined without information about competitors and the scope of competition. Scope involves a number of dimensions, including: the breadth of the institution's mission and the student and stakeholder markets it serves, the geography of the service region in which the institution competes, its infrastructure, and the attributes of rivals competing for market share in the service region. Competitive advantage is attained within a defined scope—or *context*—that effectively shapes the options an institution can pursue in establishing an advantage.[11] For example, a selective liberal arts college engaged in heavy competition for market share in affluent metropolitan regions of the Northeast will probably not choose to compete on price, convenience, or breadth of offerings. A focus on favorable pricing in relationship to competitors could be perceived as indicative of lower quality, just as a focus on convenience and increasing breadth in offerings could be perceived as indicative of a need to stem declining enrollment. Conversely, a community college competing in the same market would view low price, maximum convenience, and a comprehensive array of offerings as absolutely essential for creating a competitive advantage. Context is central to strategy because it is a determining factor in the choices institutions have in pursuing and establishing advantage.

Questions that should be asked and answered to determine possible and actual sources of advantage are the following:

- What form(s) of advantage can logically be pursued given the mission and operating context of the institution?

- How does the institution compare to competitors regarding the advantages it has chosen to pursue? What does it do better than competitors or at lower cost?

- To what extent does superior performance—doing something better or at lower cost—differentiate the institution from competitors? Does the value created differentiate the institution from its competitors?

- What must the institution do better or at lower cost to achieve an advantage over competitors? What new value must the institution create to achieve an advantage over competitors?

- Is the advantage sustainable?

These questions make it clear that the essence of strategy is choice. There is no one way to pursue advantage—there are many ways, depending on the operating context of the institution. One or two forms of advantage can be attractive, in an absolute sense, and a variety of forms may be attractive depending on the operating context. Choice is essential, however, because there are logical inconsistencies in pursuing several forms of advantage simultaneously.[12]

Assess Internal Capability

The purpose of internal assessment is to critically examine the institution's infrastructure to identify strengths and weaknesses affecting its ability to achieve advantage. The major questions that need to be addressed are

- What are the institution's core competencies?
- What are its resources?
- What capability does it have to achieve new and additional forms of advantage?

The categories of information that should be examined at this stage are resources, processes, and performance. These categories are at the center of most management information systems so they certainly will not be new to staff. In our experience, plenty of quantifiable data is organized around these categories: enrollment, revenue and expenditures, student flow in processes and systems, cost, student needs and outcomes, and much more. Institutions generally have less command over qualitative information, which describes intrinsic attributes such as their culture, as well as important features of their strategic plan or strategy, and the effectiveness of operating systems. And they typically say little, if anything, about their outputs or the effects that specific outputs have on students and stakeholders. For example, colleges and universities say a lot about their programs and services, budgets, and staff, but usually say considerably less about the effect they have on stakeholders.

Table 3.2 presents a compendium of indicators that should be examined as part of an internal assessment:

Table 3.2
Critical Indicators Describing Internal Capability

Categories of Information	Form of Information	
	Quantitative	Qualitative
Resources		
Financial/operating and capital	X	
People/faculty and staff	X	
Core competencies	X	X
Culture		X
Facilities	X	
Technology	X	
Information	X	X
Networks/partnerships	X	X
Reputation	X	X
Uniqueness	X	X
Processes		
Vision and values	X	X
Strategy	X	X
Institutional comprehensive plan	X	X
Department and unit plans	X	X
Systems and processes	X	X
Policies	X	
Communication channels	X	X
Performance		
Enrollment	X	
Degrees conferred/degree completion rate	X	
Student retention	X	
Student success	X	X
job attainment and mobility		
further education		
civic recognition/elected office		
honors and awards		
Student satisfaction	X	X
Stakeholder satisfaction	X	X
Cost efficiency	X	

The primary objective in examining these indicators is to identify the resources and distinctive competencies that an institution can draw on to achieve an advantage. These are the capabilities, tactics, and actions which it is particularly good at or the resources (broadly construed) on which it can draw easily to perform well. Without a shared understanding of its resources and competencies, a college will not be able to fully use them. Thus, the degree of consensus that attaches to this understanding is perhaps the most rudimentary test of a college's capacity to use its competencies to achieve an advantage.

In most institutions, leaders and staff have a reasonably strong sense of "what we do well and not so well around here," but they may be unable to draw a link between specific competencies and the achievement of advantage. When we have worked with institutions to help them assess their internal environments and define their core competencies, what generally happens is that an orderly well-intentioned process becomes one that is haphazard and political. The first attempt typically produces a long "laundry list" of strengths and skills—things that individuals or groups, perhaps even the institution as a whole, do well. Every participant wants to make sure that his or her unit is represented on this list because inclusion acknowledges they are making an important contribution to the institution. Said another way, every participant wants to ensure that the activities he or she manages or participates in are regarded as important within the institution. The problem is that many, if not most, of these activities are not important when viewed in the context of the whole institution. A substantial amount of effort is required to disentangle the *overarching* institutional competencies from the services, unit functions, and skills embedded in them. Indeed, the issue of core—what is central or peripheral to the mission of the institution—is probably misunderstood by many.

ARTICULATING STRATEGY

Once having determined sources of advantage and resources and competencies that can be used to pursue it, an institution has the information it needs to articulate strategy. Articulation is the process of giving definition and meaning to strategy by putting it into words that effectively express what it is. This is accomplished through the use of a *frame*: a concept or construct that identifies what type of advantage the institution is trying to achieve. A frame can take the form of a measurable concept such as *cost*, a concept that is more abstract in meaning such as *quality*, or a grouping of concepts that carry a specific meaning such as *value for students in the form of unparalleled convenience*. The critical ingredient in a frame—what it must do—is to clearly identify the type of advantage an institution is trying to achieve. For example, will advantage be pursued in the form of excellence in a particular discipline or activity? Will it take the form of some kind of unmatched value the institution will create for students? Will it take the form of convenience or lower cost?

As a concept, advantage is interesting because it can develop inclusively or exclusively of competitors. When an institution chooses to serve as its own frame of reference, advantage is realized in the form of increasing stature with stakeholders between two points in time. When competitors enter the equation, they become the frame of reference and advantage is realized as a benefit, gain, or superior position achieved in relationship to other organizations. Using these positions as end points on a continuum, an institution can pursue advantage by (1) positioning itself favorably with stakeholders, (2) changing the rules of competition, (3) anticipating structural shifts in postsecondary education and positioning itself favorably, or (4) a combination of some or all of these approaches. These approaches to advantage do not equate to or correlate in any specific way with the literature-based perspectives on strategy presented in chapter 2. Advantage is the end goal of any and all perspectives on strategy. When expressed in the form of a frame, advantage integrates elements of the various strategy perspectives into a unique position or edge that an institution is trying to build. Simply stated, a strategy *frame* and *perspective* are two different things: one involves the act of creating an advantage and the other, a framework for organizing and synthesizing the literature.

Positioning the Institution

In this approach to framing strategy, an institution takes the current structure of its relationships with stakeholders and competitors as a given and matches its strengths and weaknesses to it.[13] Strategy is incremental because it involves the achievement of advantage by doing more or better than other institutions. Important in this regard is the task of locating aspects of performance that are, or can be, superior to competitors. Examples of frames for articulating strategy include:

Frame	*Incremental advantage is achieved over competitors by*
Cost	Delivering the same or better value to students and stakeholders at lower cost
Convenience	Saving students time and energy by making access to educational services easier, faster, and more convenient

Excellence	Offering programs and services to students that are consistently recognized as superior in quality
Superior Value	Generating economic and noneconomic outcomes for stakeholders that consistently exceed those of competitors
Operational Excellence	Delivering value to stakeholders in the form of time savings, reduced cost, and need-satisfaction through superior organizational processes and systems
Strategic Alliances	Developing competencies and conserving resources through alliances with organizations that result in more and better value for stakeholders
Paradox	Adapting to change more readily than competitors through simultaneously contradictory programs and services that permit quick response to changing market conditions

Knowledge of an institution's resources and capabilities and forces in the external environment will highlight areas where advantage can be achieved and where it will not be plausible. A community college committed to open access in a turbulent market, for example, would logically build its strategy around frames of cost and convenience. Research has shown that courses and services offered at low cost and convenient times and places have a lot to do with a decision to enroll in a community college.[14] Moreover, as new options become available to students through competitors playing by different rules, the student/institution relationship will invariably change, resulting in a buyer's market and greater sensitivity to student demands. Community colleges interested in growth will have little choice but to contain costs and make services more convenient, or face the prospect of declining market share. Low cost, maximum convenience, and breadth in offerings, therefore, are likely to be at the center of a community college's strategy agenda.

Conversely, a liberal arts college would be more likely to build its strategy around a frame of superior value. Value would be realized as a significant economic and noneconomic return on investment in education. Cost and convenience would not be anchor points on its strategy agenda because any effort to reduce the price of tuition or to make access more convenient might be perceived as a sign of enrollment difficulty or diminished quality. The expression "you get what you pay for" provides a telling insight into the strategy of liberal arts colleges. In the absence of empirical information about the relationship between cost and quality, higher cost must in some way be associated with higher quality in the minds of consumers.

Finally, the visibility and allure of elite research universities such as Michigan and Stanford illustrates the coupling of frames such as excellence and superior value to forge strategy. These universities dominate

the market through brand identification associated with traditional prestige, name recognition, and mass media appeal. A message of "excellence" is driven at stakeholders through multiple venues including
high-visibility research, successful athletic teams, faculties comprised of
world-class scholars, the academic credentials of students, the accomplishments of alumni, and the sheer magnitude of their physical facilities
and holdings. Superior value is realized in the form of prestige assigned
to the institution by stakeholders who benefit directly or indirectly from
its products. They include employers who flock to their programs to recruit the "best" graduates, citizens who vote individuals into elected office on the basis of academic background, corporate officers who send
employees to their business schools for executive development, graduate
schools that include the student's undergraduate institution as a criterion
for admission, and many more.

This is not to say that community colleges offer less value or have a
different commitment to excellence than liberal arts colleges or research
universities, or that liberal arts colleges have less to offer in convenience
than community colleges. It simply means that the different contexts in
which institutions operate have a lot to do with the way they frame strategy to achieve an advantage.

Changing the Rules of Competition

In periods of turbulence, institutions are more likely to pursue advantage by developing strategies that take the offensive. This posture is designed to do more than merely cope with changing external forces or
competitors; it is meant to alter the causes of change or the rules of competition.[15] The success of for-profit colleges in student recruitment and
intake illustrates the effect that bold tactics can have in a competitive
market. Over the past decade community colleges have dominated the
adult learner market where many proprietary colleges compete for a piece
of the action. A growing number of colleges have chosen to challenge
community colleges by changing the rules of student recruitment. They
have extended the admissions process into the homes and workplaces of
potential students. In the space of a ninety-minute visit with an admissions representative, a student will be informed of the status of his/her
application, the amount of financial aid that will be awarded, the sequence of courses that will be required to complete a degree and when
they can be taken as part of a guaranteed course schedule, the type of job
that he or she will be qualified for, and companies in which he or she is
likely to be employed because of working relationships established by the

college with regional companies. Education and work are connected and there is very little left to the imagination.

This approach to strategy involves advantage that can be achieved through transformation in contrast to incremental change. Examples of frames for articulating strategy by change in the rules of competition include:

Frame	Advantage is achieved by
Uniqueness	Offering unparalleled or one-of-a-kind programs and services that create a distinctive character for an institution
Nonlinearity	Developing novel approaches to educational design and delivery that rewrite the rules of competition because rivals cannot easily duplicate them
Serial Innovation	Continuous creation of new programs, services, and delivery modes heretofore unexploited by institutions

To further understand how transformation can lead to advantage, consider the impact that new competitors are having on postsecondary education. Sensing vulnerability in the organizational culture and delivery infrastructure of traditional colleges and universities, for-profit providers like the University of Phoenix, Quest Education Corporation, and Argosy Education Group are using a strategy of serial innovation to gain market share. Their assessment of traditional providers shows that faculty who are entrusted with authority over the curriculum and who are granted a voice in decisions make traditional institutions vulnerable to competition. Bartering and negotiation are needed to effect change and this works against the climate of innovation required to maintain a cutting-edge position in the market. For-profit providers take advantage of this lapse by cultivating a climate of innovation in which continuous development of new curricula, new program offerings, and alternative approaches to instructional delivery are used to attract learners and resources. The result—as is readily apparent in the increasing visibility of institutions such as the University of Phoenix—is dynamic growth in the for-profit sector often at the expense of traditional providers.

Exploiting Structural Shifts in Postsecondary Education

The evolution of postsecondary education as an industry is important strategically because evolution brings with it changes in the sources of competition and ways of doing business. In the program life cycle, for example, new programs and services are initiated, they are copied or duplicated by competitors, and differentiation declines as programs and services offered by early adopters and copiers mature. Colleges must find new ways of designing and delivering programs or face the prospect of losing market share to competitors who have successfully duplicated their programs. Consider the example of online instruction and support services. Advancing technology and changing student needs and proficiencies have coalesced to reduce the amount of capital needed to compete in postsecondary education. New providers using part-time instructors and advanced technology can deliver online courses to students anytime, anywhere, and in any format. "Speed" is the operating idiom of these providers—identifying needs and developing and delivering courses and services faster and more flexibly than competitors. New providers using this idiom are entering the industry in volume and intensifying competition by providing learners with more choices and more pathways for postsecondary education.

Selected frames for articulating strategy that seek to exploit structural shifts are:

Frame	Advantage is achieved by
Speed	Assessing learner needs and designing and implementing new approaches to program and service design and delivery faster than competitors
Stretch	Leveraging resources to generate higher levels of staff performance that lead to growth and visibility

Consider *stretch*. In most colleges and universities, knowledge of strategic aspects of management—external forces and trends, competitor behavior, innovation and change, and the like—is limited to senior administrators or those in contact with a wide array of constituencies. Faculty and staff in day-to-day contact with students carry knowledge of their craft and their operational responsibilities, but only rarely does their knowledge (and interest) extend to strategic management. Leaders who believe in stretch—leveraging the knowledge and skills of staff to accomplish the seemingly impossible—will find ways to raise staff awareness and aspirations by imparting strategic knowledge and skills to all staff in the institution.

One of us was attempting to explain the concept of stretch to the senior management team of a teaching university as part of a strategic planning retreat. Throughout the 1980s and 1990s this institution had experienced continuous growth in enrollment and operating resources. "Of course," interrupted one vice president, "you must realize that we are successful because we have a superb leadership team. Stretch is appropriate only when your team is marginal or weak." The executive was asked about the strategic awareness and skills of staff beneath the level of vice president. The point was made: A massive investment of time and energy would be required to correct the limited understanding, monocular vision, and turf-protecting behavior of staff tied to functional responsibilities. What made stretch difficult for this institution was not its achievement of growth, but that it had not developed a capability for future growth by stretching the capabilities of its faculty and staff.

IMPLEMENTING STRATEGY

> You give an order around here, and if you can figure out what happens to it after that, you're a better person than I am.
>
> Harry Truman

The purpose of implementation is to complete the transition from formulating strategy to putting it into action by incorporating it into operations. Articulating a strategy is not enough. Developing effective action plans, programs, budgets, time lines, and implementation processes that tie strategy to operations will bring life to articulated strategy and informed understanding to those responsible for execution. The most important outcome that leaders and staff should aim for in implementation is to convert the activities of numerous administrators, faculty, and staff into coordinated action. This will be accomplished by achieving a series of instrumental steps, which are briefly described below.[16]

An important first step in implementation is the timely *introduction* of the articulated strategy to staff throughout the institution. Typically, a broad repertoire of methods is needed to bring staff onboard or at least to get them to understand the strategy and why it is important to the institution. Upon learning about the strategy, individuals and groups will, of course, want to know "what does this mean for me? what will I be expected to do?" The next step, therefore, is the *identification of tactics* that will be used to actuate the strategy and the development of a clear understanding of what needs to be done when, why, and by whom. A simple and clear *plan of implementation* that anyone can grasp, a statement of objectives and actions, resource requirements, time line, accountability, and a description of desired outcomes will help.

A third step is *analysis of the institution's capacity* to execute the plan of implementation through its administrative structure, processes and systems, and its culture. Factors that act to facilitate and constrain implementation should be carefully considered and corrective actions identified. Is the structure of the institution flexible so that staff can independently carry out activities in support of the plan? Is the cultural makeup of the institution one that embraces or resists change? Do processes and systems readily lend themselves to redesign or are they cast in concrete? These are some of the questions that need to be answered as part of an effort to determine attributes of the institution that will help as well as those that will obstruct successful strategy implementation.

Fourth, implementation should also include a design or *description of things that must change* within the institution for strategy to be successful. What changes need to be made in the structure of administration, the way decisions are made, the design of processes and systems, the allocation of resources, the outlook of staff, and more to effectively implement the strategy? A clearly stated formative evaluation process will be necessary to help staff identify obstacles and steer over, through, or around them to achieve important changes in the early stages of implementation. A good formative evaluation will also provide information that can be useful in modifying the strategy later on.

A fifth step is the *development and use of summative evaluation measures* to determine the extent to which the strategy has actually been achieved. Summative evaluations generally differentiate between outputs and outcomes. Outputs are the actual actions, behaviors, programs, services, value, or other direct consequences generated by the strategy. Outcomes are the ramifications of those outputs, their larger meaning for stakeholders inside and outside of the institution. In other words, outputs are the substantive changes while outcomes include subjective interpretation.[17] Both are important in determining whether strategy has been effective in achieving desirable results.

Finally, the *results of evaluation need to be stated* and shared with staff. The statement of results should be organized in such a way as to (1) describe the outputs and outcomes of strategy on predetermined criteria, (2) identify areas in which the strategy met, exceeded, or fell short of intended goals, and (3) indicate changes that need to be made to make the strategy more effective including, if necessary, the development of a new strategy. Leaders and staff will need to be alert to built-in bias which occludes objective judgment of strategy. They should look critically at the outcomes of strategy and work to maintain viable elements of strategy, replacing them with better ones when necessary, or terminating them when they become outmoded.

The old saying that "the proof is in the pudding" aptly describes the importance of implementation in building a successful strategy. Strategy does not exist without effective implementation. For this reason, the closing chapters in this book provide hands-on information regarding methods and techniques that can be used to articulate strategy, to develop a plan of implementation, and to evaluate its effectiveness.

Strategy in Action

We will use the example of a hypothetical liberal arts college to illustrate how leaders and staff can go about the process of formulating and articulating a strategy up to the point of implementation. Traditional College (TC) is a less-selective, nonreligious liberal arts college located in the Midwest. It has a capacity of 1,500 students, but currently enrolls 950 students and has operated at this level for several years. The cost of attending Traditional is high, approximately $25,000 for tuition and fees and room and board. With significant discounting, the average out-of-pocket cost for students is $15,000. Although TC has not conducted in-depth research on trends in the market or competitors, it knows that enrollment is up for public institutions and that liberal arts colleges in the region are investing significant resources in marketing. Like all private colleges, TC depends on tuition for most of its operating revenue.

Facing challenges of underenrollment and intensifying competition, Traditional needs a strategy. The president and executive team have learned about strategy through participation in an executive seminar sponsored by a business school at a leading university. They know that the essence of strategy is finding a way to increase TC's visibility with student markets by differentiating it from competitors. They also know that there is a discernible logic to formulating strategy and a practical method they can use to get started. This method involves activities to conceptualize the enterprise, identify stakeholders, assess value created, analyze the environment, determine sources of advantage, and assess internal resources and capabilities that can be used to enact strategy.

Conceptualizing the Enterprise

The first step toward strategy taken by Traditional is to understand the scope of the enterprise. This includes determining what business it is in and the industry of which this business is a part. TC believes that its overarching goal is the growth and transformation of its students, rather than knowledge acquisition or skill development as certified in a degree. Its second goal is to provide students with credentials that will enable them to enter a professional field or pursue graduate education. Although the executive team holds conflicting beliefs regarding whether a degree provides an accurate measure of student learning and development, it realizes that society assigns value to degrees and credentials. It also realizes that postsecondary education is an attractive industry. More and more students are going on to college after high school, more jobs are requiring college degrees, and lifelong learning is a big business in a turbulent economy. The importance of advanced education and lifelong learning is self-evident to the executive team and it affirms Traditional's role in the postsecondary education enterprise as one of preparing students for living and working in a fast-changing world.

Identifying the Stakeholders

Most of Traditional's stakeholders are internal to the institution. It receives some funding from federal and state sources, but its accountability to government is limited to a few specific reporting requirements. The stakeholders with the most direct power and sway over TC are located inside the institution, in its market service region, and in the authority to govern vested in the board of trustees. Key stakeholders, therefore, are the board, administrators, faculty, currently enrolled students and parents, prospective students and parents, and alumni. Knowing who the stakeholders are is one thing. More challenging, however, is knowing what they want and expect and the resulting implications for the college. Using data on hand plus information gathered through focus group meetings with high school teachers, counselors, and its alumni, Traditional compiled the information about its stakeholders provided in Table 3.3.

An examination of each stakeholder group reveals that numerous gaps exist between what the college actually is doing and what key stakeholders believe it should be doing. The alumni remember their residential experiences at the college and yearn for the time when the dorms were filled to capacity, the atmosphere was lively, and the town seemed as though it was an extension of campus. Faculty, reeling from the combined effect of downsizing, minimal increases in pay, and an increase in the number of students with developmental needs, suffer from low morale. They desire stability, more courses to teach, more colleagues, more opportunities for innovation, and better pay. Students are frustrated by a visible decline in the upkeep of dormitories, poor cuisine, cancellation of class sections, and the lack of the vigorous residential experience they expected in college. Alumni want and expect substantial enrollment growth in the years ahead as well as continuous improvement in Traditional's academic reputation. K–12 personnel envision more students going on to college and expect a closer relationship with TC.

Table 3.3
Identification of Stakeholder Characteristics, Needs, and Desires

Stakeholder	Characteristics	Needs	Desire Today	Desire Tomorrow
Board of Trustees	• One-third of board members are TC alumni • Business owners and corporate executives • Mostly white and affluent	• Recognition • Social networking • Feeling of being involved and, for some, in control	• Financial stability • To govern the institution responsibly	• Increase enrollment and resources • Growth in reputation and visibility for the institution
Faculty	• Low morale due to declining numbers and poor salary program • Low workload • Small class size	• Job security • Sense of belonging • Autonomy	• More students • "Brighter" students • Higher pay	• More faculty • More support for more programs • Support for new courses
Students	• Mostly white and middle class • Very few first generation • Most work 10–20 hours per week on campus or in surrounding community	• To have a good experience • Classes to fulfill degree requirements • Money • Future income, job prospects	• Better cuisine • More flexible library hours • Better orientation programs	• New and innovative programs • Expanded job opportunities • More students
Alumni	• Mostly white and upper middle class • Reconnect with the college as time and resources permit • Perception driven by memories	• Recognition of/for achievement • Relive periodically the best years of their lives • Reconnect to the college	• Growth and visibility • Enhanced academic reputation	• More growth and visibility • Successful athletic teams • New buildings and attractive campus
K-12 Personnel	• Middle class • Conservative • Financially and personally secure	• More students going to college • Improved articulation	• Recognition and outreach from TC	• More recognition and outreach

Creating Value

Traditional College has identified its stakeholders and their needs. This is an important first step, but its contribution to strategy is minimal until information about these needs is considered in relation to information about the value that TC delivers to its key stakeholders: students and alumni, the Board of Trustees, faculty, and prospective students. What is this value and is it sufficient to distinguish Traditional from competitors? Through informal conversations with these stakeholders, the executive team sized up the "value equation" in the following way:

Students and Alumni. Traditional knows through periodic research and focus group meetings carried out with students and alumni that its residential experience and dedication to holistic development deliver value to students that other providers in the region cannot match. Students who engage in active learning in small seminar classes with gifted instructors and peers consistently describe this experience as the most important part of college life. It stays with them long after they leave, an oft-expressed sentiment by alumni in correspondence and gift giving.

Board of Trustees. The primary value provided to the board is an opportunity for networking. Most board members are successful small-business owners or corporate executives who are able to provide entrée to different venues for other members. Through this and other means, their feeling of importance is reinforced by professional and personal ties on the board.

Faculty. For instructors, value is realized in the form of an opportunity to teach in a learning community comprised of committed colleagues and eager students in the intimate setting of the small classroom. Informal dialogue and formal evaluations have repeatedly disclosed this sentiment, and it is the cornerstone of the relationship between faculty and Traditional.

Prospective Students. Traditional believes that it provides an unusual opportunity to students coming out of high school. Not only do these students have the opportunity to live and learn in an academic community devoted to holistic development, they can do so at an affordable price because of TC's discounting policies.

Analysis of the Environment

Traditional College has used quantitative and qualitative information to determine the value it delivers to key stakeholders, but it lacks a benchmark against which to gauge the meaning of this information. It does not have, for example, a sense of the external trends and forces that will emerge over the next decade and how they might impact postsecondary education. It does not know how student needs and interests will change and what this could mean for the value they will want and expect from education. It knows very little about competitors, particularly those that could emerge to challenge for market share in the years to come. To answer these questions and provide a framework for assessing its capacity to differentiate itself from competitors, TC must undertake an analysis of the environment.

As part of its recently completed accreditation process, TC created a five-year strategic plan that addressed important questions about forces in the environment and competitors. Eight forces emerged through an external scan, the most important of which were

- Continuing growth within regional community colleges and for-profit providers that could impact first and second year enrollment in the college
- New high-tech industries moving into the service area
- Prestigious research universities becoming the top choice of students from affluent families in the service area
- Students caring less about holistic development and becoming more concerned about the connection between education and work and achieving financial gain
- A continuing tendency in government to favor loans over grants and fellowships in financial aid legislation
- A growing population of special-needs students requiring access to postsecondary education
- Inadequate basic-skills preparation for a growing number of high school graduates
- A growing price imbalance among regional colleges, with Traditional overpricing its primary competitors and rivaling the price of elite research universities

These trends alerted the executive team to the possibility that Traditional was losing a growing portion of its enrollment to institutions it had not considered as competitors. In addition, the team realized that while the college's curriculum and degree offerings had remained static, the demands of the market had changed dramatically over the last decade.

TC's competitor analysis revealed more troubling signs of things to come:

Peer Liberal Arts Colleges

- Cutting-edge institutions are providing a unique educational experience to adult learners in the form of nontraditional programs, organized and delivered in a way that subsidizes traditional programs without sacrificing institutional core values.

- Competition for resources will increase as colleges continue to raise prices and search for more and larger gifts as a means to enhance discounting practices.

- The more aggressive colleges are using creative approaches to imaging and marketing to differentiate themselves from traditional competitors in the hunt for students.

Community Colleges

- These colleges are experiencing steady growth and are emphasizing attributes that students find attractive: easy and convenient access, low cost, flexible program and service offerings, comprehensive programs, and responsiveness to local business and industry needs.

- The formula of low price and personalized attention in small classes, with convenient access, and market relevance used by community colleges could sift off increasing numbers of high school graduates from first- and second-year enrollment in four-year colleges.

Elite Research Universities and Four-Year Competitors

- This sector is growing and increasingly able to underprice liberal arts colleges. It is perceived as offering a more comprehensive residential experience in the form of intercollegiate athletics, student organizations, and cultural and social events.

- The increasing size and breadth of research universities and regional teaching universities contributes to an aura of success that enables them to increase efficiency through scale; that is, it works to enhance their capacity to obtain resources to absorb more students while reducing per student costs.

Sources of Advantage

By analyzing forces and competitors in the external environment, TC has put in place the last piece of information it must consider as part of its value equation: the nature of the value it will need to deliver to students and stakeholders to be competitive. TC has acquired and carefully analyzed information about (1) the current value it delivers to stakeholders, (2) the extent to which this value is similar or different from that delivered by competitors, and (3) the impact that external forces and competitor behavior would likely have on stakeholder needs in the future. This information was distilled and synthesized into a description of the value that Traditional would need to achieve an advantage. In comparison to liberal arts colleges, it was determined there were few differences among institutions in perceived value. Overall, the liberal arts colleges had similar mission statements, academic programs, emphases on residential life, and even facilities. This means that TC would need to stretch and emphasize novel ideas and practices in order to deliver value ostensibly different from peer colleges.

Conversely, the value delivered by Traditional is quite different from that delivered by community colleges. In stark contrast to the business-like approach of these institutions, TC is committed to an integrated living-and-learning experience that is designed to prepare students for life. Students become part of a learning community, and most aspects of the college experience are designed to foster this understanding. For this reason, community colleges were eliminated from further consideration in determining sources of advantage.

Perhaps the most interesting area of comparison was with the elite research universities. Traditional realized it had heretofore been ineffective in demonstrating its value relative to larger, more visible, four-year institutions. Growing numbers of students were choosing similarly priced prestigious universities over TC and it was not hard to figure out why: high school students did not know enough about the benefits of an education at TC to make a decision to enroll. Based on these results, the leadership team determined that TC needed to discernibly differentiate its value from university counterparts. Factors that would help in this regard were its small class size (twelve to fifteen students in most classes), colleaguelike working relationships between students and faculty, instruction delivered by teachers whose sole focus is teaching as opposed to research, and a residential experience that is intimate and engaging.

Overall, TC saw the greatest need for differentiation with its liberal arts competitors and research universities. Armed with this insight, the leadership team went to work to find ways to create differentiated value in relationship to these competitors. Some of its initial ideas included:

Cost as a source of advantage: Increase the discount rate on tuition as a method for reducing out-of-pocket costs for students below the level of competitors.

Nonlinearity as a source of advantage: Offer a unique and compelling undergraduate experience for students through novel approaches to teaching and learning, residential life, and service delivery:

- Create a unique first-year orientation experience operating throughout the year.

- Develop a unique residential experience with faculty living in dorms; courses and curricula integrated with student life; and special programs designed to bring students into intensive contact with social issues as a regular part of residential life.

- Expand faculty engagement through nontraditional approaches to instruction, including student-guided educational experiences and student-created majors.

- Develop an advisement system that places students at the center of a team comprised of faculty, career-field or professional-school representatives, and student-development staff.

Strategic alliances as a source of advantage: Link students with business and industry careers through special programs with national and regional corporations involving job shadowing, internships, cooperative education, and collaborative career planning with business executives.

These ideas involved building an advantage by doing things differently than other colleges. Seemingly all were feasible, but a decision as to which would yield the best result would depend on Traditional's internal capacity and resources.

Assessment of Capability

Determining the capabilities and resources TC could direct toward different sources of advantage required a rigorous assessment of its financial and human and physical resources as well as its core competencies. After careful deliberation, TC listed the following five core competencies:

- Quality instruction delivered by outstanding teachers
- Personal attention from teaching-focused instructors
- Small class sizes conducive to a more engaged learning environment
- A true residential college experience
- A values-based educational experience emphasizing holistic development

These competencies were viewed as fundamental to the mission and functioning of the college and central to any plan it would develop to differentiate itself from competitors.

While the core competencies comprise areas of strength that Traditional can draw on in building its strategy, the resource component—the financial, capital, and human assets a college can invest in pursuing advantage—is critically important. An examination of physical resources provided hope for TC. Its classrooms and residence halls had been renovated within the past decade, and they were operating at less than capacity. In addition, the college had unused land that could be used for future expansion. Examination of its human resources provided a mixture of positives and negatives. Overall, the administration and board are committed to returning the institution to the glory of its past. They are exploring new alternatives and considering some changes (i.e., new programs) that would have been considered heretical in the past. However, not all of the faculty are on board with these ideas. While many are excited about the prospect of innovation, others have been scarred by the buyouts and pay cuts of the last five years and are only interested in keeping their jobs. An examination of financial resources was less than positive. TC currently has a marginal cash flow and a small endowment that is restricted to scholarships. One area of promise is the advancement department, where a newly reorganized alumni relations office is experiencing early success in eliciting donations from heretofore untapped alumni. TC has determined the core competencies and resources it can apply toward building an advantage, and it is now ready to develop and articulate a strategy.

Articulating Strategy

Traditional College has identified several areas in which it can build an advantage over competitors, but its competencies and resources will not allow the simultaneous pursuit of all of them. It does not have sufficient slack in its operating budget or the wherewithal in fund-raising to pursue advantage in the area of cost by revising its discount policy. Moreover, it has not cultivated relationships with the corporate sector that would enable it to develop timely and efficient partnerships with business and industry for linking students with careers. Based on these findings, TC has defined its strategy as one of nonlinearity: the creation and delivery of a unique and unparalleled educational experience to students.

To deliver a unique educational experience, college leaders had to first understand what unusual experience is and how it is created. In a spontaneous conversation with several social science instructors, the president discovered an interesting book that described the concept of experience in a way that might have value for the college. Although it was developed and marketed as a business publication, *The Experience Economy: Work Is Theater and Every Business a Stage*, by Pine and Gilmore (1999), describes experience as unfolding in different realms (entertainment, educational, engagement, and transcendent) involving varying degrees of engagement (passive and active or absorptive and immersive) and leaving different imprints on people. The book's thesis is that compelling experience, that which engages the senses through active participation, transforms people.[18] On a college campus, experience becomes compelling when activities like classroom learning, collaboration with teachers and peers, concerts, and athletic contests invite students to enter and participate, to return over and over, and to remember.

Turning to its core competencies—quality instruction, personal attention, small class size, a unique residential environment, and a values-based educational experience—TC determined that with changes in its approach to classroom instruction and residential life, it could deliver experience to students that would differentiate it from competitors. It would implement this strategy using three tactics: (1) unusual approaches to classroom learning carried out by a critical nucleus of instructors in academic departments, (2) a uniquely student-centered approach to advisement and support services, and (3) living-and-learning programs in residence halls that bring students, faculty, and social issues together as part of everyday living.

CONCLUSION

Traditional College offers the quintessential example of strategy formulation in higher education. The clearly contextual process is uniquely specific to the institution. The strategy for achieving advantage will vary among institutions, depending on their internal environments and external challenges. However, while the articulated strategy will vary among institutions, the process through which it is formulated will be essentially the same for most institutions. The critical point is that the importance of context to strategy cannot be underestimated. For this reason, it is the subject of chapter 4 and the next section of this book.

NOTES

1. Michael E. Porter, "The State of Strategic Thinking," *The Economist*, May 23, 1987, 17–23.

2. Gary Hamel and C. K. Prahalad, *Competing for the Future* (Boston: Harvard Business School Press, 1994), 239.

3. Benjamin B. Tregoe and John W. Zimmerman, *Top Management Strategy: What It Is and How to Make It Work* (New York: Simon and Schuster, 1980), 19.

4. George L. Morrisey, *A Guide to Strategic Thinking: Building Your Planning Foundation* (San Francisco: Jossey-Bass, 1996), 82.

5. John M. Bryson, *Strategic Planning for Public and Nonprofit Organizations* (San Francisco: Jossey-Bass, 1995), 1–4.

6. Ibid., 29.

7. For a discussion of barriers to and incentives for the market entry of new players, see Michael E. Porter, "How Competitive Forces Shape Strategy," in *Strategy: Seeking and Securing Competitive Advantage*, eds. Cynthia A. Montgomery and Michael E. Porter (Boston: Harvard Business Review Books, 1991), 11–26.

8. Ibid.

9. Ibid.

10. For a discussion of competitive advantage, see Michael E. Porter, *Competitive Advantage: Creating and Sustaining Superior Performance* (New York: Free Press, 1985).

11. Ibid.

12. Ibid.

13. Ibid.

14. See, for example, K. Patricia Cross, "Access and Accommodation in Higher Education," *Research Reporter* 6, no. 2 (1971): 6–8; Vincent Tinto, "College Proximity and Rates of College Attendance," *American Educational Research Journal* 10, no. 4 (1973): 277–293; Richard Richardson and Louis Bender, *Fostering Minority Access and Achievement in Higher Education* (San Francisco: Jossey-Bass, 1987); and Arthur M. Cohen and Florence B. Brawer, *The American Community College* (San Francisco: Jossey-Bass, 2003).

15. Porter, *Competitive Advantage*.

16. The work of Bryson, *Strategic Planning*, 166–168, was especially helpful in building an understanding of the steps, procedures, and outcomes involved in implementation, which are described in this chapter.

17. Ibid., 167.

18. B. Joseph Pine and James H. Gilmore, *The Experience Economy: Work Is Theater and Every Business a Stage* (Boston: Harvard Business School Press, 1999), 1–25.

PART II

Situating Strategy in Colleges and Universities

CHAPTER

How Context Shapes Strategy

The financial crisis in New York City in 1975–1976 brought conventional ways of doing business in public higher education to a halt. After years of burying accumulated deficits in a "balanced," but illusionary budget, the mounting red ink finally caught up with the city and Mayor Abraham Beame. The stark reality of the massive deficit, fueled by years of rolling over debt from one budget year to the next, came to light through the media and demanded immediate action. The city controller was fired, allies of the mayor in prominent positions in city government were removed and replaced with a private-sector management team, and funding was dramatically reduced for all entities depending on the city for support. The City University of New York was one of these entities, and one of its colleges—New York City Community College (NYCCC)—was particularly hard hit. NYCCC was a comprehensive community college with a main campus in Brooklyn and a branch campus near the Port Authority in Manhattan. At its peak in 1975, it enrolled 18,500 students (mostly in career and technical programs) and had a $32 million operating budget, approximately three-quarters of which came from city funds. Its operating "strategy," loosely defined, was to "acquire all of the resources that it could and to spend everything that it acquired."[1]

Two years later, NYCCC's enrollment had plummeted to 12,500 students and its operating budget to $21 million. The context in which it operated had changed dramatically and so had its strategy and approach to business. Because most of its operating resources were tied up in high-cost career and technical programs, it had become the "oddball" in a funding formula used by the City University of New York, which favored community colleges enrolling larger numbers of students in lower cost general education programs. The 30 percent reduction in funding from 1975 was disastrous for a college with a majority of students enrolled in occupational programs. To reduce its spending to conform to the other colleges, one-of-a-kind programs would be scaled back or eliminated, money would be trimmed for equipment required to keep programs in sync with market needs, and the college would be forced to compensate faculty at a level incapable of preventing them from leaving for more attractive opportunities in the private sector. Something had to be done to infuse new resources into the college or avoid long-term damage. The city could not be part of the solution—it had nothing to offer. That left students and the state as the only sources of immediate revenue and, given the marginal socioeconomic status of most students, that meant the state. The only way out was to introduce legislation that would free the college from city funding by making it a specially funded state entity in the City University of New York. Two-thirds of its operating revenue would come from the state with the remainder coming from tuition and limited city support. The legislation was passed in 1978, and along with it came a new way of doing business and a change of name for NYCCC to New York City College of Technology.

In the space of three short years, the operating context of New York City Community College had changed dramatically. It was operating under a new name, its enrollment had plummeted and quickly recovered, and its primary source of revenue had shifted from the city to the state. With these changes came an entirely different approach to business and a new strategy. The approach to funding and budgeting used by the state varied significantly from that of the city. In contrast to the city model, in which money was allocated to the college without restriction and could be moved around freely in the operating budget, every expenditure in the new model—new and continuing staff, equipment, supplies, and so on—had to be supported by extensive documentation. Detailed plans supporting a budget request had to be drawn up long in advance and the college did not have the autonomy to move money between budget codes without the approval of the State Budget Office. A published budget, documenting every expense in every cost center, became a critical operating document in the college and long- and short-range planning became part of every manager's job description. A by-product of the new emphasis on integrated planning and budgeting was a concern about efficiency: planning and allocating resources carefully and avoiding waste by carefully monitoring the use of resources. The operating "strategy" of New York City Community College, now New York City College of Technology, had changed from "resource acquisition" to "efficiency" in the use of resources.

This chapter in the history and evolution of New York City College of Technology illustrates the effect of context on strategy. Context—the interrelated conditions in which an institution exists and operates—shapes strategy. It does so by determining strategy frames that will be appropriate or inappropriate for a college given specific forces in its external environment, unique features of its internal organization, and the values and actions of leaders. Although very few institutions experience a warp-speed transition like New York City College of Technology, every college has a discernible operating context. Understanding this context and what it means for strategy is important. This is because strategy boils down to a basic challenge facing every leader: How do you match the right strategy to the right context, at the right time, and in the right way? Whether you are the president of a small liberal arts college in Connecticut, the provost of an elite research university in California, or a community college president in Michigan, this question lies at the heart of successful strategy.

WHAT IS CONTEXT?

How does context shape strategy in a liberal arts college that has a storied history and a tradition of excellence? What elements of context interact to shape strategy options for a regionally focused community college or a national for-profit institution like the University of Phoenix? What information would leaders need to gather to accurately gauge the context and strategy options of an elite research university like Stanford? How do leaders manage conditions of turmoil and change in an operating context such as that of New York City College of Technology and create new strategy to fit context? Like all organizations, colleges and universities increasingly find themselves faced with major changes in their operating environment. They must also cope with their own internal dynamics, which, for better or worse, are influenced by the values and actions of leaders. As shown in Figure 4.1, context is shaped by *forces outside of the institution* (external drivers) that impel it to action, and *dynamics inside the institution* including the *values and actions of leaders* (internal drivers) that shape its response to the environment. Understanding these dimensions of context and the way in which they interact is essential for forging successful strategy.

Figure 4.1
Drivers of Institutional Context

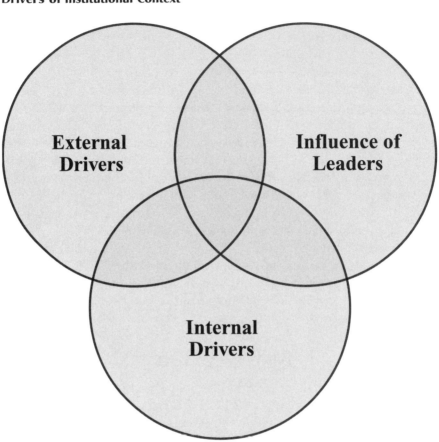

Context is also made up of fixed and variable components. Fixed components are attributes that cannot be controlled like economic conditions, public policy, and demographic trends. Variable components are aspects of context over which an institution has some control including programs and services, academic schedule, educational delivery, and costs. These components involve forces of action and reaction that shape strategy by setting boundaries for what an institution can or cannot do. Campus work groups, for example, holding strong beliefs about their role and place in the organization, may check and balance change-initiatives that an institution wants to carry out. Individual and collective beliefs in a work group involve subtle (and at times not so subtle) latitudes of acceptance and rejection that guide action in different spheres of activity. By propelling people toward or away from specific alternatives for action, the unique configuration of these latitudes limits strategy options available to the institution.

The fixed and variable components of context, furthermore, suggest that turbulence or a change in conditions outside of the institution may be met with varying degrees of resistance by people inside the institution. In periods of turbulence, faculty and staff are in constant need of touchstones—familiar ways of doing things—and may reject actions that take the institution too far or too fast from what they know. Context is a touchstone until it moves beyond individual comprehension by changing too quickly. When this happens, there is a tendency to seek comfort in known ways of doing things and to withdraw from the larger institution to the smaller department or work unit in which actions and events are predictable and more easily controlled. The effect on strategy, once again, is to limit the options available to an institution to those that fall within the comfort range of faculty and staff.

Finally, and perhaps most importantly, the components of context interact to define the nature of reality for people in the institution. In other words, they provide a lens through which faculty and staff interpret and assign value to activities and events. Professionals in higher education are part of a culture that is particularly directed toward individualism and primary-group identification.[2] As a result, colleges and universities often lack the cohesion that is found in cultures and organizations oriented toward collective welfare and shared responsibility. If leaders are to forge successful strategy, they will need to understand and fully appreciate faculty and staff conceptions of reality. They will also need to know how to inform and transform these conceptions in relation to challenges facing the institution. Any effort to formulate strategy, therefore, will need to take into account forces of change in the external environment and operating dynamics inside the institution.

EXTERNAL DRIVERS SHAPING CONTEXT

There are many aspects of the external environment that contribute to context. They are big and small, global and local, and quantitative and qualitative in nature. Ultimately, however, the drivers that are important in formulating strategy can be summarized through three questions: What are the key forces and trends in the external environment that will impact the institution? What changes can be anticipated in customers and their needs? Who are the competitors, what are they doing, and What are they apt to do?

Information gathered to address these questions will help describe factors that shape context from outside the institution. While it is not possible to provide a description of the way in which they contribute to context without constructing a customized scan for each category of institutions, it is possible to identify the drivers that all or most colleges need to consider in order to learn enough about context to formulate strategy.

Environmental Forces and Trends

A number of drivers are present in the external environment at any point in time. Only the most important are described below as *perennial drivers* (drivers that continue without interruption) and *situational drivers* (drivers that emerge under special conditions).

Perennial Drivers. What can perennial drivers such as population trends and forecasts, economic and labor market conditions, and public policy tell leaders about the context their colleges are operating in? They reveal some things that are certain and others that are in flux and never certain. Certain, for example, are the aging population and collapsing birth rate. Analysis of economic forecast data and population projections reveals that by 2100 there will be as many Americans older than 65 as there are under 18. Uncertain, however, is the impact of this trend on individual retirement programs. It could place public pensions in crisis as more workers are necessary to support more retirees. It could also result in the overhaul of existing retirement programs and creation of new programs that reflect and respond to changing demographics.

Certain also is change in the distribution of disposable income as families spend more on health care, education, leisure, and government, and less on products. Uncertain is the rate at which government spending and costs for health care and education will rise in the future and factors that will increase or constrain cost. We know through analysis of labor market data that lower paying service jobs and jobs in new industries like biotech will expand dramatically in the years ahead. Conversely, job restructuring trends in business and industry indicate that for most workers the notion of a job will change profoundly over the next twenty years. Advancing technology will require continuous upgrading of worker knowledge and skills, lower wage workers will hold several jobs simultaneously to produce a reasonable income, a progressively larger segment of the workforce will generate work through entrepreneurial skills, and electronic commuting will become more commonplace. More and more of the products we buy will be produced by workers in other countries and a growing number of the services we use will be delivered electronically by offshore workers. As the world grows smaller through advancing technology, a global community is developing in which organizations can no longer define their scope in terms of national or regional economies and boundaries. They will need to define their scope in terms of industries and services worldwide.

These trend-lines were constructed using routinely available data for ten drivers: projections of population size and composition, job projections by occupation, condition of the economy, business climate, employer workforce needs, global economic growth, trends in disposable income, technology product development, quality of life, and consumer attitudes and preferences. While other drivers (e.g., trends in education, quality of life, public policy) would also be part of an external scan, these trend-lines simply illustrate the manner in which routinely available information can be used to identify forces that institutions must contend with in their operating context. For example, the cumulative effect of a collapsing birth rate and aging population could be a decline in the pool of college-age students and in the resources available for higher education. The additional resources required to shore up pension systems and provide services for the elderly could deplete federal and state treasuries and reduce aid for colleges and universities. Similarly, globalization and the changing structure of jobs and worker skill requirements could antiquate curricula that overprepare students for jobs or do not prepare them for anything. And the requirement for continuous skill upgrading associated with advancing technology could make credentialing more important than degrees in a rapidly changing market.

Situational Drivers. Drivers are situational when circumstances in the environment coalesce to produce conditions that are unique in time and place. These drivers have important implications for organizations, and they are appearing with greater frequency on the radar screens of colleges and universities. The trick is to imagine what could be possible through analysis of current trends and to determine their effect on the institution as illustrated on the next page.[3]

These drivers will vary in impact and intensity among institutions. While all institutions will be touched in some way by many or most of them, it is unlikely that they will be touched in the same way. Elite private colleges, for example, will not feel the effects of economic downturn in the same way as public colleges and universities which rely on state appropriations. Likewise, for-profit institutions using asynchronous delivery to enter and compete in traditional markets will have a different experience with advancing technology than colleges committed to synchronous delivery. Situational drivers will play an increasingly important role in shaping the operating context of colleges and universities. The challenge for leaders will be to devise efficient and resourceful methods for tracking these drivers and assessing their impact.

Trend	Institutional Impact
Demographic Transition	
* The population is aging/ by 2020, 25% will be 18 or under and 30% will be 55 or older.	* Opportunities for lifelong learning will expand by necessity.
* We are becoming a nation of minorities. By 2100, 34% of the population will be white.	* Balancing the educational needs of young and old will become important.
* Pressure for immigration is increasing.	* Diversity will need to be reflected in staff, course offerings, and services.
* Pressure for economic mobility will increase among disenfranchised groups.	* Demand will intensify for services customized to learner needs.
Family Structure and Dynamics	
* The definition and structure of the family are changing.	* Students will follow generational norms that challenge traditional norms.
* Purchasing power is declining, giving rise to more multiple-worker families.	* Students will expect more and better service as a return on investment.
* The family is changing as an agent of socialization. Schools are expected to do more.	* More students will blend work and education while attending college.
Education	
* 1.8 million more learners will need to be absorbed in postsecondary education between 2005 and 2015.	* Pressure will increase for access to postsecondary education. Colleges will need to align resources with growth.
* K–12 and college options will expand as new competitors using advanced technology and innovative practices enter the market.	* Demand will increase for personalized programs that more fully explore students' needs, interests, and abilities.
* Learners will demand more flexible entry and exit requirements.	* Schools and colleges will redefine educational boundaries.
* Pressure will mount to redesign K–12 education.	* Semester credit hours may be replaced by flexible entry/exit processes and competency assessments.
Generational Differences	
* More age generations will be represented on college and university campuses (Silent Generation, Baby Boomers, Generation X Millennials, etc.).	* Colleges will need to prepare for tech-adept, high-expectation students who will demand customized service.
* Variation in needs, expectations, and outlook will increase among campus subcultures due to generational differences.	* Programs, services, and approaches to communication will need to be developed that bridge generational differences.

Trend	Institutional Impact

Health and Living

* Life expectancy is increasing. More people are living longer and better.
* Incremental resources will be required to provide health care and services for an aging population.
* Baby Boomers will retire in large numbers over the next decade.
* Strain will be placed on Social Security and pension funds by retirees.
* Health and energy costs are rising faster than personal income.
* The gap between haves and have-nots is growing wider.
* Discretionary spending will change as a function of decline in income.

* Patterns of state and federal support for education will change as incremental resources are required to support health, pension, and welfare systems.
* Pressure for access to higher education will increase among disenfranchised populations.
* Colleges will feel more pressure for discounting and cost containment.

Fluctuating Economy and Labor Market

* Consumer confidence is being strained by a start/stop pattern of economic growth.
* Spending on defense and national security is increasing faster than domestic spending.
* Structural shifts across key sectors of the economy will limit job growth.
* Gains in productivity are limiting job creation.
* Job restructuring in manufacturing and service industries will result in lower salaries for workers.
* Worker shortages will develop for specific professions.
* Workers possessing skills and competencies valued by employers will be in short supply.

* Appropriations to higher education will vacillate in accord with changing economic conditions.
* Federal responsibility for support of higher education will shift to the states.
* Fast-track programs will be needed to develop (a) skilled workers in rapidly growing occupations, and (b) "soft skills" valued by business and industry.

Globalization

* More jobs are moving overseas.
* Connectivity among nations is increasing through economic interdependence.
* U.S. reliance on foreign goods, workers, and capital is increasing.

* Global employment opportunities for graduates will significantly increase.
* Foreign markets will become an important source of qualified staff.
* Proficiency in foreign languages and cultural awareness will become a more important part of the curriculum.

Trend	Institutional Impact
Public Policy and Politicization	
* The U.S. population is increasingly divided by political ideology and persuasion. * Government agencies are initiating and enforcing more stringent standards.	* Campuses are becoming more politicized. * Efforts to regulate higher education will increase.
Technology	
* Continuing advances are being made in technology product development. * Technology reduces barriers to market entry for new competitors. * New approaches to learning are evolving through advanced technology. * Student expectations for technology and E-learning are growing. * 24/7 access to learning and services will become a baseline expectation for students. * Technological innovation will spur a greater demand for lifelong learning.	* More learners will enter college with advanced experience and expectations for technology. * Pressure will mount on faculty to enhance technology skills. * A larger portion of college operating budgets will be required for technology upgrading and acquisition. * Colleges will need to plan and manage technology expectations. * Technology security will become more important on campuses.

Changing Customer Needs

The *moment of truth* is a powerful idea for helping faculty and staff examine their points of view and think about the changing needs of customers. A *customer* is someone who is seeking something of value from a college—a student, an employer recruiting and hiring, alumni, townspeople attending campus events, anyone seeking a commodity or service. Because their needs and expectations are constantly in flux, they are at the center of a dynamic tension between established ways of doing things and the need for change. Following is a case in point:

An instructor in a teaching university was having difficulty reaching students in an introductory psychology class. A member of the faculty for more than thirty years, he had won numerous awards for teaching and prided himself on developing lesson plans that inspired and stimulated students. Assuming that his approach to pedagogy, crafted over a period of years, would be effective with just about any group of students, he used the same course design for the Fall 2004 Introduction to Psychology class. Lectures were interspersed with clinical case studies and small group work, a course pack was used to provide up-to-date supplementary readings, and the instructor made himself readily available to students outside of class through e-mail and published office hours. He asked for student feedback via e-mail following each class meeting to determine how the course was going. Instead of expressions of satisfaction and praise for his teaching, however, he received a steady stream of ideas as to how he could improve the content of the course and his approach to teaching. His e-mail box was overloaded with replies from critical, but engaged 18–19-year-old students suggesting everything from incorporating a focus on breaking research in psychology via the Internet, to conversations with field practitioners, to realignment of course material for more effective learning, to using more and better technology, to updating case studies, to scheduling flexible hours for the course to permit time for fieldwork. With his experience and prior track record of success all but thrown to the wind, he could feel the course slipping away.

This was the moment of truth, one of many that would happen in a course packed with students who comprise the Millennial generation now entering colleges and universities. Programmed since birth by watchful Baby Boomer parents, Millennials have been part of the day-to-day negotiations about their lives since they were old enough to point.[4] With technology and the media blurring the difference between fantasy and reality, this generation of students has needs and expectations that are entirely different from previous generations and certainly from those of a veteran instructor with a "different" view of the world. This is a generation that has had access to cell phones, personal pagers, and computers at an early age. Through the Internet they can visit virtually every corner of the globe and choose between learning in a real classroom or a virtual classroom. What knowledge and skills would a caring instructor be able to convey to them that they could not find on their own on the Internet? How can an instructor engage and inspire students who are so intimately connected with the world and one another through technology? How can institutions, instructors, and staff stay abreast of rapidly changing student needs in a world turned topsy-turvy by change and instantaneous communication?

Students have more choices from a wider variety of providers than ever before in American higher education. Their range of choice is expanding as new providers using innovative practices and more and better technologies enter the market. Each successive innovation raises the bar for providers by elevating customer expectations. Whereas in prior years students would have been satisfied with expanded hours of service, they now expect services to be available 24/7 on the Internet. Whereas a comprehensive schedule of course offerings would have satisfied most learners five years ago, they now expect to be able to take courses anywhere, anyplace, and anytime to fit their schedule. They expect that a significant portion of their coursework will be taken electronically and that they will be able to take courses at several institutions and apply them to a "home" institution for the degree. Very few students enter college, progress through the curriculum in a linear fashion, and leave four years later with a degree. They swirl back and forth through multiple institutions and attendance modes, which puts pressure on colleges to implement common learning goals, standards, and competency assessments to determine student attainment.

Students are arriving on campuses much better informed about what to expect and with significantly higher expectations of the college experience than earlier generations. Some come armed with cell phones, smaller and faster computers, smart cameras, and personal data assistants that put them a click away from oceans of information. Others come with high expectations and limited academic and financial resources. Regardless of background or resources, however, they share one thing in common: they expect to engage in an experience that is meaningful when it happens and beneficial later on in terms of improved quality of life. Many factors underlie this expectation. Chief among them is the changing frame of reference for student experience in colleges and universities. Through growing exposure to best practices in different types of organizations, students have changed their frame of reference for performance from the institution itself to a host of organizations. They generalize experiences from one organization to another as shown in Figure 4.2.

The similarities in processes such as flight check-in, hotel registration, seating and table service at a restaurant, customer service in a department store, or course registration in a college probably outweigh the differences, for a student expecting outstanding service. A service is needed, and it is delivered in a manner that is good or poor, fast or slow, or courteous or rude. The common ingredient is that it is evaluated—by a student, not a consumer—and compared to a similar service received elsewhere. This evaluation becomes the basis for raising or lowering expectations for experience provided by a college. A favorable experience with one organization means that an equivalent or better experience can be provided by another. If not, something is wrong.

Listed below are selected attributes of learners as "customers" that shape the context in which colleges and universities operate. These attributes lie beyond the range of student characteristics that are routinely assessed. They are presented here to provide insight into some of the more intrinsic factors related to learner needs and expectations that colleges and universities will need to consider in formulating strategy.

Figure 4.2
Changing Customer Dynamic: Blended Experience and Expectations

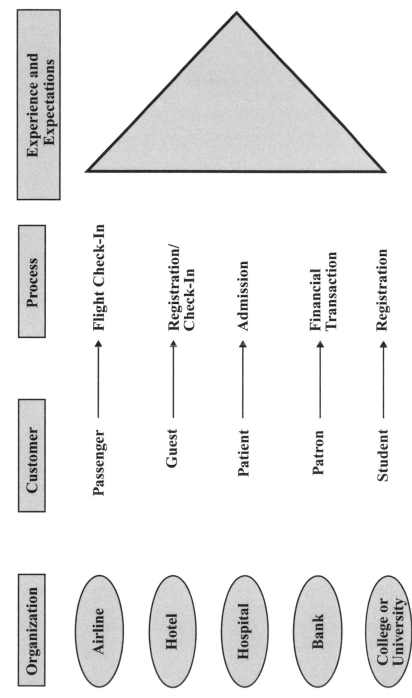

Customer Attribute	Source of Information
Needs for assistance during and after enrollment	Survey research
Expectations for quality and convenience	Personal contact
Exposure to best practices in profit and nonprofit organizations	Personal contact
Technology experience and expectations	Survey research
Preferred medium for course, program, and service delivery	Survey research
Course-taking plans inside and outside of the institution ("swirling")	Personal contact
Expectations for "experience" in courses and services	Personal contact
Plans for work while enrolled in college	Survey research

These factors illustrate the changing customer context on college and university campuses. Beyond expecting more and better service, students seek engaging experience inside and outside of the classroom, and clear connectivity between academic processes and requirements and personal goals and aspirations. As Davis and Botkin recognize in *The Monster Under the Bed*:

> The industrial approach to education . . . [made] teachers the actors and students the passive recipients. In contrast, the emerging new model takes the market perspective. By making students the active players, the focus will shift from the provider to the user, from educat-*ors* (teachers) to learn-*ers* (students) and the *educating act will reside increasingly in the active learner, rather than the teacher-manager.* In the new learning marketplace, customers, employees, and students are all active learners or, even more accurately, interactive learners.[5]

Judith Rodin, president of the University of Pennsylvania, recognizes the active nature of education that will be sought by current and future generations of learners as well as the fact that learning can take place anywhere, anyplace, and anytime. In her 1994 inaugural address, she proclaimed: "We will design a new Penn undergraduate experience. It will involve not only curriculum, but new types of housing, student services, and mentoring, to create a seamless experience between the classroom and the residence, from the playing field to the laboratory."[6] Encounters of this kind immerse students in engaging experiences that cut across all aspects of academic life. Each aspect provides multiple opportunities for learning, including communication and group interaction skills in residence life, team and project management skills in a classroom project, and even principles of physics as part of weight training for athletes.

Competitors

> We believe education represents the most fertile new market for in-
> vestors in many years. It has a combination of large size (approxi-
> mately the same size as health care), disgruntled users, low utilization
> of technology, and the highest strategic importance of any activity
> in which this country engages. . . . Finally, existing managements are
> sleepy after years of monopoly.
>
> Anonymous quote from a venture capital prospectus

Just a few years ago, competition in postsecondary education could be
likened to a marathon in which colleges playing by established rules jock-
eyed for market share. Consistent with this metaphor, the institutions
with the fastest and strongest runners (in other words, the most resources) usually finished first, but every runner finished the race. Today,
however, a soccer game played without rules could also be a metaphor
for competition. The rules of engagement are changing and the realities
of the game are in constant flux—so expect the unexpected, as described
by Fahey in *Outwitting, Outmaneuvering, and Outperforming Competitors*.
If one applies the soccer metaphor to the current marketplace, the following disclaimers and warnings to the players would be required:[7]

- All rules are subject to change without notice.
- The field for the game is round and sloped.
- The size of the field and boundary lines will change after the game starts.
- New entrants may join or leave the game at any time.
- A game can start anytime, anyplace, anywhere, and the game strategy can change based on the most current information.
- Players can throw balls in and claim goals whenever they want to.
- Players may form alliances.
- All creative strategies that are not specifically against the law are al-lowed.
- The game is played as if it makes sense.

The nature of the game changes as new players enter the contest and
rules change to advantage different players at different points in competition. More and more, the advantage is going to institutions that can
most quickly develop a winning strategy or rethink their strategy while
adapting to frequent changes in the market. And forces which heretofore were considered to have minimal impact on college and university

enrollments are now recognized as formidable. Economic growth and military conflict, for example, divert students from college campuses in sufficient numbers to warrant attention from admission offices.

Interestingly, many basics of the soccer game still apply. Players (the institutions and organizations delivering educational programs and services) develop and use marketing strategies that will gain an advantage with those who control the resources (students and stakeholders). Winning is measured in terms of acquiring and keeping students and resources from current and future rivals (competitors). As the game progresses, institutions adapt and amend their strategies as they observe, and anticipate, the actions and reactions of stakeholders and competitors. Stakeholders (those with an interest in the institution and the game) watch the game and are influenced by its outcome. The institutions playing in the game need to convince stakeholders that they have the wherewithal to compete effectively. The game boils down to the actions taken by players based on information they have been able to gather.[8] To devise successful strategy, institutions must have a thorough understanding of competitors and stakeholders, and they must be able to convert this intelligence into timely action.

What do institutions need to know about competition and competitors? The interplay of five conditions determines the extent to which competition will exist among institutions. Competition evolves when organizations pursue the same student and resource markets at the same time, when one institution achieves growth at the expense of another, when institutions use aggressive tactics to increase market share, when one institution feels it is in a vulnerable position relative to another institution, and when rapidly changing external conditions (e.g., economic growth or decline, war, public policy) constrict resource markets and impel institutions toward drastic action. Colleges need to know who their competitors are, the dimensions on which they compete, and their advantage or disadvantage relative to the strengths and weaknesses of competitors. They also need to know what information to gather about competitors and where and how to get it.

Who are the competitors? The "who" involved in competition can be as simple as two institutions in proximity competing for students in the same market or as complex as an array of providers throughout the world using multimodal delivery techniques to reach a global market. Competition can be conceptualized as occurring on different levels and in different dimensions as depicted in Figure 4.3. Competition takes place at three levels with institutions competing in systems involving multiple competitors, as whole organizations, or as parts of an organization. Com-

Figure 4.3
Structure of Competition

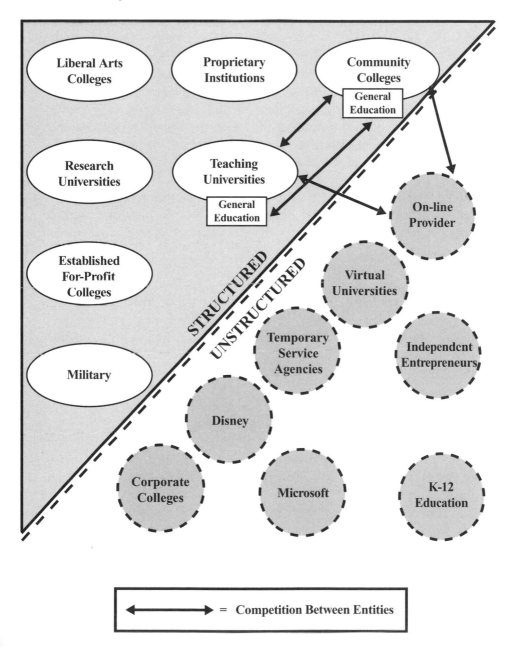

petition also occurs in two dimensions with relationships among competitors either structured or unstructured, depending on how much they know about one another. Each level and dimension constitutes a unique focus on competition.

At what levels do institutions compete? Competition at the system level involves a variety of institutions striving for market share in an industry (postsecondary education) or a segment of the industry such as undergraduate education, continuing education, or professional education. At the institutional and department levels, the playing field is much smaller. It is made up of institutions or departments within institutions competing for the same pool of students in a boundaried market. For example, a regional teaching university and adjacent community colleges competing for graduating high school seniors, or a physics department in a research university competing for the best students with rival departments at peer institutions. Competition is structured because the rivals know one another and their behavior is predictable. It would become unstructured if new players entered the market and changed the rules of engagement.

The success of Baker College in Michigan in growing market share using innovative student recruitment techniques is a good illustration of unstructured competition. Baker's student intake process is based on rapid admission and financial aid decisions, guaranteed course schedules, and close working relationships with regional business and industry employers that guarantee job placements for students. Baker challenges providers using traditional procedures by going the extra mile with students and exceeding their efforts in every phase of student intake. It sustains this advantage by maintaining close scrutiny over information about its intake process and maintaining an aura of uncertainty about its behavior. College representatives will not be seen on conference programs or in workshops describing Baker's intake process nor are they interested in marketing their system to other institutions as a way of enhancing institutional prestige.

On what dimensions do institutions compete? Competition is not as simple as a contest between rivals for a valued resource. Institutions interact with one another and with the environment on two dimensions that are integral to competition. As illustrated in Table 4.1, the first dimension is the *Source of Competition* (entities, forces, or conditions outside of the institution from which competition evolves) and the second is the *Arena of Competition* (areas inside the institution on which institutions compete).

In its simplest form, competition for colleges and universities can be seen as evolving from the five following sources:[9]

Table 4.1
Dimensions of Competition

| | Source of Competition | | | | |
Arena of Competition	Existing Competitors	Threat of Entry	Stakeholder Expectations	Pressure from Substitutes	External Conditions
Students					
Resources					
Programs/Services					
Delivery Systems					
Operating Processes					
Networks					
Convenience					
Cost					

1. *Rivalry with Existing Competitors.* Competition in postsecondary education continues to be shaped by rivals that are visible and known. It draws the attention of leaders when numerous institutions with equivalent resources are competing in the same market, the market is growing slowly, education is perceived as a commodity for which students have many options, the costs of switching from one institution to another are minimal, and competitors have diverse strategies and personalities.[10]

2. *Threat of Entry.* The second force is new competitors who bring vigor, new ideas, and resources to gain a foothold in the market. These competitors may be start-up organizations seeking to carve out a niche, but more often than not they are established for-profit organizations pursuing new opportunities in a growth industry. The ease or difficulty a competitor may experience in gaining market share has a lot to do with the decision about market entry. The more difficult entry is, or appears to be, because of financial and capital requirements, regulations, stakeholder preferences, and the like, the less the competition and the greater the likelihood of success for current players.[11]

3. *Stakeholder Expectations.* Students and stakeholders become a significant force in competition when they exert pressure on institutions to meet or respond to changes in need, interest, and expectation. They exercise maximum leverage when they have a significant interest in convenience and cost savings, are concerned about the quality of education, have multiple pathways for accomplishing the same end, have full information, and are willing to play institutions off one an-

other to achieve their aims. This source of competition is not fully acknowledged by institutions because it is perceived as putting too much power into the hands of stakeholders, yet it is always present and becomes troublesome when stakeholders look elsewhere for service.[12]

4. *Pressure from Substitutes.* The fourth competitive force relates to the ease with which students and stakeholders can substitute one type of service for another.[13] For example, educational credentials offered by for-profit organizations are substitutes for degrees offered by colleges and universities. Substitutes become a visible threat when they provide not only an alternative choice for the student, but also a significant improvement in price and performance. For example, foundation courses offered by Sylvan Learning Systems could have an adverse effect on remedial programs in community colleges if they produce superior outcomes at moderate cost.

5. *External Conditions and Circumstances.* Whether acknowledged or not, some institutions are in competition with environmental forces and circumstances for students and resources. Increased demand for workers and on-the-job training in periods of economic growth is a case in point. As demand increases and wages rise to attract workers to jobs, jobs compete with enrollment. The same would be true in periods of military conflict when incentives such as training, education, and income enhancement are used to draw recruits to the armed services.

The arenas of competition identified in Table 4.1 are basic in that they represent only the most obvious areas in which institutions compete. Jockeying among established institutions for students and resources is an all too familiar arena of competition for college and university administrators. Cost is another arena in which institutions compete, each trying to position itself favorably in pricing compared to rivals.

How is advantage achieved? A college achieves an advantage over its rivals by detecting and acting on changes in customer needs and expectations more quickly, by anticipating the behavior of rivals and taking action before they do, by ascertaining how to create value for stakeholders beyond that provided by competitors, and by learning from the actions of rivals and converting this knowledge into new initiatives. A number of indicators can be used to determine whether advantage has been achieved. Among them are factors such as the number of new programs and services introduced, enhancement of market share, improvement in student satisfaction, and enhancement of image and reputation.

Gathering information about competitors. Information about competitors can be acquired from multiple sources ranging from published industry reports to "shopping the competition." Institutional marketing publications and published reports, state agency statistical reports, and U.S. Office of Education data can be used to gauge enrollment strength and market share. Newspaper clipping services and information produced through media in competitors' home locations can be used to gauge current and future capacity and the nature and direction of long-term plans. Vendors, suppliers, and marketing consultants are excellent sources of information about tactics competitors use to gain an advantage. Another prime source of information is ex-employees. Finally, "shopping the competition" is another useful source of information. This may include participating in a competitor's systems (e.g., student intake), enrolling in courses, or using a competitor's services and technology.

INTERNAL DRIVERS SHAPING CONTEXT

Most institutions have plenty of quantitative information describing resources available to educate students, such as their programs and curricula, course offerings, student services, facilities, faculty and staff, learning resources, technology, and so on. They typically have much less of a command over qualitative information. Factors such as the nature and makeup of an institution's culture, faculty and staff satisfaction, the quality of its programs and services, and the effectiveness of its systems and processes have a lot to do with its success—actual or perceived—in meeting stakeholder needs. The same could be said of the ability of institutions to articulate their development strategy. One of the most important steps in strategy formulation is the identification of institutional capability. To do this, leaders and staff must be able to define the institution's development path and its core competencies. The strategic thinking involved provides an informed basis for understanding the way in which *internal drivers*—attributes, capabilities, and resources of the institution—contribute to context.

An array of drivers are present in the internal environment at any one time. Four major categories of drivers that leaders and staff should routinely understand are resources; organizational architecture, systems, and processes; culture; and climate. Not only are these categories basic to understanding the impact of internal drivers on context, they are also the fundamental categories around which institutional capability is determined.

Resources

Drivers in this category relate to the different types of resources institutions have available to serve students and stakeholders. Most of the information in this category can be accessed through institutional data systems and reports. Questions to ask and answer about institutional resources are

What are the institution's mission, vision, and core values?

What resources does the institution have available to meet customer needs?

- educational programs, curricula, and courses
- learning resources
- support services
- faculty and staff (number and capability)
- operating revenue
- technology
- facilities

To what extent are the institution's resources fixed or discretionary?

How effectively does the institution deploy its resources?

Organizational Architecture

Drivers in this category relate to the administrative structure of the organization and its effect on individual, group, and organizational behavior. Of particular interest is information about the formal and informal structure of the organization and the way in which authority, power, and influence work. Questions to ask and answer about organizational architecture are

What is the administrative structure of the institution?

- levels and functional areas in the formal organization
- distribution of staff in the formal organization

How is authority vested in the formal organization?

What is the informal structure of the organization?

- distribution of power and influence
- channels of communication

To what extent does the informal organization differ from the formal organization?

Systems and Processes

Drivers in this category relate to institutional performance in service to students, for example, the experiences students have while enrolled in a course, when using a service, or when moving through institutional processes and systems (e.g., registering for courses). They also describe institutional operations and the extent to which they are efficient (save time), meet user needs (satisfy), and advantage or disadvantage the institution. Some of the information in this category can be acquired through institutional data systems and reports. Much of it, however, must be gathered directly with client groups through surveys and face-to-face interaction. Questions to ask and answer about processes and systems are

How current are institutional processes and systems?
- frequency of review by users and clients
- actions taken to break down and redesign processes and systems
- success in implementation of redesigned processes and systems

Who are the actual and desired customers for institutional processes and systems?

Are the actual and desired customers the same, or are they different?

To what extent is state-of-the-art technology being used in institutional systems and processes?

How do institutional processes and systems compare with those of competitors in terms of cost, speed, efficiency, and client satisfaction and benefit?

Culture and Climate

Drivers in this category relate to the distinctive beliefs and patterns of behavior that develop in institutions over time. *Culture* refers to deeply held values, beliefs, and ideologies of staff that have superordinate meaning while *climate* refers to common perceptions, attitudes, and feelings of staff about organizational life.[14] Patterns of behavior implicit in culture and climate are unconscious and taken for granted. They are reflected in shared perceptions, values, understanding, outlook, stories, ceremonies, and other symbolic forms. Leaders who understand the power of culture and climate have a better chance of influencing their institutions than do those who focus on other aspects of organizational behavior. Information in this category can only be obtained through direct interaction with staff. Questions to ask and answer about culture and climate are

Does the institution comprise a single culture or is it made up of multiple cultures?

What is/are the dominant culture(s) in the institution?

What are the shared values of the dominant culture(s)? What do they mean for the institution?

The nature of internal drivers varies in important ways across institutions. Colleges and universities have different missions and cultures, serve different types of students, develop different structures and coordinating systems, and have different relationships with resource providers. Of course, there are elements common to the internal operation of institutions, but no two institutions are the same. To understand the context in which institutions operate, leaders must know the internal drivers that are at work and the way in which they impel an institution toward or away from specific strategy alternatives.

THE INFLUENCE OF LEADERS

Leadership is offered as a solution for many of the problems of colleges and universities. Institutions will work, we are told, if presidents and executive teams provide vision, direction, and strong leadership. Though the call for leadership is universal, there are lingering concerns about what it means and the capacity of leaders to shape the direction of an institution. Changing notions of the heroic leader have led to a shift in emphasis from the assumption that "leaders make things happen" to the proposition that "things make leaders happen." Perhaps a more accurate proposition is that through word and deed, leaders contribute in some way to context, while context influences what leaders can and must do. In this way, the interplay between leaders and context shapes the strategy options that are desirable for an institution.

An example from the current period of resource decline in higher education will illustrate the relationship between leadership and context. The problems facing leaders of public colleges and universities in states with low capacity and explosive growth (Florida and California) are very different from those facing leaders in states with high capacity and slow growth. The problem faced by presidents in states where enrollment demand exceeds capacity is how to persuade legislators to provide the resources institutions need to educate more students. Presidents in states with excess capacity face a different problem: how to align their institutions with increasingly competitive markets. The contexts for leadership are as different as are the strategy options for institutions.

In each context, the actions of leaders generate responses from constituents which shape, and are shaped by, the context in which strategy is formulated. It is important to distinguish carefully here among the interplay between leaders, context, and strategy. Successful strategy is not simply a matter of what leaders want to do, but of what is possible given attributes of the context in which the institution is operating. For example, a public college or university president committed to growth as a method for acquiring resources will approach strategy differently depending on the context. In periods of expansion, he or she will be able to match a personal commitment to growth with situational characteristics that reward growth. A change in context (e.g., an economic downturn or a shift in public policy) will serve to encourage the president to suspend his or her commitment to growth in favor of a more suitable strategy. In this way leadership and strategy are situational; that is, what works in one context will not necessarily work in another one.

The challenge of developing a strategy that will work in a specific context is a primary task of leaders. In many institutions, leading has transitioned into managing, in other words, tending the board, balancing the budget, cultivating donors, orchestrating capital and operational improvements, and making deals. The role of leaders is much more than stewardship of specific functions. A core responsibility of leaders is strategy: defining and communicating the institution's unique position, making choices and trade-offs, and forging a fit between needs and resources. Leaders who understand the relationship between context and strategy have the capacity to decide which market forces and stakeholder needs the institution will respond to while avoiding distractions and maintaining distinctiveness. They also have the capacity to make choices about what not to do. Deciding which markets to serve and how to serve them is fundamental to developing a strategy, but so is deciding which markets not to serve. Thus an important role of leaders is to provide the intellectual discipline needed to formulate strategy and the communication skills needed to implement it. Indeed, one of the benchmarks of a successful strategy is the extent to which staff in different parts of the organization use it to guide their actions and behavior.

HOW CONTEXT SHAPES STRATEGY

Context is the bedrock of strategy. It helps to define the nature of reality for those who are part of an organization. It provides a background against which people envision possibilities, test ideas, and make decisions. It shapes strategy by providing a lens through which leaders and staff interpret and assign value to various development alternatives for the institution. Recognizing that strategy can only be fully understood in the unique configuration of people, events, and dynamics that make up an institution's context, we offer a description of the relationship between strategy and context in four different settings.

Private Liberal Arts College. Prestige College is a venerable college of the liberal arts located in the Northeast. Its sticker price is rising faster than the Consumer Price Index, and its fund balance is being eroded by the discounting practices of competitors that it must match in order to maintain market share. Competition for students and donor support is keen. The uncertain economy is compounding an already difficult situation by encouraging Prestige to reduce out-of-pocket cost for students and families through enhanced discounting. A strategy option focused on revenue enhancement (relaxing admissions policies and extending services to new markets) will not work because it could give the appearance of lowering standards. A strategy option focused on cost containment (deferred maintenance, a conservative salary program, or outsourcing of services) could put the institution at risk because it might cut into its ability to put its best foot forward. Peeling paint on buildings, overgrown lawns, overburdened staff, and unhappy instructors are not becoming for any college.

Facing a need to maintain its position in a context marked by intensifying competition, economic uncertainty, and commitment to tradition, Prestige settled on a strategy of *quality through growth*. Quality would be defined in terms of the academic credentials (GPA, achievement test scores, National Merit scholars, etc.) of entering students. Prestige would raise the level of quality by enlarging the applicant pool and, within this pool, the number of academically and financially capable students. In so doing, it would reduce the level of discounting by getting more students to pay for more of the cost. For this to happen, however, Prestige would first have to generate a perception of scarcity among students and families—that is, a sense of intense competition for a limited number of spaces in its freshman class. Prestige altered its curriculum to improve the connection between general education and the professions. It focused, in particular, on the soft skills (competencies in oral and written expression, critical thinking, persuasional skills, team skills, workplace understanding, project management, etc.) valued by employers. Leaders reasoned that if all or most courses in the general education curriculum included a soft skills component, Prestige would produce better graduates, who would be hired in better jobs by better firms. Graduates and employers would laud the performance of the college—testimony that would eventually trickle down to high school students and parents and add to Prestige's reputation. The overall effect would be to impel more and better students to apply for admission thereby further enhancing the perception of quality and the willingness of students to pay for more of their education.

Community College. Opportunity Community College (OCC) is a rapidly growing urban multicampus institution in the Southwest. The increasing presence of Hispanic and immigrant populations in the region has fueled a rise in educational demand, which, when combined with declining state support, has forced Opportunity to stretch its resources to the breaking point. The college has absorbed most of the demand by increasing class size, hiring additional part-time instructors, and increasing the workload of support staff. This has worked well over the short term, but regional employers and four-year colleges are beginning to voice dissatisfaction with the level of student preparation. Basic and critical thinking skills are not in place when students enter the workforce or transfer to a senior institution. Strategy options of low cost, convenience, and comprehensiveness are necessary if OCC is to remain true to its mission, but they will not be enough to resolve its quality problem.

A task force comprising members of the executive team, planning and research personnel, and selected social science instructors studied the problem and discovered that it was rooted in three phenomena: (1) the changing structure of families and a lack of parental discourse with children about education and careers, (2) reduced expectations of youth moving through K–12 schools resulting from parental disengagement and overextended teachers and counselors, and (3) employers needing and expecting top-quality skills in workers in order to compete in a global market. Essentially families, schools, and employers were found to be working on different playing fields with OCC as the nexus of all of the fields. Recognizing this, the task force recommended a strategy of *collaboration*: a K–20 initiative integrating the efforts of schools, families, employers, and colleges and universities in a laddered curriculum to produce world-class workers. Children would be exposed to careers at a young age through the combined effort of all parties. OCC would serve as the hub for this effort. Its faculty and staff would interact with employers to identify valued workplace skills and, in turn, represent these skill requirements to families and schools. Curricula at all levels would be organized in a seamless progression to produce these skills and continuous assessment would be used to determine the level of skill attainment.

Teaching University. High Performing University (HPU) is a large teaching university in a southeastern state experiencing rapid growth and a projected shortage of workers in occupations vital to its economic base. Demand for postsecondary education is increasing geometrically while capacity is limited because the state lacks the resources to mount a major capital program. Further, state support for education is declining and tuition is capped thereby constraining HPU's ability to "grow its way out of austerity." In order to ensure that the most qualified students are admitted and workers are produced in sufficient number for high-demand occupations, the state has issued guidelines that require HPU and other public four-year institutions to "sculpt" their enrollments, that is, to admit students in greater numbers to specific majors to produce the graduates needed to fill worker shortages.

The conventional strategy of growth to produce additional revenue will not work because the state has capped enrollment. Recognizing this and realizing that few, if any, viable options were available, HPU's president was ready to think outside of the box and try something new. A conversation with a corporate executive who had revolutionized the information technology industry by changing the way computers are ordered, produced, and delivered, led to the development of a new strategy. HPU would *reinvent* the way funding flows to the university by entering into a partnership with corporations and government to change the way students are prepared for occupations. Corporations would partially offset costs by underwriting the cost of educating students who would become employed in the organization directly after graduation. In turn, HPU would work closely with employers via advisory boards to integrate industry knowledge and skill requirements into the curriculum, and state government would agree to buffer the institution from further reductions in funding. Using innovations in program design and delivery co-created with corporate professionals, the length of time required to prepare a skilled professional would change from four years to three years. More professionals would be graduated in a shorter amount of time, thereby enabling the state to assemble a labor force capable of attracting new industries and companies. Industry growth would translate into additional revenue that would find its way into the operating budgets of public universities such as HPU.

For-Profit Provider. Enterprise College is a newly established for-profit institution in the Midwest specializing in the health sciences and information technology. It is entering a market saturated with institutions that have been around a long time and have a comfortable familiarity with one another. Through shared programs and services, carefully constructed articulation agreements, and lobbying with local and state representatives, existing players operate as part of an informal alliance that renders market entry difficult for new players. This has resulted in a false sense of security, which manifests itself in the deliberate manner in which institutions seek and act on information related to customer needs. Nothing changes without extensive consultation, and when change is proposed it must successfully navigate many barriers before it is enacted.

Prior to making a decision on start up, Enterprise studied the structure of the market. It concentrated on regional trends and institutional strengths and weaknesses and found five areas in which it could establish an advantage over current players. They were institutional processes and systems (e.g., curriculum development and approval), responsiveness to customer needs, application of advanced technology to programs and services, convenience, and marketing. Each of these areas pointed to a lapse in serving the customer, and collectively they led to the identification of *speed* as the strategy Enterprise would use to enter and succeed in the market. By gathering and acting quickly on information related to customer needs (potential students, employers, communities, and government agencies), the college would open and fill new programs at a much faster pace than existing players. It helped that Enterprise did not have to deal with obstacles such as state agency policies guiding program approval, unions, and resistance by long-serving staff.

CONCLUSION

An informed understanding of context makes an important contribution to strategy by bringing viable options into focus and eliminating those that are inappropriate. Leaders and staff without an understanding of context lack a framework for creating strategy; it is difficult to craft strategy to fit an organization that is not understood. So the important act of understanding context and fitting strategy to context is indispensable in strategy formulation.

Understanding the context, however, may be necessary but not sufficient to beat the odds against successful strategy creation. From working with leaders in different types of institutions, we have learned that strategy is successful when context is matched with institutional capabilities and resources by informed and insightful leaders. This relationship is the topic of discussion in the next three chapters which focus on strategy formulation in different institutional contexts: liberal arts colleges, institutions with a comprehensive mission, and for-profit providers.

NOTES

1. The budgetary figures reported for New York City and New York City Community College are approximate. They are based on the recollection and

experience of Richard Alfred, who was dean of finance, planning, and management services at New York City Community College from 1977 to 1980.

2. William H. Bergquist, *The Four Cultures of the Academy* (San Francisco: Jossey-Bass, 1992), 1–13.

3. The data and information supporting these trends were abstracted by the authors from routinely available reports and forecasts issued by for-profit organizations and agencies of local, state, and federal government. Trends were constructed by aggregating data from multiple sources into themes that appeared to provide a forecast of the future.

4. See, for example, Lynne C. Lancaster and David Stillman, *When Generations Collide* (New York: Harper Business, 2002).

5. Stan Davis and Jim Botkin, *The Monster Under the Bed: How Business Is Mastering the Opportunity of Knowledge for Profit* (New York: Simon and Schuster, 1994), 125.

6. Judith Rodin, "A Summons to the 21st Century," *Pennsylvania Gazette*, December 1994.

7. Liam Fahey, *Outwitting, Outmaneuvering and Outperforming Competitors* (New York: John Wiley and Sons, 2000), 3–4.

8. Ibid., 4–6.

9. Sources of competition are derived from Michael E. Porter, *On Competition* (Boston: Harvard Business School Press, 1996), 21–37.

10. Ibid., 33–34.

11. Ibid., 23–28.

12. Ibid., 28–32.

13. Ibid., 32.

14. Bergquist, *The Four Cultures*, 1–4.

CHAPTER 5

Strategy in Colleges Committed to the Liberal Arts

For all of their strengths—specifically, their commitment to education that prepares students for life—liberal arts colleges are not readily understood by broad segments of society. They are not particularly responsive to rapidly unfolding events and public opinion. And, unlike their public-sector counterparts, they are driven more by internal stakeholders than by external constituencies. They are inclusive of a broad range of institutions, from elite, highly selective colleges like Swarthmore College in the East to Buddhist-influenced Soka University in the West and values-based Olivet College in the Midwest. At first glance, they seem to be more different than alike. As a group, however, they face similar competitive challenges and employ similar strategies regardless of their history, selectivity, size, or location.

In this chapter, strategy is examined in institutions committed to the liberal arts. The settings that are used to explore the relationship between context and strategy vary among institutions according to prestige, cost, tradition, selectivity, commitment to religious principles, the makeup of internal stakeholders, and more. These points of variation are important because they propel institutions toward strategy alternatives that fit specific circumstances and situations. The same is true of leaders. They are impelled to think and act in ways that fit the context in which their institutions operate.

ROOTS OF A STRATEGIC DILEMMA

As we look at liberal arts colleges and the competitive challenges they face, a dilemma is apparent for many, if not most, of these institutions. It can be described as follows:

> Colleges dedicated to traditional curricula and synchronous delivery may encounter difficulty in a market rife with lower-cost competitors. Cost, convenience, quality, and market relevance are factors that weigh heavily in student decisions about where they will go and what they will pay.

Colleges that do not recognize this dynamic and move to differentiate their product could experience difficulty in maintaining market share. Let's see how this could happen through the experience of two fictitious, but all-too-real institutions: Prestige University and Denominational College.

Prestige University

Prestige University is a venerable institution of the liberal arts located on the eastern seaboard. Founded in 1835, it is loosely affiliated with the Methodist Church and prides itself on the quality and durability of its core curriculum. Its enrollment has remained stable at 1,600 students for more than a decade. Prestige is ambitious; its vision is to compete with the best colleges in the region and, in so doing, to become one of the nation's top liberal arts colleges. It is familiar with the criteria used for ranking liberal arts colleges: peer assessment, rejection rate, entering student ACT/SAT scores, faculty resources, student/faculty ratio, retention, alumni giving, financial resources, graduation rate, and the like. Unfortunately, Prestige is not faring as well as its competitors on several of these indicators. Its rejection rate is lower than that of other colleges; its alumni do not donate in proportion to their income; and it is having difficulty attracting and retaining top faculty in competition with peer institutions.

Anxious to improve Prestige's position, but uncertain as to the payoff associated with different initiatives, the president and executive team have opted to minimize risk by putting their eggs in a number of different baskets. They have sought and received an invitation to join an athletic conference comprised of elite institutions—what might be called prestige by association. They have increased the price of tuition to reinforce the notion that price is correlated with quality. And they have decided to overhaul the core curriculum by creating a Prestige College Compact—a move designed to link courses and curricula directly with executive skills valued by Fortune 500 companies. The revenue needed to resource the compact would come from a $50 million Prestige Challenge campaign targeted to donors and alumni who want to put the college over the top.

Almost immediately, the team encounters difficulty with several aspects of the plan. Prestige was admitted to the athletic conference, but its teams fared poorly in competition and contributed little to its effort to gain recognition as a top tier school. The parents of prospective students reacted with displeasure to the tuition increase. They felt that "although Prestige costs as much if not more than other colleges, it did not match them in quality or reputation." Their technology-savvy progeny, the first wave of Millennial or Now Generation students entering Prestige, were challenging as well. Synchronous delivery of prescribed courses in the compact's core curriculum did not appeal to them. Accustomed to high-tech convenience, these students wanted 24/7 access to services on the Internet, access to a bevy of distance delivery courses at Prestige and other institutions, and the capacity to "swirl" credits from multiple institutions together into a degree from Prestige. A recent move by regional community colleges and teaching universities to partner in the delivery of lower-cost general education courses on the Internet further complicated the college's position by opening up additional choices for students. And then there was the faculty—the backbone of the institution. Feeling that traditional values endemic to the liberal arts were being compromised by the injection of a "corporate dimension" into the curriculum, they resisted the move to restructure the core curriculum.

The failure of Prestige to fully anticipate and comprehend the changing needs of students, the mind-set of its faculty, and the behavior of competitors marginalized the success of many of its initiatives. If leaders had moved earlier, and in concert with faculty, to restructure the curriculum using robust information about changing student needs and preferences, the college might have been able to differentiate its product. Lacking a distinctive product, Prestige sealed its reputation as a second-tier college, at least for the short term.

Denominational College

A small religious college in the South, Denominational has watched its resource base erode after years of successful operation. At its peak in the 1980s, the college enrolled more than 1,000 students. Now it enrolls fewer than 500 students, and it is rapidly running out of money. Over the past few years, it has spent much of its limited endowment on operations. The church is no longer in a position to allocate additional resources, and the college is maxed out on contributions from the board. For the short term, there are only two ways out of the dilemma: increase enrollment and secure private funding.

Knowing that time is limited, the president has asked members of the executive committee of the board for help in securing private funding to address the enrollment problem. The executive committee members agreed to lend support, but will only do so if three conditions are met: (1) membership on the board must double in number with new trustees added on the basis of personal income, influence, and connections; (2) the executive team must develop a realistic plan for increasing enrollment including target markets and projections, action steps, a timeline, and resource requirements; and (3) the college must show a significant gain in enrollment and operate in the black within two years. As part of the business plan, the president hired a new admissions director and a marketing consultant was brought on board. They took immediate steps to rectify the enrollment problem, but the damage had been done. Word had leaked out about the college's financial problems and new student recruitment became much more difficult as competitors took advantage of the situation. With only a short time to increase enrollment and achieve financial solvency, the president huddled with the executive team to determine what could be done to turn the situation around.

The obvious solution was to work harder to recruit students. A "market it and they will come strategy" was implemented. Efforts were made to expand the recruitment base, to offer more scholarships, and to attractively market the best the college had to offer. The early results were discouraging. At the end of the first year, enrollment had not risen appreciably despite the additional resources spent on recruitment. Frustrated and determined to put the college on a better path, the president met with the admissions director. She put the problem into perspective by describing a conversation with a prospective student in which an offer of admission and a scholarship had been declined. When the student was asked why he would not be attending Denominational, he responded, "For the same price, I can go to five other colleges just like yours, which are closer to home. For half the price, I can go to the University of Georgia, and for a third of the price to Georgia State University. Even though I like your campus and your programs of study, they are not different enough from other schools to justify paying more to go to Denominational."

The president immediately realized the problem: he was unable to answer the prospect's question in a convincing way, and he was certain that no one else on campus had a good answer. Denominational's problem was not in *how* it was marketing and recruiting, but rather in *what* it was marketing. It did not have a clear idea of what it was trying to sell.

When it comes to competition, liberal arts colleges do very little to differentiate themselves from other colleges. Consider for a moment the following attributes and ask yourself if they are not part of a dilemma facing liberal arts colleges:

- nearly all are tuition dependent and susceptible to downward swings in enrollment that can seriously impact the bottom line;
- with a few notable exceptions, they tend to cost appreciably more than public colleges and universities;
- they share a common commitment to holistic student development and critical thinking through a core curriculum;
- they operate in a steady state changing as necessary to adjust to substantiated trends in the external environment; and
- they benchmark themselves against institutions they consider to be their peers.

These attributes distance liberal arts colleges from the mainstream of competition. In so doing, they contribute to a strategic problem: how to convince prospective students that a liberal arts education is worth the additional expense because it is *better than or different from* the education provided by other institutions. Denominational College was awakened to the reality of its broad competitive environment when it used data from its new admissions-tracking software and discovered that the top three institutions chosen by students who decided to go elsewhere were not other liberal arts colleges, but rather research universities and state teaching universities. Denominational was losing more students to institutions dissimilar in purpose and cost than to institutions it benchmarked against. Even more surprising was the realization that two community colleges were in the top-ten list of institutions that prospective students were choosing from. A large number of students who left Denominational College without a degree were taking classes at a community college, and over half of the graduating students had completed at least one course at a community college during one of their summer breaks.

The lesson of Denominational and Prestige is that liberal arts colleges must acknowledge and confront market forces that are broader than their immediate peers. Thirty years ago, attending a small private college was an easy choice for a high-performing student from an affluent home. Today, however, student interest is growing in institutions that are affordable and convenient, offer an eclectic curriculum, and provide a comprehensive out-of-class experience.

THE CUSTOMER IS THE PRODUCT

Pine and Gilmore argue in their book, *The Experience Economy*, that the market is moving away from a commodities, goods, or service-driven economy to a market that values experience.[1] People are more than just consumers—they are themselves both the product and the customer. The applicability of this concept to liberal arts colleges is both interesting and compelling. The minimum product that any institution of higher education offers is preparation for further education or a job with reasonable compensation. Liberal arts colleges provide impressive credentials (a tangible good) along with job placement (a service), but more importantly, they provide—or should provide—a unique, transformative experience.

Students interested in liberal arts colleges are not merely looking for the goods or services that a college education can provide. They are interested in both the tangible and intangible outcomes of a transformative college education: one that is unique from the experience that another college can provide. As such, liberal arts colleges are not in the business of offering credits and degrees; they are in the business of transforming students at an important stage in life. To provide this transformative experience, colleges must recognize the personal nature of their relationship with students—a relationship involving personnel in every part of the institution. The experience they provide must be meaningful and unique since the student, as both the consumer and the product, determines the value of the experience.

Commoditization Through Declaration

Many colleges believe that their declarations have strategic value but, in reality, they do very little to distinguish a college from its peers. When viewed across institutions, the most common forms of declaration—mission and vision statements—look and sound remarkably alike. They all mention a commitment to quality, a supportive environment, social or civic engagement, lifelong learning, and an appreciation for diversity. Carroll (2003) labels this "a discordant melody of sameness" in which institutions become part of a snakelike procession in mission, marketing, and behavior that leads to a common image presented over and over to the same audience.[2] There are exceptions, of course, such as when an institution's unique mission is stated and executed in a way that differentiates it from competitors. For example, Olivet College in Michigan promotes "Education for Social Responsibility." Its mission and vision are built around a commitment to education for individual and social responsibility that is articulated through the Olivet College Compact:[3]

- I am responsible for my own learning and personal development.
- I am responsible for contributing to the learning of others.
- I am responsible for service to Olivet College and the larger community.
- I am responsible for contributing to the quality of the physical environment.
- I am responsible for treating all people with respect.
- I am responsible for behaving and communicating with honesty and integrity.
- I am responsible for the development and growth of Olivet College.

The Olivet College Compact affects the entire campus experience, from scheduling classes to planning and structuring student activities. Because of Olivet's emphasis on the relational nature of education, there are no classes scheduled on Wednesdays, which are reserved for guest lectures, campus symposia, and required weekly meetings of students with their faculty advisors. Advising at Olivet sets it apart from other colleges in that, in addition to having faculty advisors, each student also has career and clinical advisors. The career advisors are on-campus counselors while the clinical advisors are professionals working in the field that the student is interested in pursuing. In order to graduate, all students must complete a senior portfolio that is assessed by all three of their advisors. In this way, they make intentional linkages between their liberal arts education for social responsibility and its applicability to their developing career.

In its unique approach to education, Olivet is not better or worse than other colleges; it is *different*. Look at the college mission statements below and compare and contrast them with Olivet's. The message in each is essentially the same.

Grinnell College (Iowa)

The College pursues a mission of educating young men and women in the liberal arts through free inquiry and the open exchange of ideas. As a teaching and learning community, the College holds that knowledge is a good to be pursued both for its own sake and for the

intellectual, moral, and physical well-being of individuals and of society at large. The College exists to provide a lively academic community of students and teachers of high scholarly qualifications from
diverse social and cultural circumstances. The College aims to graduate women and men who can think clearly, who can speak and
write persuasively and even eloquently, who can evaluate critically
both their own and others' ideas, who can acquire new knowledge,
and who are prepared in life and work to use their knowledge and
their abilities to serve the common good.[4]

Aquinas College (Michigan)

Aquinas College, an inclusive educational community rooted in
Catholic Dominican tradition, provides a liberal arts education with
a global perspective. At Aquinas, we emphasize career preparation
with a focus on leadership and service to others. An Aquinas education fosters a commitment to lifelong learning dedicated to the
pursuit of truth and the common good.[5]

Swarthmore College (Pennsylvania)

Swarthmore students are expected to prepare themselves for full,
balanced lives as individuals and as responsible citizens through exacting intellectual study supplemented by a varied program of sports
and other extracurricular activities. [Swarthmore College's mission]
is to make its students more valuable human beings and more useful members of society. Although Swarthmore shares this purpose
with other educational institutions, each school, college, and university seeks to realize that purpose in its own way; . . . Swarthmore
seeks to help its students realize their fullest intellectual and personal potential, combined with a deep sense of ethical and social
concern.[6]

These mission statements communicate values, ideals, and purpose,
but they do little to distinguish these institutions from one another. By
focusing on what the institution seeks to provide to students, in contrast
to what it actually delivers, they commoditize the liberal arts. Recall that
the difference between *strategy* and *strategic* is determined, in part,
through four questions: Who are the stakeholders? What kind of value
is created for these stakeholders? Does the value created lead to advantage by differentiating the institution from its competitors? Is the advantage sustainable? The mission statements from Grinnell, Aquinas,
Swarthmore, and many other liberal arts colleges do not address these
questions.

Value Added Through Tactics

The tradition of a core curriculum and emphasis on community are fundamental elements of the liberal arts experience. Faculty and staff are the caretakers of this tradition, and they are also its primary customers. In their devotion to the liberal arts and belief in the empowering ideal of the core curriculum, they may have put the product before the customer by failing to ask how the product must change to meet or exceed changing student needs and interests. It is a tactical error to assume that the inherent value of the curriculum and the power of community will attract more and better students. Generations are turning over more quickly than ever, and students are changing in needs, preferences, and expectations. Tomorrow's students will almost certainly differ from today's in needs and expectations for service, preferred approaches to learning, and expectations of the college experience. Without a full understanding of who the students are, what they are thinking and why, and what they want, a college cannot expect to offer a truly contemporary educational experience.

The *core curriculum* of liberal arts colleges pervades the design of their pedagogy and curriculum. It is enduring and traditional, but in a world of turbulent change and global competition, its real value lies beyond the walls of the institution. In keeping with the emphasis that business and industry leaders place on the importance of critical thinking and the ability to understand multiple perspectives, the core curriculum may differentiate liberal arts colleges from other institutions. Employers publicly and privately decry the lack of soft skills and critical thinking capability in workers in profit and nonprofit organizations. They portray a gap between what is permitted in education and what is required in work that may subliminally set workers up to fail. Showing up late or not at all, missing deadlines, and asking for an opportunity to redo poor work are options in the world of education, but they are not options in the world of work. By educating the whole person, liberal arts colleges may prepare students who are better equipped for the workforce upon graduation.

The intangible notion of *community* is one of a liberal arts college's most important tools in differentiating itself from its peers. Students on liberal arts college campuses develop indelible memories of space and architecture, tradition and ritual, interaction with instructors, relationships with friends, and experience in formal and informal groups. They commonly explain their college choice by describing the institution as an extension of home. "When I came to visit, I just felt at home here. People were friendly. They knew my name." A liberal arts experience provides both a family and an affiliative community that is experienced through the personal nature of interaction within small groups on campus. Upon graduation, community is experienced as membership in a privileged body of alumni.

BUILDING DISTINCTIVENESS THROUGH STRATEGY

Declarations make the case for liberal arts colleges as a unique educational entity, but fail to distinguish them from one another. Tactics, such as the core curriculum and the power of community, add value to the lives of students and, in so doing, distinguish the liberal arts experience from other forms of college experience. Together, however, they do not differentiate liberal arts colleges from other institutions sufficiently to make a convincing argument for investment. From the perspective of strategy, what is it about liberal arts colleges that makes them unique and distinctive? What attributes and capabilities differentiate them from other institutions and lead to advantage? Four approaches to strategy can be considered in response to these questions: (1) distinctive mission, (2) institutional prestige, (3) cost, and (4) unique experience. All of them are potentially useful, but only the last is universally applicable to liberal arts colleges; therefore, it will receive the most attention,

Distinctive Mission

As previously discussed, very few liberal arts colleges have a truly distinctive mission. In general, they tend to use the same broad language to describe institutional purpose and commitment. If one was to take the mission statements of five colleges and remove the names from each, it might be difficult for even the presidents of the institutions to pick their own mission from the mix. However, the declared missions of some colleges are so unique that they represent a distinctive approach to strategy in their own right. Consider, for example, the mission and purpose of Berea College in Kentucky:

> Berea's contemporary mission is to educate students "primarily from Appalachia, black and white, who have great promise and limited economic resources."[7]

Since its founding in 1855, Berea College has been guided by a vision of a college and a community committed to interracial education, to the Appalachian region, and to the equality of all persons regardless of race, creed, color, gender, or class. Today, 80 percent of Berea's students come from Kentucky and the Appalachian region; the remainder come from the rest of the United States and from around the world. Approximately 12 percent of the college's students are African American, and international students representing 68 countries comprise 7 percent of the student population. Such diversity strategically places Berea to prepare students for living in a multicultural world.

Guided by a self-help philosophy, Berea's distinctive character has long been its commitment to provide a tuition-free education. Each of the college's 1,500 students receives a full-tuition scholarship. A significant distinction in the Berea tuition model is a work program in which each student receives a job. Whether assisting in the computer center or maintaining the campus grounds, students integrate productive work, disciplined learning, career exploration, and personal development by working ten to fifteen hours per week in any of 130 labor departments that range from food service, to handicrafts, to technology, to academic research. Beyond the practical goal of self-help, the work program is grounded in Berea's belief that all work has "dignity as well as utility" and that work is done in service to the community. Witness the following comment from a student.

> Berea's work study program is wonderful. Through work, I have become more disciplined and have learned to manage my time better. I also contribute my talent to the college. When I make a Berea College broom, I have an intense feeling of self-accomplishment. When I sell a broom, I have the added bonus of meeting a customer who is appreciative of my work. I enjoy talking with customers about my jobs. I also talk with alumni, and they tell me about their days at Berea, with many of their stories revolving around their labor positions. I know that, like them, I will never forget how my work contributes to my education.[8]

As unique as Berea is, it does not stand alone among institutions whose mission differentiates them from rivals. Denominational institutions with a stated purpose of preparing church workers have a strategic advantage through their mission. If a pre-seminary degree from a denominational institution is a prerequisite for acceptance into a denomination's seminary or its church service positions, then the mission of preparing church workers distinguishes it from its competition. For most liberal arts colleges, however, the mission is but one means of creating an advantage over competitors. Factors such as prestige, cost, and the college experience also enter the equation as described below.

Institutional Prestige

While institutional prestige is particularly useful for highly selective established colleges, even less-selective colleges can find utility in prestige as a strategic frame. Institutions like Amherst, Colgate, and Swarthmore have national prestige, but many liberal arts colleges have regional or niche prestige. Regional prestige is evident in colleges like Kalamazoo College (Michigan), Hendrix College (Arkansas), and Wittenberg College (Ohio). Niche prestige is easily evident in religious institutions such as Wheaton College (Illinois), Taylor University (Indiana), and Bryan College (Tennessee). Regardless of whether an institution has a national, regional, or niche reputation, prestige is a viable frame for strategy. By seeking to position itself as the crème de la crème among its competitors, an institution can gain a competitive advantage. The value of prestige is in its relative sustainability. It takes decades or even centuries to attain an elite status. Once this status is achieved, it takes time for current performance to catch up with reputation and for decline to become apparent to the public.

The benchmarks of reputation and prestige are all too familiar for liberal arts colleges. They begin with attributes that can be easily seen and measured—institutional history, campus appearance, value of the physical plant, financial resources, size of endowment, and selectivity—and extend to attributes that are less easily measured including faculty credentials, student quality, peer-institution perceptions, student retention, graduation rate, student outcomes in work and further education, and the accomplishments of alumni. Using these indicators for the purpose of illustration, Vassar College provides an interesting example of the relationship between prestige and strategy. Located seventy miles north of New York City in the picturesque Hudson Valley, Vassar was founded as a women's college in 1861. It originally served as the sister school to Yale University, but Vassar was established with an entirely different objective than to provide women with the finishing experience often associated with women's colleges at the time. It was envisioned as an elite women's institution that would rival the education provided by elite men's colleges.

Today this vision is communicated in virtually everything that Vassar does, beginning with the architecture of the campus, which introduces students and families to the "Vassar experience." The 1,000-acre campus is both a national arboretum and a showcase of architectural history with a three-foot-high stone wall separating it from the surrounding city. Every tree, garden, lake, and building is kept in pristine condition and is part of a story that connects to the founding of the institution.[9] The $840 million physical plant and grounds *are* Vassar. Beyond the architecture is a tradition of prestige manifested in exclusivity and affluence: an average SAT score of 1377 for entering students (2004), an admission rate of 28.7 percent (Class of 2008), a $608 million endowment, and a $120 million general fund operating budget.[10]

Vassar has developed an eccentric and individualistic ambiance, providing the intimacy and nurturing typical of a liberal arts college, while also being decidedly different. The Vassar student does not fit the typical college student profile. It is rare to find groups of students in jeans, sweatshirts, and baseball caps. Rather, Vassar students express their individuality through artistic self-expression and uniquely conceived apparel. This is reinforced by an affirming environment for students of diverse background and persuasion, ideology, and learning preferences. Individual preference and choice extend into the curriculum as well. A popular option is the self-designed major, which has an unlimited horizon. It is not unusual for students to work individually and in teams on long-term interdisciplinary projects that involve unusual approaches to research. More than half of the junior class elects to diversify their knowledge and intercultural skills by studying abroad.

The residential experience at Vassar is traditional, with over 95 percent of the students living in residence halls or college apartments. Selected members of the faculty and their families live alongside the students in residence halls. Classes are small and opportunities for interaction with faculty are frequent. Students are on a first-name basis with their professors, who they routinely encounter in the classroom, as partners on research projects, in the residence halls and dining facilities, and in campus activities. Undergraduates are exposed to opportunities for research throughout their academic career. One-on-one mentoring relationships are developed around research, which often culminates in a required thesis in the senior year. Tightly established advising relationships and personal connections make it difficult for a student to slip through the cracks. Faltering performance in the classroom is monitored directly by a faculty member, who helps the student develop a strategy to get back on track.

Faculty are the mainstay of Vassar and set the intellectual and creative tone of the institution. Value to them is the opportunity to reside and raise their families in an exclusive physical and intellectual environment. Personal ideologies often align with institutional values, but challenges to the norm are invited and encouraged. Faculty enjoy the same opportunities for personal, academic, and professional explorations that students experience. Creative approaches to academic disciplines are explored with a level of freedom that is not found at other institutions.

Teaching and mentorship are highly valued and there is extensive support for academic research. Students develop confidence and expertise early in their college career, which is strengthened by opportunities to participate directly in faculty research and departmental projects. The creative thinking and problem-solving skills that evolve make Vassar graduates highly sought after by graduate schools and corporate employers. Many graduates assume leadership positions in profit and nonprofit organizations, government, health care, and socially oriented foundations.

Is the value that Vassar offers unique? Yes and no. Value similar in form and expression can certainly be described for other colleges, particularly those with a similar pedigree. As with any and all colleges, however, it is difficult to find metrics that can answer this question. Certainly graduation rates, advanced degrees, employment trends, and achievements of graduates can be tracked and compared to students enrolled in other colleges. Movement into leadership positions and unusual contributions to community and society can also be determined. But it is the name recognition associated with being a Vassar graduate that is inherently unique, and this uniqueness is sustainable. Vassar is what it is precisely because its value is inherently sustainable.

Cost

Most liberal arts colleges operate under a high-tuition, high-discount model, in which actual tuition costs are reduced through scholarships and non-loan assistance that provide anywhere from 40 to 60 percent of the published tuition rate.[11] A select few colleges have chosen to use lower cost as a strategy for attracting students from specific target markets. For example, Grove City College in Pennsylvania deliberately keeps tuition and fees low and offers less in scholarships than peer institutions. Instead of using a high sticker price and discount package as a measure of prestige, it uses reduced tuition to attract the students it wants. With tuition, fees, room and board, and a notebook computer priced at less than $14,300 a year, Grove City has been able to attract so many students that *Barron's Guide to the Most Competitive Colleges* (2003) lists it as one of the fifty most selective institutions in the country.[12]

The Grove City example suggests that there are two viable pricing strategies for liberal arts colleges. The first is a high-price, high-discount strategy designed to conform to consumer perception that price is a correlate of quality—that is, "you get what you pay for." In this approach to strategy, an institution seeks to convey more prestige than its immediate peers through higher pricing. The second pricing strategy—keeping costs low and providing less in scholarship assistance—results in a perception of getting significant value through a liberal arts education for less money. The institution builds a reputation for quality and an advantage over peers by attracting more and better students through an attractive education offered at a lower price.

Unique Experience

Perhaps the very essence of strategy for liberal arts colleges is the unique nature of the liberal arts experience. Despite the growing popularity of large research universities, for many Americans a small, private, liberal arts education still represents the ideal college experience. If Pine and Gilmore's (1999) assessment of the economy's migration toward the growing value of experience is correct, then liberal arts colleges should be able to capitalize on the way in which they provide a unique educational experience.[13] A simple experiment that can be carried out on any campus at any time will reveal the power of experience and its essential difference from education as a commodity. Engage instructors on college and university campus in a conversation and ask them what business their college is in. The first response will probably be, "We are in the business of imparting knowledge and skills to students through courses that lead to a degree and enable them to achieve important goals." Upon further reflection, one might ask, "Aren't we really in the business of making a difference for students, of transforming their lives?" Liberal arts colleges are in the business of transforming lives. They have a natural advantage over larger, more impersonal institutions in creating value for their students in three important ways: engagement, intimacy, and connectedness.

By engaging small groups of students in classroom and co-curricular activities in unique and distinctive ways, liberal arts colleges create an experience that goes beyond the more generic one that other institutions provide. Intimacy is a second important means through which value is created. Small class sizes, residential campuses, and personal relationships with faculty, staff, and administrators set liberal arts colleges apart from larger colleges. Finally, students' need for connectedness adds to the appeal of liberal arts colleges. Personal connection is experienced through a campus community that provides an extended "family" where "everybody knows your name," in which students can experience unparalleled connections with both peers and professors. This is evident in the words of a student reflecting on her choice of St. Edward's College in Texas:[14]

> I chose St. Edward's because I was looking for smaller classes and more personalized service. At the larger universities I considered I would have been just a number. After waiting in line for over an hour at one university to meet with a counselor, I was told that most first-year classes have on average 150 students in them. I couldn't fathom how anyone can learn in a class with 150 people in it. . . . While at St. Edward's, I never had a class with more than forty students and all my professors knew me by name. I also developed relationships with my professors whose real life experiences fostered my intellectual growth and pushed me to be a better student. I looked forward to going to class—that was something I had never experienced before.

Connectedness is also maintained through lifelong friendships formed during college and reinforced through alumni communications, programs, and activities after college. Liberal arts colleges, more than any other form of postsecondary education, appeal to those who value connectedness.

Using the ideas of Pine and Gilmore, let's see how the concept of experience could work in a liberal arts college. What follows is derived directly from the conceptual work of Pine and Gilmore in *The Experience Economy* (1999). According to the authors, an experience can engage students on any number of dimensions. Consider two of the most important as depicted in the axes of Figure 5.1.[15] The first (on the horizontal axis) corresponds to the level of student *participation*. At one end of the spectrum lies *passive* participation, where students do not directly affect or influence the activity. A student moving through a highly organized registration process controlled by staff or sitting in a classroom with sixty other students listening to a lecture delivered by a professor would be an example of passive participation. At the other end of the spectrum lies *active* participation, in which students personally affect the activity. Examples would include a seminar or a small-group activity in which students actively participate in creating their own experience.

The second (vertical) dimension of experience describes the kind of *connection* or *context relationship* that ties students to the activity. At one end of this spectrum lies *absorption*—occupying a student's attention by bringing the experience into the mind. At the other end *immersion*—becoming physically (or virtually) a part of the experience. In other words, if the experience goes into the student, as when watching a video, then he is absorbing the experience. If, on the other hand, the student goes into the experience, as when organizing and leading a classroom discussion, then he is immersed in the experience. Students watching a play in a performing arts center absorb the event taking place before them from a distance. Meanwhile, the students who are acting in the play are

Figure 5.1
Realms of Experience

Experience Realms

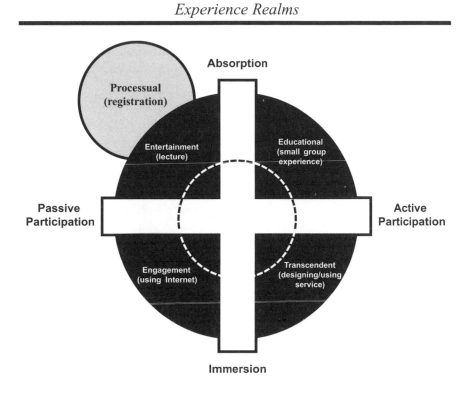

immersed in the experience. A student inside a lab during a physics experiment will be immersed more than when she just listens to a lecture; creating a work of art in a studio will immerse a student in the experience far more than looking at the artwork in a gallery.

The coupling of these dimensions defines five realms of experience: processual, entertainment, educational, engagement, and transcendent, as shown in Figure 5.1—mutually compatible domains at work in a liberal arts college that form uniquely personal experience. The kinds of activities that students experience as *processual* or *entertainment* occur when they passively absorb the experience through their senses, as generally occurs when they participate in an orderly process (registration, orientation, academic advising) or listen to a classroom lecture. Similar to entertainment, with *educational* experiences the student absorbs the activities unfolding before him. Unlike entertainment, however, educational experience involves active participation on the part of the student. To truly engage a student, the activity must draw him in such as small-group work in a classroom or intensive discussion in a seminar. Memorable experiences in the fourth realm, *transcendent*, involve much greater immersion than processual, entertainment, or educational experiences. The student in the transcendent experience is completely immersed in it, and actually creates the activity through his involvement in it. Examples of campus experiences that are transcendent include chat rooms in which students share conceptions of campus life, research projects involving collaboration between students and professors, and participation in athletic events. The fifth and last experiential realm is *engagement*. In such experiences, students immerse themselves in an activity, but have little or no effect on it, leaving the activity (but not themselves) essentially untouched. Engagement experiences include visiting an art gallery or museum on campus, browsing in the campus bookstore, sitting in a coffee house in the college union and watching people interact. While students partaking of an educational experience want to *learn* by absorbing information, and those involved in a transcendent experience want to *do*, those partaking of an engagement experience just want to *be* there.

Putting these ideas to work in a liberal arts college as part of a strategy to differentiate the institution from competitors, would entail creating as much experience as possible in the engagement and transcendent realms. To accomplish this, leaders will need to draw on the principles of engagement, intimacy, and connectedness mentioned earlier to forge a community in which students are empowered to create experience through what they do inside and outside of class. Immersion most readily occurs in small groups where students create the experience by becoming part of it, by leading or participating in classroom discussion, collaborating with professors on research, organizing a campus activity, carrying out an academic project, creating a work of art, or participating in an athletic event. Liberal arts colleges that embrace connectivity through small class size, extensive interaction with peers and professors, innovative living and learning experiences, and student involvement in campus activities will have a natural advantage in creating experience that sets them apart from other colleges. The trick is how to describe this experience and its implications for students during and after college in a way that can be easily understood by prospective students.

Measuring Experience

The quality of experience is almost impossible to measure objectively, therefore other indicators or proxies are necessary. An institution's *total enrollment* is generally a good starting point for determining the nature of the experience a college will have the potential to offer. Students seeking a smaller liberal arts environment will think twice about an institution perceived to be too large to provide an environment of intimacy. However, if enrollment is too small, a college may be viewed as having inadequate academic and social opportunities.

The *student/faculty ratio* is also a viable indicator of opportunities for engagement. A preference for small class size, interaction with peers and professors inside and outside of class, and mentorship opportunities shapes prospective students' opinions about what their experience would be like on a campus with a high or low student/faculty ratio. Similarly, *student characteristics* are an important indicator of the experience a student will encounter on campus. Prospective students who are looking for opportunities to join an intimate, connected "family" are naturally concerned about who will be part of the "family" they will join. Student characteristics that define the community include community of origin; background experience; average standardized test scores and GPAs; racial, ethnic, religious, and gender composition of the student body; and student interests and achievement.

A fourth and closely related indicator of experience is the *residential nature of the campus*. The percentage of students living on campus, the size and architecture of residence halls and floors, the number of student and staff residential advisors, rules and community norms (such as alcohol and smoking policies), and the number of dining halls and informal social spaces are all indicators of the residential experience. Conclusive judgments about the quality of a liberal arts experience cannot be based solely on individual pieces of information, but students do use this information in forming perceptions about institutions in the process of college choice.

THE SACRED AND THE SECULAR

Given the religious orientation of many liberal arts colleges, we would be remiss not to address unique opportunities for strategy inherent in the mission and characteristics of religiously affiliated institutions. Religious institutions face both the challenge of demonstrating relevance that will attract students in an increasingly secular society, and the opportunity afforded by the current trend in values-based, socially responsible education. Although church attendance is on the decline, particularly among young people, a curriculum that is grounded in moral and ethical training is attractive, both to prospective students and to potential employers.[16] In a post-Enron, post-WorldCom, post–Martha Stewart world, many religiously affiliated institutions may have the advantage of appealing to students looking for a curriculum and a community that can promote spiritual and ethical development. Clearly, the transformative nature of this type of college experience may have reached a new level of importance in a changing social context.

In their approach to strategy, religiously affiliated institutions typically begin with an understanding of the students they are trying to recruit and the competitors who share the same market space. Although students considering religious colleges are seeking an experience unduplicated by a secular institution, a religious institution's competitors are much broader than its immediate religious peers. Prospective students are constantly weighing the value of an expensive religious educational experience against a more affordable secular college experience. Thus, religious institutions must be deliberate in communicating how the education that they provide is indeed superior to that of other religious and secular competitors.

Another consideration for strategy in religious institutions is that, in a religious context, parents generally play a more important role in decision making than they do in a secular context. A more stringent in loco parentis philosophy provides reassurance to families that the institution will continue to guide their children in a manner consistent with their religious traditions. The religious educational experience sought by parents and prospective students is part of the curriculum, extracurricular activities, and the campus culture. Embedded in the process of choice-making by parents and students are deeper interests in theology, sexuality, and other social issues that have a values-base in the classroom. The nature of social interactions with like-minded individuals also provides opportunities to form meaningful relationships, including the potential for meeting a spouse. This is a source of advantage for religiously affiliated colleges.

The King's College in New York City offers an interesting illustration of how strategy can work in a religiously affiliated college. It is without parallel when it comes to creating an unduplicated college experience. Housed on the fifteenth floor of the Empire State Building, The King's College is one of a handful of Christian undergraduate colleges in New York City, and one of a small number of urban religious institutions in the United States. Its 8:1 student-to-faculty ratio is lower than any of its competitors, and its facilities in the Empire State Building are technologically and aesthetically top-notch. It does not attempt to use price as a competitive advantage—its tuition and fees are close to $17,000 per year, far from the most affordable on the market.[17] Residence arrangements are provided to students through buildings and apartments purchased by the college and leased to its students, at an average cost of over

$7,000 per year. With tuition, board, books, and miscellaneous expenses, The King's College annual cost to students is over $28,000 per year.

Even with this high ticket price, the college has been able to attract one of the most diverse student bodies of all Christian colleges, with over 50 percent nonwhite students. The capacity of The King's College to attract minority populations that are so elusive to many of its peer religious institutions takes us back to the question issued at the beginning of this chapter. Why would students pay so much to attend The King's College? The college's success is achieved through a strategy of differentiated mission and unique experience to create distinctive and sustainable value for its students.

The King's College mission is to integrate a Christian liberal arts curriculum with internships on Wall Street and in New York media outlets in a manner that is unduplicated by any other college. The student experience of an intimate, engaged, and connected community in the heart of the nation's busiest city provides an unparalleled experience. This competitive advantage is sustainable because the cost (financial and sustained effort) of competing in the same market as The King's College deters competitors from going head-to-head with it. Thus, The King's College exemplifies how an institution can understand its stakeholders and create value in a way that results in a sustainable advantage.

CONCLUSION

In the fast-changing, competitive market they operate in, liberal arts colleges must realize that the real business they are involved in is transforming lives, not providing programs and services. It is a business of immersing students in experiences that set the stage for realizing their most important goals, not conferring degrees. The strategic advantage for liberal arts colleges in the future will be in the realm of experience, because degrees, programs, and services are no longer enough. Students want engaging experience, and they are willing to pay for it. There is much work involved in creating and staging experience as well as in measuring and marketing its outcomes. The colleges that perform this work in a way that truly engages students are the most likely to succeed.

NOTES

1. B. Joseph Pine and James H. Gilmore, *The Experience Economy: Work Is Theater and Every Business a Stage* (Boston: Harvard Business School Press, 1999).

2. William J. Carroll, "A Discordant Melody of Sameness," *Trusteeship* 11, no. 2 (2003): 13–17.

3. Information derived through campus visitations and conversations with college personnel in 2003 and Web site exploration, www.olivetcollege.edu.

4. Information derived from the Web site of Grinnell College, www. grinnell.edu.

5. Information derived from the Web site of Aquinas College, www. aquinas.edu.

6. Information derived from the Web site of Swarthmore College, www. swarthmore.edu.

7. Information derived from the Web site of Berea College, www.berea.edu.

8. Ibid.

9. Karen Van Lengen and Lisa Reilly, *Vassar College: The Campus Guide* (New York: Princeton Architectural Press, 2004).

10. Telephone and electronic communications with Susan DeKrey, vice president for College Relations at Vassar College on January 14, 2004, and June 14, 2004.

11. National Association of Independent Colleges and Universities, *Independent Colleges and Universities: A National Profile* (Washington, DC: NAICU, 2004).

12. Barron's Educational Series, Inc., College Division, *Barron's Guide to the Most Competitive Colleges*, 3rd ed. (Hauppauge, NY: Barron's, 2003).

13. Pine and Gilmore, *The Experience Economy*, 1–23.

14. Electronic communication with Michelle Tam, executive director of marketing at Cy-Fair College in Cypress, Texas.

15. Figure 5.1 and the discussion related to different realms of experience is adapted directly from the work of Pine and Gilmore, *The Experience Economy*, 28–32.

16. The Barna Group, *Church Attendance*, http://www.barna.org/FlexPage. aspx?Page=Topic&TopicID=10 (accessed May 3, 2004).

17. Information derived from the Web site of The King's College, www. tkc.edu.

CHAPTER

Strategy in Institutions with a Comprehensive Mission

Although community colleges and teaching and research universities are rarely thought of as occupying the same niche within higher education, a closer examination reveals important similarities among these institutions. They enroll and serve diverse student populations, they provide an array of programs and services, and they pursue a broad mission with multiple stakeholders. In addition, they are expected to be more involved in regional and local communities than other segments of higher education. They are *comprehensive* institutions in word and deed, scope and reach, and impact and effect.

Comprehensive institutions are large when compared to other sectors of higher education. They serve multiple audiences, they acquire revenue from multiple sources, they are responsible to multiple stakeholders, and they use multiple venues for educational delivery. Whether it is a research university serving 65,000 students on three campuses, a teaching university serving 30,000 students on a main campus and multiple off-site locations, or a community college district serving 90,000 students through a variety of venues including traditional campuses, off-site centers, and one-stop locations, they are corporate entities unto themselves. Each has a particular identity, but collectively they account for the lion's share of enrollment in postsecondary education. Among their identifying characteristics are size and complexity; comprehensive program and service mix; commitment and service to a diverse population of students including traditional college-age youth, adult learners, and racial and ethnic minorities; accountability to a broad array of internal and external stakeholders; and durability.

The breadth and diversity of these institutions can be an advantage or disadvantage depending on the issue and the stakeholder. Their comprehensive nature allows for greater flexibility in offerings and services, sources of support, and the creation and pursuit of opportunity. Comprehensiveness can become a disadvantage, however, when it renders institutions slow to change, difficult to guide and manage, and incapable of responding to customer needs. Whether advantaged or disadvantaged by their size and complexity, comprehensive institutions have accumulated a considerable amount of leverage with and through the constituencies they serve. They are visible, their actions are noticed, and they are a source of great pride for those who are, or have been, associated with them.

The colleges and universities operating under the mantle of comprehensive institutions are varied and diverse. The market forces buffeting them and their organizational characteristics predispose them toward certain strategy alternatives. Let's see how these strategy alternatives take form through an examination of the context in which these institutions operate.

RESEARCH UNIVERSITIES

Research universities are comprehensive in mission and purpose, but their primary emphasis is on research for the creation, application, and perpetuation of knowledge. Control can be public or private, with ultimate authority residing with a governing board that is either elected or appointed. The boards at private research universities are generally large, often numbering more than fifty persons, with the members recommended by executive officers and elected by the existing members of the board. Because of the shear size of these boards, involvement in internal affairs is limited and executive officers are relied upon to run the institution. Public university boards are quite different. They are small (eight to fifteen members) and elected by voters of the state, appointed by the governor, or elected by alumni of the institution. The board of trustees at a public institution is more likely to be involved in the business of the university. However, control is determined, in large part, by policies and coordinating mechanisms established by the state. It also resides with those who have access to, or control over, money: alumni, corporate benefactors, and elected officials who can influence the flow of resources to the institution.

Multiple sources of revenue including state appropriations, tuition, and federal and state research grants support the operation of research universities They rely heavily on endowment and gift income as well as research grants from the corporate sector. Tuition is typically a small portion of overall income in public universities with federal financial aid comprising much of what is received. The support that research universities receive is somewhat of a double-edged sword. It provides revenue that enables them to expand their commitment to education, research, and service. However, a significant portion comes with political or economic strings attached whether they be those of state or federal government, or of a private corporation.

Organizational Dynamics

A broad-based organizational structure is required to perform the many functions of a research university. The administrative structure of these institutions is complex with executives that oversee academics, business and finance, student development, enrollment management, the board of trustees/regents, development and alumni affairs, individual campuses, legal counsel, athletics, government relations, and public relations/communication. Like most institutions, there is an implicit hierarchy within and among functional areas. Research universities are built on academics, and in keeping with this tradition, the provost or vice president for academic affairs is generally second in command. However, as operating dollars have declined, the business-and-finance function has begun to take on a larger role. Student affairs, fairly or unfairly, are perceived as performing functions that do not directly generate revenue, therefore they are not accorded the same level of clout within the institution as are other areas.

The role of the president is divided into three primary functions: development, government relations, and board of trustee relations. Reliance on endowment and donated resources is growing, and therefore an increasing portion of the president's time is devoted to fund-raising. Guided by the development function, the president is responsible for courting major donors or fronting an endowment campaign. At public institutions the relationship of the institution with the state government is crucial, and the president's time is often dually focused on building these relationships and advocating for the needs of the institution. Finally, the board of trustees is a primary focus of the president; it does, after all, exercise ultimate authority. Trustees are often benefactors in private institutions through the resources they donate, and influence purveyors in public institutions, through their relationship with government officials. The demanding roles and responsibilities shouldered by the president mean that many functions within the institution operate independently and autonomously. On paper, the president has responsibility

for oversight, but has very little time to devote to the day-to-day operations of the university.

Those at research universities are not unaware that money and influence can buy almost anything. While people at these institutions are dedicated to the creation, application, and perpetuation of knowledge,
knowledge production in some areas is more lucrative than in others.
There is a hierarchy among disciplines that reveals itself in the everyday
behavior of the institution. For example, because of the newness of and
the premium placed on research in the life sciences, there would likely
be an excitement surrounding the construction of an elaborate life sciences complex while the Slavic language department might be housed in
the basement of an old residence hall. Institutions deal with differences
in revenue generated by academic programs in different ways. Some
choose to use the general fund budget as a central pool of funds that is
divided among programs without regard to the amount of revenue generated by individual programs. Others follow a practice of responsibility-
centered management, in which each function, department, or school is
required to be financially independent. Typically this means that revenue
streams are taken into account when allocating money to departments,
and each department is responsible for operating within that allotment.

Culture and Climate

The climate and culture of research universities differs from institution to institution because of variation in size, control, location, endowment, and governance. One unifying characteristic of these institutions
is their status as places where critical questions are asked and answered
and where life-changing discoveries are made. Accordingly, academic
programs and disciplines, and the faculty who teach within them, have
a lot to do with the makeup of institutional culture. Institutions take on
the flavor of their programmatic emphases. For example, the prestige of
liberal arts disciplines is felt across campus at the University of Michigan and MIT has developed a bigger-than-life reputation for excellence
in technology and engineering.

The faculty are varied and difficult to characterize. Those who are full-
time occupy tenured or on tenure-track lines, although more and more
courses are being taught by nontenure-track lecturers, teaching assistants,
and clinical practitioners. Professors are acutely aware of the reward system that guides tenure and promotion decisions and, accordingly, place
a strong emphasis on research and scholarship. Many are entrepreneurs
who bring resources to the university through grants they receive from

outside sources. Autonomy is valued, and in general academics would prefer to lead rather than be led. Many, if not most, are content to conduct their research and teach their courses, and choose not to involve themselves in the affairs of the university. Others choose to engage themselves in the life of the institution through service they perform in administrative roles or through membership on committees, task forces, and so forth.

Like faculty, the characteristics of students who attend research universities are varied, making it difficult to describe a typical student. Most are undergraduates, but there is a sizable graduate-student population that absorbs a significant portion of the instructional resources these institutions spend. Students enroll in research universities for many reasons. Some are attracted by a specific area of interest, while others are drawn by the opportunity to explore a myriad of academic options. Some are drawn to the prestige of academics, while others are drawn to athletic programs. Some are attracted by a reputation for quality, while others are attracted by the social and cultural opportunities that are part of campus life. Some prefer urban environments, while others prefer pastoral settings. Some are drawn because of the opportunity to become part of a long-standing tradition, while others are looking for an institution that will allow them some level of anonymity.

Research universities are almost always residential campuses, which expose students to peers from different racial and ethnic groups, nationalities, socioeconomic backgrounds, and life experience. Athletics and social activities are a large part of the culture at many of these institutions. In recent years these schools have poured money into sports programs, which have contributed in significant ways to their identity. At a school like Indiana, which is known for its basketball tradition, or the University of Florida, known for its football tradition, athletics make a definitive contribution to culture and climate.

Internal Challenges

While research universities are among the most durable and sustainable of higher education institutions, they are not without challenges. Internally, some of the more salient challenges include size and complexity, balancing institutional priorities, maintaining faculty vitality, and enhancing quality.

From the standpoint of size and complexity, research universities are massive organizations. Michigan State University, one of the largest institutions in the country, has[1]

- 7 trustees, 1 president, and 11 executive officers
- 200 programs of study in 14 degree-granting colleges
- over 44,000 students and almost 320,000 alumni
- approximately 4,500 faculty and academic staff, 6,000 support staff
- extensions in 83 countries and 200 study-abroad programs
- 660 buildings and 26 residential facilities
- over $870 million in operating revenues, $295 million in sponsored research, almost $400 million in state appropriations, and $60 million in gifts
- 4.5 million volumes in the library
- 12 intercollegiate sports for men and 13 intercollegiate sports for women
- 500 registered student organizations and 53 Greek-letter organizations

In an organization of this size and complexity, strategic and operational management are complicated processes. There are always too many priorities to balance, too many people involved in decisions, and too many moving pieces to manage day to day. Academics compete for attention with social activities and athletics; government relations and development campaigns compete with programmatic issues for time from administrators; and employee groups vie for attention to unique needs that require different approaches to problem solving. Tuition-paying students think their needs should come first; faculty members think their individual research agendas are most important; government officials express concerns about positions taken by professors and institutional activities and costs; employees want better benefits; schools and colleges believe they should get more resources; and alumni want a better football team or renovated performing arts center. Creating and carrying out change in a research university is like turning an ocean liner to avoid an iceberg—it takes time, people, and a lot of open water to successfully accomplish.

Priority disputes are part of organizational life at research universities, and balancing priorities is a constant challenge. On the academic side, the program that is most lucrative may be among the most controversial, the program that is smallest may be world renowned, and the program that is most prestigious may be losing money.

Academics, however, are not the only game in the university: athletics bring money, notoriety, applicants, spirit, and persona to the institution. There is always a question regarding a healthy balance between academics and athletics and of where the line should be drawn between education and business. Finally, there is the balancing act involving the priorities of different constituencies. Students, alumni, politicians, trustees, and donors are attracted to the institution for different reasons.

Decisions regarding which interests to serve, what to do and when to do it, and what not to do are difficult for leaders. The comprehensive mission suggests that the university should respond to a variety of interests, but available resources may force it to choose among them.

Faculty are pivotal to the strategy and operations of research universities. Attracting and retaining "stars" and promising young faculty is an important part of reputation building. Considerable resources therefore are invested in activities that promote and maintain faculty vitality. Professors armed with tenure, research dollars, and visibility can wield considerable power in university affairs. If for some reason, they believe that a new initiative or program is not in keeping with their own or the university's interests, they can slow the decision process and bring change to a walk. Consequently, a lot of time is spent on attracting the best faculty and putting into place conditions—salary, benefits, research support, facilities and technology, and more—that will favorably dispose them to stay.

Research universities are constantly challenged to stay on the leading edge. Many parts of society look to these institutions to produce progressive and sometimes life-changing research results. Not only are they expected to carry out a broad mission, they are expected to perform at a high level in anything they do. Many of these institutions strive to be among the best in every field. They often use their own performance as the yardstick for measuring success. Once a business school achieves top-five status, it is expected to maintain that status over an extended period. To do so, however, it must constantly improve, which means it must always be looking for the next great idea.

External Challenges

Research universities are in a unique position because, unlike other institutions, they are resilient to market fluctuations. Many are so well established that it would take a major event to change their overall market position. This is not to say that research universities are invulner-able to market forces. Among their most pressing challenges are the rapidly increasing population of potential students and the sputtering domestic economy—conditions that threaten to place demand vastly beyond capacity and imbalance the entire postsecondary education industry.

Population of Eligible Students. As the number of students in K–12 education changes, the number of students seeking higher education also fluctuates in a delayed pattern. The children of Baby Boomers are moving through K–12 education in record numbers, resulting in dramatic growth in the number of students available to research universities. More of these children are interested in pursuing some form of postsecondary education, which puts added pressure on overextended and underfinanced public universities. In high-growth states where the number of available students is used as a gross measure of the capacity required in colleges and universities, the picture is especially grim. Many institutions have not built or renovated substantially since the end of World War II and still more have not done so since the end of the Vietnam War. With buildings that are out of date and a general lack of capacity, most universities are struggling to ramp up for the next wave of students.

Domestic Economy. In recent years, public and private research universities have been heavily impacted by the continuing erosion of the economy. Publicly supported institutions have suffered from a dip in state aid and private institutions from a decline in gift income. Some have even lost a substantial portion of their endowment. Because research institutions rely so heavily on revenue other than tuition, the increase in potential students will only marginally affect their bottom line as the dollars required to enroll more students will exceed those generated through increased enrollment. An upward turn in the economy will help, but it will not solve the problem of capacity for most institutions. The focus of government spending will be on economic growth, and income generated by for-profit organizations will be invested in research and product development. Not until federal and state government budgets have recovered and private investors have expendable discretionary income will research institutions be able to fully recover. And even then, the loss of years of private giving and government appropriations will not be recovered overnight.

Competition. Primary competition for research universities comes from other research universities. Their rivalry is multifaceted, encompassing competition for students, government appropriations, sponsored grants, prestige, faculty, and staff. To a limited extent, research universities compete with elite liberal arts colleges. These colleges employ discounting practices that bring an intimate and unique educational experience within the financial reach of many students and families. For those students who find advantages in small size, liberal arts colleges are a sound investment. For students looking to save money or to stay close to home, teaching universities and community colleges have become an attractive alternative to the research university. Transfer is always a possibility and the savings students receive through enrollment in a lower-cost institution can be used to offset the cost of upper-level education in a research university. Finally, during good economic times, research universities may find themselves in competition with business and industry. A prime example of this occurred in the late 1990s when top students were lured away from education by wage incentives in the lucrative dot.com industry.

Sources of Advantage

Traditional Prestige. Despite greater competition, research universities have multiple weapons in their arsenal that lead to advantage in the higher education market. First and foremost, they have an aura of prestige and credibility. They are large, well-known institutions with significant name recognition. Durable in structure and function, many have a reputation for quality that has lasted through wars, other world events, and societal transformation. The prestige and credibility of these institutions draw stakeholders who want to study at, work at, donate money to, or otherwise be part of "the best." Traditional prestige, therefore, is both a source of advantage and a frame for strategy in research universities.

The faculty at these institutions are among some of the finest in the world and their work is often at the cutting edge. This is a draw for students looking to learn from the best, but it is also a draw for individuals and organizations seeking to commit resources to institutions that provide a significant return on investment. The name of an individual or corporate donor on a building or school at a major university can bring a return vastly beyond the original investment. For example, the Kellogg School of Management at Northwestern University has provided the Kellogg Company with name recognition worth considerably more than the dollars donated, simply because it is a prestigious business school at one of the best-known research universities in the nation. Likewise, the recently named Steven M. Ross School of Business at the University of Michigan provides continuing visibility to the individual donor beyond the value of the initial gift.

Size and Durability. Like any organization large enough to be in the public eye, research universities are always vulnerable to changing perceptions of their programs, operations, and behavior. Many of these organizations are so large in size and scale, however, that they can make mistakes and not suffer any loss to their reputation or prestige. In the words of a university president who will remain anonymous, they have a capacity to "bleed profusely and survive—a capacity that encourages [the] innovation and risk that are essential for growth." Over time research universities have created a physical and material infrastructure that is beyond the comprehension of the public, let alone the leaders of the institutions themselves. Add to this a reputation for financial soundness and durability (universities are a good investment because they have always been and will be part of the American landscape) and the result is a juggernaut that is immovable in place and time. These institutions are among the longest surviving of organizations—they have survived war, anarchy, and the ravages of public policy and continued to grow and flourish.

Comprehensiveness. The full range of academic programs research universities offer gives them an advantage over niche providers. The inherent efficiency of scale in comprehensiveness attracts students seeking multiple options. For example, a student interested in merging liberal arts with career preparation can pursue a major in psychology while gaining significant research experience in organizational behavior or labor studies as part of a dual-degree program. In addition to the wide range of programs offered, research universities offer students the opportunity to pursue multiple degree and program options. For example, a student completing a bachelor's degree in chemistry has the option of securing program-related employment, enrolling in a graduate program in chemistry, pursuing a master's degree in secondary science education, or even an advanced degree in environmental science. Comprehensive institutions can facilitate student engagement in any one of these tracks—a real convenience for students who prefer the efficiency of completing their education in one institution.

Experience. Students are drawn to the wide-ranging opportunities that are part of co-curricular life at a research university. A panorama of events can be underway at any point in time—a football game, a concert or social gathering, a museum tour, a campus lecture, intramural sports—the list is endless. Students looking for the prototypical academic environment complete with residence halls, co-curricular activities, and Division One sports can easily find it at a research university. Whether it is the ivy-covered walls of Harvard Yard or a football-Saturday at UCLA, many research universities exude a tradition that cannot be imitated. This combination of academic offerings and campus tradition can be attractive to prospective students and alumni alike who view the collegiate experience as an important part of life.

Cost/Benefit. In addition to offering the benefit of experience, for many students public research universities are affordable and academically accessible. As the changing economy and workplace demand more from students in the way of preparation, the value of an education at a research institution increases proportionally. The greater the prestige and the higher the cost, the more significant the benefits, as studies that compare lifetime earnings for students graduating from different types of institutions have shown.

Institutional Strategy Illustrations

Washington University

Washington University in St. Louis, Missouri, is a midsize research university that excels in teaching and research. Founded in 1853, it enrolls 6,500 undergraduate students and 5,500 graduate students in more than 90 academic programs and 1,500 courses per year.[2] The primary goals of the institution are to foster excellence in teaching, research, scholarship, and service; to prepare students to be productive citizens of a global society; and to be an exemplary institution in St. Louis, across the country, and throughout the world.

Washington embraces three frames that constitute its approach to strategy: experience, change, and exceptional teaching and research. From the standpoint of experience, the campus ambiance at Washington is one that is described as involving an "intangible excitement" that can be felt around campus. Students exude this quality whether studying, socializing, or participating in activities, and the University has used it to attract a uniquely talented mix of faculty, staff, and students. The propensity for change at Washington University can best be understood through the writings of Ralph E. Morrow, a former provost at the university. In his book, *Washington University in St. Louis: A History*, Morrow indicates that Eliot, the first president of Washington University, "offered not an academic plan that he wanted to impose upon history, but a pocket compendium of strategies for building an institution over time by cooperating with history. . . . The incorporators, therefore, were at a threshold "of a . . . great work, capable of indefinite extension."[3] The university still abides by this strategy today and is constantly looking to change and improve itself.

The third frame in the approach to strategy at Washington is exceptional teaching and research. In 1996, the university opened an initiative to enhance teaching and research dubbed "Project 21."[4] The goal of Project 21 was to move the university to a level of preeminence in teaching and research achieved by only a handful of institutions worldwide, within the first decade of the twenty-first century. Toward this goal, university leaders set four objectives to be achieved within a decade: to attract and retain outstanding faculty and students, to provide the best learning environment possible, to enhance programs and fields in which the university already enjoyed a strong leadership position, and to develop new areas of scholarly significance with a potential for world leadership in research.

Washington University established one overarching metric to evaluate its success in executing this arm of strategy: movement of the university to a level of preeminence achieved by only a handful of institutions worldwide, by the beginning of the twenty-first century. Apparently the university has been at least partially successful in achieving this goal. In 1996, the year Project 21 began, Washington University was ranked twentieth in university ratings by *U.S. News and World Report*. In 1998, it was ranked seventeenth, and in 2004 it was ranked ninth.

DePaul University

DePaul University is a large private institution in Chicago enrolling more than 20,000 students, most of whom are full-time. Its seven campuses are strategically located throughout the metropolitan area. It does not have the national focus or elite reputation of many research universities, but it is similar to these universities in comprehensiveness and its focus on teaching, research, and co-curricular experiences.

In the mid 1990s, DePaul was an institution of moderate visibility with two campuses, one downtown and one in a more residential area of the city. It was respected, but not considered exemplary. Realizing this, DePaul's leaders looked into options for enhancing the institution's brand and visibility and charted a new course. They elected to increase its size by increasing the number of campuses and making education more accessible and convenient. Their overarching strategy was to become the dominant provider of professional education in Chicago through growth in undergraduate and graduate enrollment.[5]

DePaul identified four tactics for executing its growth strategy:

- *Expediency*: It would be aggressive in its development of delivery systems to meet the needs of prospective and continuing students. Originally only a single campus institution, its most notable venture toward expedience became the opening of six regional campuses.
- *Practicality*: It would strive to provide an education relevant to the everyday lives of its students. With 80 percent of its student population working while in college, practical application (internships, case studies, simulations, etc.) became an important part of courses and curricula.
- *Entrepreneurialism*: It would embrace principles of innovation and risk taking and move beyond the box of traditional education.

- *Diversity*: It would establish and sustain a diverse and inclusive environment of faculty, staff, and students.

The most remarkable nuance of DePaul's new strategy was the way in which leaders introduced it to faculty and staff in the institution. This was not a strategy that sat on a desk and collected dust. A full internal marketing plan was developed and the strategy was introduced to the university community in grand fashion. The leadership team developed measurable goals that would indicate the extent to which DePaul accomplished its strategy of becoming the dominant provider of professional education in the city. Each vice president tracked specific goals, and every division and department developed its own performance goals tied directly to the university's goals. As part of the internal marketing plan, a poster showing progress toward each and all of the goals was created and updated quarterly. As the goals began to permeate the institution, the poster became a centerpiece of attention, often turning up on cubicle walls and cork boards. This action literally unified all of the departments, both academic and administrative, in pursuit of a common strategy within the university.[6]

DePaul has been so successful in executing its strategy it has surpassed its own expectations. Within five years—and five years ahead of schedule—it had met its enrollment target. In 1995, it enrolled just over 17,000, students; today it enrolls 23,500 students. DePaul is currently the largest provider of professional education in the Chicago metropolitan area.[7]

COMMUNITY COLLEGES

Community colleges began as junior colleges and high school extensions a little more than a century ago. They are now among the largest and most comprehensive institutions in the higher education knowledge industry. From serving legions of students in transfer, occupational, and adult education programs, to contracting with business and industry, to serving as a hub for community development, the mission of community colleges is to meet the educational needs of a region, locality, or community. The uniqueness of these institutions and the breadth of their mission means that strategy must be viewed through a lens unlike that of any other organization.

Profiling Community Colleges

As distinct from two-year colleges, community colleges are open-access institutions with a comprehensive mission focused on serving the needs of a local community. Their comprehensive nature is obvious when examining the variety of programs and degrees available to students. A student may be (1) seeking an associate of arts degree in preparation for transfer to a four-year college or university, (2) working toward career entry in an associate of science or associate of science in technology program, (3) a high school student dually enrolled in K–12 and postsecondary coursework, (4) taking a course to keep up with changing workforce demands, (5) a senior citizen taking a leisure course, (6) an employee in a local company receiving industry-specific coursework at the workplace, (7) a four-year college student taking courses to accelerate completion of a baccalaureate degree, or (8) a reverse-transfer student with a bachelor's degree who is interested in skill training for a specific occupation. A growing number of community colleges have established centers on campus where students can take undergraduate or graduate courses from four-year colleges. In special instances, community colleges have received approval to offer bachelor's degree programs in specific fields.

Not only is the mission of community colleges varied and diverse, the student population is as well. Roughly half of all first-time students enrolled in postsecondary institutions attend community colleges. They are diverse in racial and ethnic background as well as academic preparedness. To succeed in navigating the educational system, many of these students need personal attention. Unlike research universities, the focus of community colleges is on the whole student. Flexible programs and learner-centered courses are provided in the comfortable setting of small classes and customer-friendly offices. The faculty-reward system is focused on teaching and learning, which provides an incentive to attend to the individual needs of learners. The student/faculty ratio averages 20:1 on many campuses, and students enrolled in introductory courses are taught by experienced instructors, in contrast to graduate assistants.

Growth in community colleges is fueled by factors of convenience and cost. Estimates indicate that 90 percent of the U.S. population is within a forty-five-minute drive of a community college. With learning opportunities provided through multicampus districts, extension centers, and online education, it is likely that most citizens are within a keystroke of a community college education. Cost is an important consideration for students unable to afford more expensive institutions or who are reluctant to commit to a bachelor's degree institution. Through articulation agreements, specialized arrangements, and university centers, community colleges provide a proving ground for students to build skills and confidence and, ultimately, to test their readiness for advanced education.

Community colleges have a long history of serving the developmental needs of communities through activities such as regional planning and business/industry attraction and retention. Communities depend upon firefighters, police officers, and EMTs trained by community colleges to ensure their safety. Hospitals depend upon associate degree nurses to provide excellent patient care. In addition to preparing civil employees, community colleges open their facilities to the public. Whether for local high school sports, public debates on social issues, or meetings of community-based organizations, they are an extension of the community. Their reach is not restricted to a campus. Much of what they do is delivered off-site in community gathering points such as libraries, shopping malls, K–12 schools, and civic buildings. From courses providing skills in computer basics to learning a language, citizens can learn new skills in the comfort of known surroundings. Community colleges have become a hub for community development and, in so doing, have redefined the notion of community outreach in American higher education.

Finally, because of their role in workforce development, community colleges have a natural linkage to business and industry. More and more businesses require workers to have at least some postsecondary experience. Through credit and noncredit offerings custom crafted to workforce needs, community colleges collaborate with local business and industry to increase occupational opportunities for residents. Working as partners they share facilities and technology, co-create courses and curricula, and underwrite the cost of education to improve the earning power and quality of life of citizens. There are numerous examples of corporate decisions (e.g., Saturn in Tennessee and Mercedes-Benz in South Carolina) to locate in a community because of the opportunity to partner with a community college in developing skilled workers.

Challenges to Vitality

As successful as they have been as a growth enterprise, community colleges are not without challenges. Three, in particular, are on the radar screen of most colleges: increasing demand, declining support, and competition. Among the factors contributing to demand are the record number of students graduating from the nation's high schools, and the rising tide of adult learners requiring education to gain a foothold in the economy. A formula of open access, low cost, and quick response makes community colleges attractive to these learners. Add to this their growing importance in providing customized training for employers and in promoting economic development for communities, and the result is a prescription for growth. With growth comes new problems, however: Where will the resources come from to serve the rising tide of new learners? What capabilities will colleges need to develop to meet the needs of these learners?

While funding has ebbed and flowed in recent years, many believe that the current downturn is part of a pattern of progressive erosion in public support of higher education. When state appropriations lag behind enrollment, operating budgets are rendered incapable of supporting growth and quality. Alternative sources of revenue must be found or reductions must be made to bring expenditures into line with revenue. The mission of community colleges does little to soften the impact of declining appropriations; funding from sources such as research dollars and donor and alumni gifts is not a major source of income in the operating budget. This picture is likely to get worse before it gets better. Community colleges experiencing dynamic growth will need to increase their efficiency or find new ways to support programs. The alternative—which is unpalatable to many colleges—is to close the open door and deliver service to targeted constituencies.

The entry of new players offering advantages of convenience and speed has changed the competitive equation for community colleges. Whereas these colleges have always held an advantage in convenience, fast-moving competitors have replicated this advantage for their own gain. For-profit institutions and online providers offering flexible courses and services have made education remarkably convenient for adult learners. Proprietary institutions holding close working relationships with employers have experienced great success in attracting learners desiring a tight connection between education and work. For-profit institutions operate on a business model designed to anticipate and adjust to market shifts. To keep up with them, a college must have a capacity for rapid and continuous intake of information and an infrastructure that encourages timely conversion of information into action with programs, services, and delivery systems.

Sources of Advantage

Based on this analysis of challenges facing community colleges, it should come as no surprise that there are approaches to strategy uniquely suited to these institutions as illustrated in Table 6.1.

Since their establishment, community colleges have generally relied on low cost and unparalleled convenience to build an advantage over competitors. This has been accomplished by keeping tuition low and providing ready access to programs and services. Environmental turbulence

Table 6.1
Approaches to Strategy in Community Colleges

Approach	Stakeholder	Value Provided	Competitive Advantage	Sustainable?
Convenience	Neighborhood residents benefit from an educational center in the community	Time saved through easy access to conveniently located facilities	Ease of access to programs, facilities, and services exceeds that of competitors	Yes, if competitors do not change their approach to educational delivery
Cost	Students benefit through lower cost of tuition	Money is saved and foregone earnings are minimized	Out-of-pocket costs for students are considerably lower than competitors' costs	Yes, if competitors choose not to adjust their cost structure
Collaboration (K–12)	K–12 students dually enrolled in community college courses	Early start on college at affordable cost/reduced time to degree	Community colleges are the preferred provider of this option	Yes, if collaboration continues with K–12 school systems
Collaboration (University)	Students taking undergraduate courses on a community college campus	Convenience of BA degree program in accessible location	Competitors cannot offer the same level of convenience and efficiency	Yes, if competitors do not follow suit
Collaboration (Business)	Employees receive onsite training through community colleges	Savings in time and efficiency/relevance of courses to job	Courses are more relevant to the workplace than those of competitors	Yes, if competitors fail to develop comparable offerings
Paradox	Students changing career and educational goals	Ability to move among programs without penalty	Niche providers lack the breadth to accommodate change in student plans	Yes, if competitors do not increase program options

caused by contradictory forces, however, has changed the strategy dynamic for these institutions. Cost and convenience may no longer be sufficient to guarantee advantage. Rising tuition associated with double-digit decreases in state aid has brought some community colleges to a point where they are approaching public university tuition levels, which will nullify cost as an effective strategy. The viability of convenience is also under question. Colleges choosing to promote growth through convenience at the expense of quality now find themselves facing serious questions about the integrity of their offerings and the quality of their product.

Challenged by competitors and constrained by tight finances, community colleges are turning to concepts such as stretch, collaboration, and responsiveness as a basis for strategy. *Stretch* is the ability to leverage limited resources to achieve lofty goals. As resources dwindle, community colleges will need to find new sources of revenue or increase operating efficiency to avoid reduction. This reality will encourage leaders to adopt a strategy of *collaboration* with business and industry, K–12, and technology partners. A key idiom in these partnerships will be *responsiveness* to stakeholder needs. Pressure from competitors similarly invested in collaboration will push community colleges to move quickly in responding to needs or face the prospect of diminished market share. This may require colleges to expand noncredit offerings and off-site delivery to provide more convenient access.

Environmental turbulence and shifting strategy options could open the door to contradictory development paths for community colleges. One path would involve limiting the scope of the enterprise to bring operations into line with resources; its converse would involve leveraging resources to support growth. Limiting scope would mean tailoring the mission to the constituencies and functions considered most vital. Strategy would be expressed in the form of a move to build advantage by concentrating resources on selected stakeholders. Given their commitment to open access, most community colleges will resist moving in this direction. Capping growth will have the effect of diminishing opportunity for learners who already have limited access to education and meaningful participation in the economy. For this reason, most colleges will choose to stretch and leverage resources to ensure maximum service to community and stakeholder needs.

Case-Study Illustrations

To probe more deeply into the inner-workings of strategy in community colleges, we turn to illustrations developed for the Community College of Denver and hypothetical community colleges located in the Midwest and the Southeast.

Community College of Denver

Founded in 1967, the Community College of Denver (CCD) is the only community college serving the more than 550,000 residents of the city of Denver. By legislative mandate, the downtown campus (Auraria) shares land and facilities with Metropolitan State College and the University of Colorado at Denver. CCD offers 125 programs of study that include noncredit courses, certificates, and a variety of associate degrees including the associate of arts, associate of science, associate of applied science, and associate of general studies degrees. As the largest provider of developmental education in the state, it is dedicated to preparing disenfranchised learners for further education and for work. In so doing, it is committed to becoming an exemplar of urban education for the nation's community colleges.[8]

The City of Denver is 56 percent minority, and the student population of CCD is a mirror of the community.[9] CCD serves a large population of low-income students (67 percent) and first-generation students (more than 50 percent). The central constructs underlying CCD's ideology of service to underprepared learners can be found in its mission and philosophy, the cultural pluralism of its students and staff, and its commitment to teaching excellence. CCD lists six categories of responsibility to the students it serves. These include

- Transfer programs for the bachelor's degree
- Occupational programs for job-entry skills or upgrading
- General-education courses
- Remedial instruction and GED preparation
- Continuing education and community service
- Cooperative inter-institutional programs

Its focus on cultural pluralism can be summed up in one word: inclusiveness. CCD exists to prepare multiethnic students for living, working, and learning in a diverse community. Everything that CCD does—its support services, programming and delivery, administrative policies and practices, and more—is designed to promote the ideal of inclusiveness. This ideal is further elaborated through a Statement of Values for Teaching Excellence that defines a commitment to

- Enable students to become independent learners
- Demonstrate a commitment to student outcomes

- Provide an opportunity for critical thinking and problem solving
- Demonstrate excitement about teaching and learning
- Maintain high, but realistic expectations
- Demonstrate an appreciation and understanding of a diverse student population
- Practice an individualized, student-centered approach to encourage growth in self-esteem

The overarching strategy of CCD is *paradox*—the provision of programs and services that possess seemingly contradictory qualities and aims. The college seeks to engage a racially and ethnically diverse population in postsecondary education through program and service offerings, teaching and learning methodologies, and delivery systems that are "simultaneously contradictory." That is, CCD seeks to be inclusive by providing program, service, and delivery options to students that are in seeming opposition to one another: general-education versus career-training curricula, credit versus noncredit offerings, synchronous versus asynchronous delivery, self-paced versus traditional instruction, and so forth. To execute this strategy, CCD uses four frames: uniqueness, collaboration, stretch, and convenience.

Uniqueness. In promoting access to postsecondary education for academically underprepared learners, CCD adds value that no other college in the region can duplicate. *Value-added* refers to the difference between prospects for a career, earnings, and educational achievement at entry and exit from college. Most of CCD's students enroll in developmental courses at entry because of marginal basic skills and limited prospects for success in college-credit courses. Successful completion of developmental-skills courses has become a barometer for success at CCD. Among full-time students entering in 1999, 52 percent were enrolled in developmental courses, 59 percent were minorities, and 58 percent were women. Of the students completing developmental courses within one year, 72 percent passed the college-level English composition class, 76 percent passed college algebra, and their cumulative GPA was 2.94. CCD not only provides access to postsecondary education for underprepared learners, it also adds value by enabling students to acquire advanced degrees and better paying jobs.

Collaboration. To fulfill the lofty principles expressed in its Statement of Values for Teaching Excellence, CCD collaborates with the Denver Public Schools, regional colleges and universities, and business and industry. The objective of collaboration is to create a seamless transition between education and work, thereby enhancing the likelihood that youth will enter meaningful careers and become productive citizens. CCD's long-range goal is to partner with virtually every high school in the Denver Public Schools with the shared objectives of increasing high school retention and graduation rates and increasing college entrance and persistence with a focus on underprepared/underserved urban students. Collaboration is accomplished through a number of programs. Primary among them is the Eleventh and Twelfth Grade Experience at the Middle College of Denver, the Southwest Early College, and Bridge to College Labs. These programs enable high school students to earn credits toward a college degree while satisfying high school graduation requirements. Additionally, they bring underprepared students into direct contact with CCD faculty and staff, who use techniques such as "intrusive advising," case management, and tutoring to individually prepare students for college study. Further enrichment is provided through Summer@CCD, which enrolls 300 public school students in summer-school classes at the college for basic skills enhancement.

CCD is perpetually engaged in efforts to craft innovative programs with Metropolitan State College and the University of Colorado at Denver and is moving to expand articulation agreements with the University of Phoenix, Regis University, and the University of Denver. It also works extensively with regional business and industry in contract training. A business advisory committee is used as a vehicle to acquire state-of-the-art information about workforce training needs, and CCD offers a variety of contract-training opportunities for business and industry including computer training, consulting, and coaching and mentoring services designed to enhance staff and organizational performance.

Stretch. The concept of *stretch* can be understood as a gap between resources and aspirations. In the case of Community College of Denver, it describes an ability to do more with less, fueled by a shared commitment to provide exceptional learning opportunities for students. Programs such as the Online Writing Library (OWL) were created by faculty as an extension of their teaching role to provide assistance to students in writing, grammar usage, and language. The *Paper Bank* provides access to sample papers and paragraphs written by undergraduate students and ranges in level from beginning native and ESL speakers to advanced students. *Darling's Guide to Grammar* provides an extensive section on basic grammar and punctuation guides to an "Ask Grammar" option, which allows for individualized responses to specific questions. Another resource available through OWL is *Dave's ESL café*. This chat room enables interaction among ESL students around the world to learn about culture and language.

While most colleges provide nominal services to students with disabilities, CCD has stretched its resources to ensure that disabled students have access to the full educational experience. One way CCD increases access is through an alternative-materials program, a program designed to provide course materials on cassette and disk, and in large print or Braille. Assistance available within the classroom includes sign language and oral interpreting, a note-taking service, and a classroom assistant. The classroom assistant is able to assist in full classroom participation. For example, a student unable to use a keyboard can request and receive an assistant in a computer course so that he or she can participate fully in the experience. The capacity for stretch enables CCD to provide an unparalleled educational experience for students who cannot expect to receive the equivalent from other institutions. It sets CCD apart from competitors who will not work as hard to serve students and thereby becomes an advantage.

Convenience. The Community College of Denver makes education convenient by putting educational opportunities within easy reach of learners. With six campuses that include the downtown campus (Auraria), three Denver neighborhood-branch campuses, a Health Sciences Center (Lowery), and a downtown Corporate Training Center (Parkway), CCD is able to offer a range of programs, certificates, and associate degrees on-site. Credit offerings have also been expanded into local hospitals to enable students to pursue a variety of health-related certificates and degrees at the location of employment. Other forms of delivery affording convenience are

- CCC Online: a consortium of colleges pooling courses on the Internet to provide students with an array of distance-learning opportunities. This service allows a student in Denver to take courses from colleges throughout the state.
- Evening and Weekend College: aimed at working adults unable to take college courses during the workday. The majority of classes meet one day a week, enrollment can be continuous or episodic, as many as six courses can be taken at a time, and certificates generally take less than a year to complete.

The convenience provided through these options enables CCD to reach a wider audience and provide offerings specific to the population served.

Synthesis: CCD has been able to establish an advantage over competitors through a strategy of *paradox.* It offers a variety of programs that appeal to multiple stakeholders and it collaborates with profit and non-profit partners to enhance learner outcomes. Rather than relying on the tried and true in instruction, CCD uses an array of pedagogical techniques to reach learners with different needs, backgrounds, and skills. If a true measure of paradox is the number of people whose lives are touched in different ways by a community college, CCD is an exemplar of this strategy.

Suburban Community College

Suburban Community College (SCC) is located in a heavily populated county adjacent to a major city in the Midwest. Affluent County is among the 100 wealthiest counties in the United States and has a large property-tax base from which the college draws a substantial portion of its revenue. There are a variety of educational options for learners in the county including Mid-America Research University (MARU), Rustbelt Teaching University (RTU), a denominational liberal arts college (Divinity College), and several for-profit business colleges. Business is a key player in the regional economy with strong biotechnology, pharmaceutical, and robotics industries. Because of the array of educational opportunities available to traditional students, SCC draws only 20 percent of the graduating seniors from county high schools. The majority of its students are working adults, nearly two-thirds are first-generation, and 30 percent are from minority groups.

To better serve residents, Suburban has established campuses in the northern, western, and eastern sections of the county. It has also opened outreach centers in high schools, libraries, and shopping malls. Evening, weekend, and accelerated courses are offered to working adults and services are available 24/7/365 on the Internet. The combination of accessible facilities, courses, and services has made SCC the county's postsecondary education provider of choice. Its primary advantage is *convenience* and it expects to maintain this advantage by working harder than competitors in program and service delivery. Another advantage is the *cost* of education in comparison to the other providers. SCC's annual cost is $1,750 while the cost of attending MARU is $13,000 (including room and board); at RTU it is $8,000, and tuition and fees at the business colleges average $6,000. Additionally, SCC offers students the benefit of a more personalized education through small classes taught by experienced instructors. SCC's student-to-faculty ratio is 18:1, whereas at MARU and RTU it exceeds 30:1. The combination of low cost and personalized education offers unparalleled value for students that competitors cannot match.

Like all community colleges, Suburban provides for a variety of needs within the community through comprehensive programs. These include education and training programs for business and industry, social service agencies, K–12 school districts, and government workers. Occupational offerings have been strengthened by the completion of a complex for Innovation in the Economy: a 75,000-square-foot building designed to offer the latest training in manufacturing, allied health, technology, and a host of other occupational fields. Transfer students are assisted by articulation agreements established with twenty colleges, including proprietary institutions. The list of noncredit offerings includes courses in basic computer training, soft-skills development, and family health. No college in the region offers this variety of educational opportunities to so many different stakeholders. *Responsiveness* is a strategic frame for Suburban Community College in addition to *convenience* and *cost*.

Synthesis: Convenience, cost, and responsiveness are important ingredients of strategy at SCC, and each contributes to growth, which is central to everything the college does. Suburban's overarching strategy, therefore, is *growth* measured in terms of enrollment and resources.

Rural Community College

Located in a southeastern state, Rural Community College (RCC) serves a sparsely populated three-county area. The service area is larger than the state of Connecticut and three colleges are located within its borders: RCC, a teaching university (Progressive University), and a private denominational college (Rose Hill College). The various campuses and extension centers of RCC are located so that all residents within the region are no more than thirty minutes from any site. The average family income for a family of four is $27,000, and the tuition at RCC is $1,300 a year. Progressive's tuition is $7,500, and Rose Hill's is $12,000. Rural stresses that its goal is to better serve students, but leaders readily admit there is no institutional strategy. The cost of attending RCC is so low compared to other institutions that there is no need for a strategy.

Conversations with college leaders indicate that Rural uses a tactic of *convenience* to attract and hold students. The service area is large with mostly rural routes, so it is difficult for students, most of whom work, to travel great distances to attend college. Online education is not an option because many families cannot afford a computer. Therefore, putting courses within easy reach of learners is imperative if RCC wants to grow and thrive. College leaders recognize this and have taken steps to simplify access within the limits of geography and technology. Not only are campuses located within easy reach of learners, but steps have been taken to bring education directly to them through a self-paced curriculum, credit and noncredit programs in the workplace, and courses delivered through community centers and the public library system. Students attending RCC are able to earn a degree without ever setting foot on campus.

A new dimension of Rural's strategy of convenience is a collaborative program with Progressive University that enables students to complete a bachelor's degree at any of RCC's campuses. Recognizing that collaboration might be a smarter course of action than competition, leaders of the two institutions came together and carved out an arrangement that would profit both institutions. Progressive's leaders recognized that time and cost constraints would limit the enrollment of regional students in its traditional programs. RCC's leaders recognized that expanded access to the bachelor's degree among area residents was essential for enhancement of the regional economy. The site-based program for bachelor's degree completion on Rural's campuses was a win-win for both institutions as well as for regional citizens.

TEACHING UNIVERSITIES

A regional teaching university (RTU) can generally be defined as a moderate to large-size public institution serving primarily undergraduate students from a limited geographic region within a state. These institutions tend to have a long-standing focus on preparing students to meet the employment needs of their region and state. Many started as Normal Schools, while others were established to fill the needs of students who were denied access to, or could not afford, more prestigious institutions. Others evolved from small colleges that outgrew their initial structure, and some were satellites of larger educational systems.

Today's RTUs have links to research, the business community, and national and international initiatives. Their funding is heavily dependent on state appropriations, but income derived from endowment is becoming more important as part of the operating budget. Governance is through constitutionally appointed or elected boards that reflect the makeup of the regional population. Through increasing selectivity, RTUs have positioned themselves at the upper end of a snakelike procession, with research universities and elite liberal arts colleges at the top. However, while knowledge production is the primary aim of research universities, transmission of knowledge is the goal of teaching universities.

External Challenges

Three forces pose unique challenges to regional teaching universities in today's market: public policy, demographics, and changing finances. Each presents a unique set of demands that institutions will need to address and resolve to solidify their position.

Public Policy. The prevailing political ideologies of the 1990s strongly supported higher education as a national priority. However, with the 2000 election of George Bush, the World Trade Center tragedy of 2001, and the ensuing "war on terror," federal funds have been diverted from higher education and other social programs in order to support national security initiatives and military action. Higher education has been relegated to the states as yet another public service for which they must shoulder more of the funding burden. The reality for teaching universities is that the trillion-dollar federal budget deficit will mean less money to distribute to states and correspondingly less to allocate in support of institutional general-fund budgets. Such policy issues will necessarily call upon RTUs to become more creative in delivering services to constituents while holding costs constant.

Demographic Issues. The U.S. Department of Education projects that by 2013, enrollment of 18 to 24-year-olds in degree-granting institutions will increase by 11.2 percent over 2000 enrollment.[10] Over the next ten years, undergraduate enrollment in four-year institutions is expected to outpace enrollment in two-year institutions, women will enroll in greater numbers than men, and full-time undergraduate enrollment will increase at a faster rate than part-time enrollment.[11] These and other data suggest there will be no shortage of learners seeking higher education over the next decade. The number of high school graduates will peak with the classes of 2008 and 2009, but increasing demand for postsecondary education will fuel continuing enrollment growth in colleges and universities.[12]

Steadily growing K–12 and college enrollment can create a double-edged sword for teaching universities. On the one hand, growth is a desirable position for institutions seeking to stabilize finances and to enhance stature. On the other hand, each institution has a discrete capacity to meet demand and not all students can be accommodated in periods of rapid growth. The dimensions of this challenge are illustrated by the projected distribution of public high school graduates by family income for 2006–2007. Although the number of graduates from high-income families is expected to grow, they will do so at a slower rate than students from low-income families.[13] More students will seek access to teaching universities and will require some form of aid to offset the increased cost of attendance, a circumstance that suggests two questions for institutional leaders: (1) How can more students be accommodated if revenue from traditional funding sources lags behind growth? and (2) Will students have the wherewithal to enter and succeed in college at a time when financial aid options are being severely reduced by government agencies?

Changing Finances. Between 2000 and 2004, the nation's economy weakened and the financial condition of states plummeted to depths not seen in decades. Most states were forced into deficit budgeting and many raised taxes to offset the gap caused by reduced federal funding. Appropriations to public colleges and universities were reduced, and institutions adjusted by passing costs on to students in the form of increased tuition. The net effects have been (1) to reduce student capability to acquire a college education and (2) to increase competition among institutions. Students driven away by rising costs reduce the size of the enrollment pool and create difficulty for less-selective institutions caught in a squeeze between more affordable community colleges and prestigious research universities. This circumstance is especially challenging for teaching universities that lack a distinctive identity and cannot count on quality, reputation, or cost to distinguish themselves from competitors.

Institutional Responses to Changing Conditions

An external challenge such as changing policy, demographics, and economic decline can each place a significant demand on an institution in almost any operating context. When all three converge at the same time, however, an institution is severely tested. Regional teaching universities are among the first to feel the challenge of rapidly changing conditions, and they feel it deeply as illustrated in the case-examples below.

Western Regional University (WRU)

Western Regional University is part of the California State University (CSU) system. It is located in Citrus Grove, a city in the northeastern section of the state with a population of 100,000, which includes the surrounding metropolitan area. Citrus Grove is a scenic community of primarily Caucasian middle-class residents. In recent years, it has become a destination for companies in the burgeoning biomedical and information-technology industries.

Western was founded in 1920, as a Normal School and over the ensuing decades evolved into a State College as its mission expanded to include a commitment to agriculture, business, health, and teacher education. Almost 60 percent of its students come from a twelve-county service area with the remaining students coming primarily from northern California. Two out of three of its 15,000 enrolled students are Caucasian, 14 percent are Latino, 9 percent are Asian American, 7 percent are African American, and 6 percent are Other. In recent years, WRU has been criticized for its relatively homogeneous population, and considerable effort has been invested in expanding recruitment efforts into the larger and more diverse communities of central and southern California.

Stakeholders and Market Environment. As identified in its strategic plan, Western serves three primary stakeholder groups: (1) traditional-age students, (2) professionals seeking bachelor's and advanced degree preparation in specific fields, and (3) profit and nonprofit organizations. Over time WRU has served these groups with distinction, but its ability to do so in the future has been compromised by budget cuts in the California State University system. WRU has fared better than its sister schools as an influx of new industries and a strong economic base has helped to offset the impact of declining state appropriations. Additionally, post–9/11 has found WRU experiencing an increase in demand for enrollment among native and transfer students seeking the safety and security of a quiet community away from the din and clatter of urban centers. Unfortunately, these vehicles for growth only provide a slim buffer against the downward spiral of an ailing economy.

On May 26, 2004, the Associated Press reported that the CSU governing board had passed a 14 percent increase in student fees and agreed to support Republican Gov. Arnold Schwarzenegger's request for a 10 percent cut in enrollments for the 2004–2005 academic year. In return, the governor promised that state money for enrollment growth would be increased in 2005. Under this plan, the California State University system would have the resources to realize an enrollment gain of nearly 8,000 students across the system. Students who could not be absorbed by the state university campuses, would be channeled into community colleges. As a sign of good faith, CSU offered guaranteed admission to colleges if students maintained satisfactory grades during their tenure in the community college system.

Competition and Distinctiveness. An essential premise of the California Master Plan for Higher Education is that competition between institutions is a nonissue because each tier within the system has a unique mission and enrolls from an unlimited pool of applicants. The plan also encourages each tier to establish distinctiveness within its mission rather than among individual schools. This approach to differentiation tends to minimize or negate the distinctiveness that would develop for any one institution over time as part of its history, tradition, programs, and accomplishments. In theory, competitors and competition are nonexistent—what students see is a university system with a number of campuses that can be accessed to pursue a college degree.

Students do, however, have a voice in selecting the schools they will ultimately attend. In the process of considering the pros and cons of different institutions, they place the tiers, and the individual institutions within them, into competition with one another and the winners are determined through answers to questions such as How much does it cost to attend College A versus College B? What are the opportunities for a social life at College A compared to College B? Which college graduates get higher-paying jobs: those from College A or from College B? For parents, the critical question might be Why would I want to pay for my son or daughter to attend WRU instead of Cal Poly Tech? The reality is that like competition in the profit sector, colleges and universities must develop an identity in a defined marketplace, or face the prospect of decline. WRU may never experience a downturn in its student pool, but in the absence of strategy, the composition of this pool could change in ways that would stretch the capabilities of the institution. For example, the entry of more underprepared learners could strain institutional resources by requiring a depth and scope of support services beyond institutional capacity. To succeed in this context, WRU must acknowledge that competition exists and that it will need to distinguish itself in the minds of stakeholders in order to come out ahead.

Framing Strategy. Prior to the formulation and release of Governor Schwarzenegger's budget plan, a WRU task force was hard at work devising a plan to reduce costs and maximize resources. The goals of this plan were to enroll more students and to maintain a high level of customer service through cost savings and resource reallocation. As details of the plan emerged, it became apparent that it was more than a series of actions to achieve specific goals. It was, in fact, a strategy built upon a principle of *stretch*. WRU would stretch or leverage its resources by redesigning processes to provide more and better service to students while holding costs constant. This would be accomplished by (1) streamlining services to move students more quickly through them and (2) making services available on the Internet to free up staff for behind-the-scenes administrative processing and systems tasks.

Much to the delight of administrators, the stretch strategy, if successfully implemented, would lead to immediate advantage for Western. Given the bureaucratic approach to business within the California State University system and the traditional architecture and approach to governance within its colleges, change of any type is resisted on campuses. The administrative organization of most CSU colleges is grounded in a traditional model of departmental specialization that resists institution-wide initiatives. What on the surface appears to be a unified structure for each college is, in reality, a series of decentralized units, each acting independently of one another. This fragmentation is encouraged by the existence of parallel vertical structures, or chimneys, for academic and nonacademic functions. This results in a system that is rigid, costly, and labor intensive—a perfect target for an institution seeking to develop an advantage by *streamlining systems*. Since many, if not most, universities in the system subscribe to this traditional model, any effort by WRU to increase efficiency through system and process redesign will lead to advantage. Interestingly, advantage will be obtained not only through increased efficiency, but also through the added *convenience* afforded to students. Streamlined processes save time by enabling students to electronically complete transactions, avoid long lines, and bypass wasteful duplication caused by administrative processing. This can work to enhance satisfaction by channeling student time into more productive activities.

Mid-American University (MAU)

Mid-American University is located in the city of Plainview in the heart of the Great Lakes region. Its central location places it equidistant from the two largest cities in the state and the state capitol. Plainview's population has remained stable over the last few decades at a level of 25,000 residents. Most of its residents are white, but an important part of its heritage is a Native American culture that is widely embraced and celebrated. The community is surrounded by rich farmlands, and this, together with the hospitality and ecotourism industry, makes for a vital and progressive community. The city is one of the top-five tourist destinations in the state, due largely to an expansive gambling casino built and owned by the Chippewa tribe. Plainview's small-town atmosphere and midsize-city energy makes it a popular environment in which to settle.

MAU was founded in 1892 as a Normal School enrolling thirty-one students. By 1918 it had become a four-year public college with an enrollment of 850. Throughout its history, Mid-American has remained true to its roots in teacher preparation, but it has also expanded its academic offerings to keep pace with growth and change in the economy. Today, MAU enrolls more than 22,000 students and offers twenty-four undergraduate degrees from five different colleges, which are committed to developing and adapting programs to match career opportunities. It is easily accessed because of its central location. Students come from every county in the state as well as from the neighboring states of Illinois, Ohio, and Indiana. Its College of Extended Learning, which offers undergraduate and graduate programs, enrolls 8,000 students in more than sixty service centers throughout the United States, Canada, and Mexico. For the 2003–2004 academic year, 85 percent of MAU's on-campus students were Caucasian, 4 percent were African American, 2 percent Hispanic, 2 percent "International," 1 percent Native American, 1 percent Asian American, and 5 percent were "Unknown."

Stakeholders and Market Environment. Mid-American's primary stakeholders are students and parents, elected officials, donors, high schools and community colleges, foundations and granting agencies, and the public. Over the past four years, enrollments have continued to grow while appropriations have been cut, including critical dollars earmarked for scholarships and financial aid. Tuition has increased by 25 percent and spending has been reduced by $15 million from its 2002–2003 level. MAU has successfully avoided cutting faculty positions, but in the past year it laid off thirteen staff members and cut fifty-five full- and part-time staff positions. Rising energy, health care, and pension costs, compounded by a weakened state economy, portend a poor budget picture for several years to come.

Framing Strategy. In the late 1990s, MAU's leadership team embarked on a path that brought the institution to the forefront of innovation in postsecondary education. Moving beyond the traditional planning model of establishing goals and priorities, the team adopted a multilayered approach to strategy involving partnerships in the design and delivery of curricula and services customized to employer needs. Essentially a strategy of *collaboration,* MAU's unique approach to partnering involved opportunities for students to practice the skills they were learning in class in field placements. A long-standing example is the student-teaching experience. Students, in the role of apprentice, are matched with K–12 community partners, in the role of expert or master, from whom they learn and practice skills and crafts in a safe and structured environment. An evaluation or feedback mechanism is used in the apprenticeship to make it a true learning experience. Other forms of collaborative programs developed by MAU include internships, job shadowing, clinical experience, study-abroad programs, and research projects. Many, if not most, institutions offer some form of experiential learning to students, but MAU makes the experience distinctive over competitors by establishing relationships with leading-edge partners in high-tech industries.

Recognizing that it does not have the capability or resources to compete with large research universities, Mid-American sought to actuate its strategy in small specialty markets and to become the preferred provider within these markets. An example of this stratagem is a joint venture with technology partners in nanoscience and data mining initiated in 2002.

Campus leaders opened this initiative with a series of internal forums to identify niche-building opportunities in the state's high-tech infrastructure. Through a confluence of circumstances, the governor established Smart Zones in 2002 to promote the development of research initiatives around cutting-edge technologies. While the convergence of institutional planning and state policy was, in part, a matter of coincidence, it was also a function of the way in which MAU had positioned itself as a nimble organization capable of seizing opportunities as they emerged.

To move the nanoscience initiative into high gear, MAU established a private nonprofit company, the Center for Applied Research and Technology (CART), to interface with external partners. CART was designed to function as a joint venture between MAU, the city of Plainview, the Mid-America Development Corporation, and the state as one of eleven Smart Zones designated by the State Economic Development Corporation. The Plainview Smart Zone was established to attract and stimulate high-tech industries that require a synergistic relationship with a college or university partner to design and deliver new products. The newly emerging field of dendrimer nanoscience was one of its first initiatives along with biotechnology and data mining.

As a strategy, collaboration cannot be executed without risk-taking and initiative. Collaboration between MAU and its partners on the dendrimer nanoscience initiative began with brainstorming sessions to address questions that would shape the dimensions and dynamics of the partnership. Results from these sessions included the following:

- Imagination: What kinds of jobs are essential for the growth and vitality of this industry? What experiences best prepare students to step into careers that meet industry needs? What are the industry's long- and short-term needs and how can MAU contribute in a way that also leads to opportunities for students?

- Collaboration: Which organizations offer the greatest opportunity for students in this industry? Which organizations recognize and have a need for student talent? What win-win benefits will be realized by students, MAU, and its partners?

- Leveraging: What resources, financial and nonfinancial, can be leveraged for students and MAU through collaboration? How can MAU generate resources through investment in collaborative efforts?

Forthcoming from discussion were a series of decisions that determined the direction of the initiative and the roles and responsibilities of partners. Land and a physical plant were purchased by MAU and developed into a state-of-the-art facility including wet laboratories and a biolevel 2 lab to meet the needs of industry partners. MAU faculty and students would have the opportunity to collaborate in hands-on research with leading scientists in biology, chemistry, and physics. Established and start-up companies would benefit from the intellectual capital of the partnership, and students would hire into career positions—a key objective of MAU's participation in the initiative. Other groups and organizations would benefit as well. Regional K–12 teachers would learn about nanotechnology and interest students in high-demand science careers at an early point in their education. High school and college students would acquire versatile problem-solving and research skills that would enhance their value in the job market. And women would be encouraged to enter science careers.

Mid-American uses *collaboration* to build relationships with partners at the local, state, national, and international levels. These partnerships include research and business support for corporations, nature and environmental learning and conferencing centers, educational and technology resources operations, an extensive charter-school program, a communication-disorders clinic, and a Special Olympics program. Each partnership is grounded in relationship building between students and external stakeholders, which elicits substantial private-sector support for MAU. Potential donors are much more interested in extending support to projects and tangible results than a general list of institutional needs. MAU's relentless pursuit of partnerships enables it to strengthen its position and remain nimble in a highly competitive market.

CONCLUSION

Comprehensive institutions are remarkably stable organizations. Their faculty, curricula, and students change little from year to year, and to a much greater extent than other institutions, they reflect the makeup of the communities they serve. The form and structure of these institutions is not likely to change. The courses and services they deliver and the degrees they award have become institutionalized in the public mind as well as in the policy deliberations of funding and coordinating agencies. For most of these institutions, change in the future will be in emphasis, not in kind, although some institutions will break the rules and carve out new realms of experience for students, new ways of delivering programs and services, and new approaches to deploying resources.

What will change for many, if not all, of the institutions in this category is their interest in, and involvement with, strategy as they seek to differentiate themselves from increasingly aggressive competitors. Research universities that have traditionally relied on size, prestige, and visibility to achieve advantage will be pushed by peers working with a different set of rules to find new forms of advantage. One needs only to look at the recent move by Harvard to offer tuition-free education to highly qualified students from low-income families to understand the implications of rule-breaking behavior for institutions in the same category. Similarly, community colleges will encounter stiff competition from proprietary institutions for the adult-learner market while competing aggressively for the high school market with teaching and research universities. All of this would seem to point to a volatile new era of competition in which the deftness of an institution's strategy will have a lot to do with its success.

NOTES

1. Information derived from the Web site of Michigan State University, www.msu.edu.

2. Information derived from the Web site of Washington University in St. Louis, www.wustl.edu.

3. Ralph E. Morrow, *Washington University in St. Louis: A History* (St. Louis: Missouri Historical Society Press, 1996).

4. Web site of Washington University.

5. Information obtained through Web site exploration, www.depaul.edu, and professional experience on the staff of DePaul University. During the 2001–2002 academic year, Tara Sullivan served as an assistant director of Alumni Relations at DePaul University. In this role, she participated in the implementation of DePaul's growth strategy.

6. Ibid.

7. Ibid.

8. The case illustration for Community College of Denver was developed in cooperation with Christine Johnson, president of Community College of Denver.

9. Statistics provided by the Greater Denver Chamber of Commerce.

10. Andrea Livingston and John Wirt, eds., *The Condition of Education in Brief*, www.nces.ed.gov/pubs2004/2004076.pdf, National Center for Educational Statistics, U.S. Department of Education.

11. Western Interstate Commission for Higher Education, *The Class of 2008 and Beyond* (Denver: WICHE, 2004).

12. Western Interstate Commission for Higher Education, *Knocking at the Door—2003: Projections of High School Graduates by State, Income and Race/Ethnicity, 1988–2018* (Denver: WICHE, 2004).

13. Ibid.

CHAPTER 7

Strategy in For-Profit Institutions

While the traditional image of a college involves a picturesque campus with residence halls, lecture halls, and youthful students, an alternative organization offering a very different experience is making its presence felt. Institutions in this category include for-profit providers such as the University of Phoenix and DeVry University, virtual universities engaged in distance education, corporate universities such as Sprint and Motorola, and proprietary institutions like the art institutes run by Education Management Corporation. As a group, they are known as special-purpose institutions and they operate in a manner unlike traditional colleges and universities.

Whereas traditional providers may debate the value of a liberal education versus career preparation, special purpose institutions focus on higher education as a knowledge industry—one in which curriculum content is determined by the needs of business and industry. Their overarching goal is to deliver education and training programs that lead to a meaningful job for students while meeting the workplace needs of employers. As such, students and employers are their *customers* and everything they do is dedicated to identifying and serving customer needs. Curricula are designed to impart practical skills, classes are run around the clock, and input from business and industry stakeholders is used to design and modify programs—all toward the goal of connecting students and employers. The business model employed by these institutions may seem foreign, if not offensive, to traditional academicians. Profit is their bottom line and growth is the measure of their success. Special-purpose institutions depend on customer satisfaction for growth, and they are more capable than traditional institutions of demonstrating value-added. Indeed, their corporate environment requires such measurement as a routine part of operations.

The profile of special-purpose institutions varies dramatically when compared to traditional providers. This chapter examines the business model and strategy of these institutions through one category of institutions, for-profit providers, as a way of illustrating some of these differences. Working descriptions from three institutions—DeVry University, Quest Career College, and Strayer University—and business practices common to for-profit providers are presented to show how strategy is used to build advantage in this sector of higher education.

PROFILE OF FOR-PROFIT PROVIDERS

The term *for-profit* refers to a group of institutions known variously as niche providers, proprietary institutions, business colleges, corporate universities, and electronic providers offering sub-bachelor's, bachelor's, graduate, and/or nondegree education. These institutions offer a variety of programs. For example, degree credit courses, noncredit competency-based training, certification focused on technical skills, and occupationally based associate or bachelor's degrees in fields such as business, management, or computer technology. Some offer graduate training, typically in business and management, through special programs designed internally or purchased from specialized providers. The curriculum is the lifeblood of these institutions and it must be current to the market. For this reason, responsibility for curriculum development is often centralized in the hands of a class of administrators known as *curriculum managers*, and instructors are hired to deliver an approved curriculum, not one of their own making. Curriculum development is an ongoing process involving input from business and industry to ensure currency and relevance.

Student success in for-profit institutions is viewed as a shared responsibility and services are organized around this philosophy. In *Higher Ed, Inc.: The Rise of the For-Profit University*, Richard Ruch (2001) argues that for-profit and nonprofit institutions are both after two essential goals: academic quality and a healthy bottom line. But for-profit institutions "change the center of gravity by radically shifting the balance between academics and business in favor of sound business practices."[1] Using this business model, the organization thrives when exceptional products are delivered and the customer is satisfied. A major aspect of "customer service" is providing education when, where, and how the customer wants it—anytime learning. Learning can occur in on-campus classes during traditional hours, at night, on weekends, on a personal calendar as opposed to an academic calendar, and through distance delivery. Instructors and staff understand that it is the customer who will determine when and how instruction is accessed as well as the approach to pedagogy. Customers move through coursework and programs with the major focus being preparation for a job or career. They are supported by a battery of curricular and co-curricular services designed to prepare for the workplace. These services include training in workplace deportment, ethics, human relations and soft skills, interviewing techniques, résumé writing, job placement, and other skills deemed necessary to connect customers with a career.

While many view business practices and principles as an unwanted intrusion into academe, the market-driven curriculum of for-profits sets them apart from other institutions. The curriculum closely parallels business and industry needs, instructors are knowledgeable about current practices in industry, and they are intimately involved with the subject matter they teach. Ruch describes the faculty in a typical for-profit institution as having "significant industry experience at the professional level."[2] They are focused on teaching and do not have to apportion their time among multiple assignments (e.g., committee work, curriculum development, research). Moreover, they understand and practice a basic rule in customer service: A customer that believes he or she is getting something of value is more likely to be satisfied and to return.

Finally, revenue streams in the for-profit sector differ from most other academic institutions. These institutions are privately owned and operated and, therefore, are not eligible for state or local funding. They are purely customer-driven, with tuition accounting for more than 90 percent of their operating revenue. Governance is top-down through a defined hierarchy, and stockholders are part of the governance equation. The lack of tenure, stringent evaluation processes, and increased accountability define the role and responsibilities of instructors. One of the realities of working in a for-profit institution is the presence of bosses, and there is no doubt about who the boss is.[3] Stockholders hold a vested interest in the success of the institution, in addition to corporations that provide investment capital. Many for-profits provide employees with the opportunity for ownership through stock-purchase programs such as 401Ks or stock options. As the enterprise grows and achieves financial success, a portion of income may be returned to stockholders as an incentive for future investment.

CHALLENGES TO VITALITY

The business model of for-profit institutions places customers at the center of a dynamic relationship between programs, services, and market needs. When this relationship is working properly, customer needs are anticipated and satisfied and profit is generated through growth. This cannot happen in institutions that are static in place and time. For-profits must be constantly positioning themselves for opportunities, or face the prospect of decline. This means that to grow, they must be nimble and capable of continuous change.

As "change or die" institutions, for-profits are facing three challenges that require attention in order to ensure growth. These are (1) managing the relationship between growth and quality, (2) creating added value for customers, and (3) outmaneuvering competitors. Opportunities for growth will be rampant in a market loaded with learners that need new and updated skills to acquire and hold a job. The career-program courses of for-profit institutions have always attracted adult learners who need job training and retraining. Over the next several years, however, record numbers of students will graduate from the nation's high schools and most will require postsecondary education to prepare for a job or career. Many of these students will choose for-profit institutions as their first entrée into higher education in order to receive a quick return on investment.

The combination of returning adult learners and first-time high school graduates will challenge for-profits to find ways to manage *growth and quality*. Balancing the two is a simpler task in traditional institutions, which operate on a linear academic model. For-profits, however, operate in a hierarchical mode with one side of the house making decisions and the other side carrying them out. The "business" or back-office side (administration) is responsible for growth and financial stability, program and curriculum development, and operational management including relationships with stakeholders. The front-office or "customer" side is made up of staff and part-time instructors who have maximum contact with customers, but little input into curriculum and operational procedures. Administrators responsible for strategic management can let the profit motive shape and control major decisions if they are not sensitive to the relationship between growth and quality. Similarly, teachers and staff who desire, but do not have, a voice in matters that affect their work can suffer a loss of esteem and unintentionally diminish service to customers. When either or both of these conditions prevail, quality can be sacrificed in favor of growth and profit, and the reputation of the institution tarnished.

One of the challenges of working in a for-profit institution is that the senior managers, and those to whom they report, are basically operations managers, not academic leaders.[4] As a result, the academic voice at the top of these institutions is silent, or at best, a whisper. Executives who are business people bring a pragmatic and straightforward approach to supervising teachers and staff that alters the nature of the academic conversation within an institution. According to Ruch, "a discussion about effective teaching, for example, is basically reduced to a conversation about grade distributions, failure rates, withdrawal rates, and student progression to next-level course, rather than, say, a conversation about teaching people how to think critically".[5] Curriculum conversations are centered on how the arrangement of courses contributes to student success in staying enrolled, completing the program, and getting a job. Discipline-based issues, such as whether students should take microeconomics before macroeconomics or financial accounting before managerial accounting, are grounded in the question of what contributes to student success rather than in the question of what constitutes proper academic tradition.

The lack of an academic voice at the top of the institution can have an impact on *value-added for customers*. Academic standards could be shunned in favor of business principles such as growth and profit. Achieving growth by putting more students into classrooms and moving them through courses more quickly could become more important than preparing them fully for jobs. Never has this been more apparent than in conversations with employers decrying the lack of soft-skills preparation in college graduates. The absence of an academic perspective may encourage curriculum managers to emphasize technical skills, which are more easily measured than soft skills such as ethics, analytic ability, and the art of persuasion. If the academic perspective is not carefully integrated into the culture of the organization, the result could be a narrow and shortsighted view of the skills that students will need to obtain a job and maintain a career.

Competition will play an increasingly important role in shaping the nature of for-profit institutions. As federal and state funding continues to diminish, public-sector competitors will change how they do business and become more agile in pursuit of new student and resource markets. Community colleges with links to local business and industry will move to calibrate curricula and services to changing customer needs. They will gather information from stakeholders more quickly and adjust programs and services at more frequent intervals to meet customer needs. Similarly, less selective four-year colleges will develop closer ties with K–12 school systems to gain the upper hand in recruiting. They will make their presence known at an early age—perhaps as early as the sixth grade—to imprint the idea of college attendance on impressionable youth. To maintain their current advantages of speed and flexibility, for-profits will need to compete in specialized ways. They will need to continually reinvent the market for career education.

SOURCES OF ADVANTAGE

For-profit institutions operate in much the same manner as business organizations in that best practices are used, scanning and evaluation are ongoing, resources are efficiently used, and the ability to adapt is a prerequisite for survival. They achieve advantage by looking "outside the box" for new ideas. Demographers and economists are consulted to identify future trends, and the corporate sector is studied for innovative ideas about management practice. Decisions about resources are guided by pinpoint information and *efficiency* is stressed in every operational area. Whereas traditional institutions tend to duplicate services in departments and units that operate independently of one other, *centralization* within for-profits limits duplication. Centralization also helps to control costs and increase the *speed* at which change occurs. In contrast to the experience of traditional providers, for-profits have the capacity to implement change in weeks or months because resistance from internal fiefdoms is limited.

Pricing and cost benefits are also advantages when compared to traditional higher education institutions. Ruch defines *pricing* as "the tuition level and strategy used for setting it" and *cost* as "how much it costs the institution to educate students and how those costs are controlled."[6] While tuition and fees rarely cover the cost of educating a student in a traditional institution, the negligible difference between pricing and cost enables for-profits to remain financially viable. For-profits can lower the cost of education by limiting waste and funneling resources into expenses directly associated with instructional delivery as opposed to underwriting amenities and auxiliary services. To illustrate the differential cost of educating a student at a public, private, and for-profit institution, Ruch provides the following breakdown for two semesters of education:[7]

Public four-year: $17,026
Private four-year: $23,063
For-profit: $6,940

From these numbers it is evident why for-profit providers are able to hold down tuition pricing: their costs are substantially lower. By controlling costs that are not directly related to instruction and instructional support, for-profits create the opportunity for profitability and are less dependent on price increases to cover costs. Ruch describes the business value of this tactic as the ability to "stabilize the relationship between the cost of educating a student and the tuition charge, so tuition actually covers the full cost of the education provided. . . . Then by taking advantage of economies of scale, for-profits are able to leverage a profit by enrolling a sufficient volume of students in each academic program. . . . Sufficient enrollment volume combined with enrollment growth results in stable costs and predictable revenues."[8]

Framing Strategy

For-profit institutions occupy a market niche in which strategy is of paramount importance. Institutions live and die in this niche. Those that are successful operate on the basis of strategy, those aspiring to success need to formulate strategy or face challenges to their survival, and those that are unsuccessful somehow fail to connect with strategy. Table 7.1 illustrates viable strategy frames for for-profit institutions.

A review of these frames reveals that the overarching strategy of most for-profits is growth. This can be achieved through different frames working individually or in combination. For example, if an institution chooses to build advantage using a frame of *collaboration*, it will seek to partner with local businesses in the design, development, and implementation of industry-specific curricula. It will continuously monitor current and emerging industry needs, develop and modify curricula accordingly, and assess outcomes to ensure that performance meets or exceeds stakeholder expectations. Similarly, an institution seeking to build advantage through *speed* will move faster than competitors to develop or modify programs, courses, and services in response to student and/or market needs. The remainder of this chapter examines strategy frames in use at three for-profit institutions that have successfully carved out a niche in the market.

DeVry University

Since its establishment in 1931 as DeVry Institute of Technology, DeVry University has become one of the largest for-profit providers of higher and postsecondary education in the United States. Roughly 52,000 students receive a DeVry education each day through its sixty campuses in nineteen states and Canada, as well as its corporate training programs and its online offerings. DeVry is a comprehensive institu-

Table 7.1
Strategy Frames in For-Profit Institutions

Strategy Frame	Stakeholder(s)	Value Delivered	Differentiation from Competitors	Sustainable Advantage
Collaboration with Business and Industry	Local businesses	Highly skilled workers through job- and industry-specific training	Cutting-edge and expertly designed training	Yes, through continuous assessment of business/industry needs
Relevance	Students and employers	Competency in high-demand skills in employer market	Curricula that are constantly modified to meet changing employer needs	Yes, because traditional providers do not engage in continuous assessment
Speed	Students and employers	Rapid response to market needs	Ability to adjust programs on a business timetable	Yes, because traditional providers lack capacity for fast change
Efficiency	Students	Savings in cost and time	Pricing limited to the cost of direct program delivery; students save money and time	Yes, because traditional providers incorporate amenities into price of tuition
Convenience	Students	Savings in time and effort	Ease of access to programs, services, and facilities	No, this form of advantage can be duplicated by competitors

tion as reflected in the "university" designation it adopted in 2002. It is market-driven, as the following mission statement illustrates:

> To foster student learning through high-quality, career-oriented undergraduate and graduate programs in technology, business, and management. The University delivers its programs at campuses, centers, and online to meet the needs of a diverse and geographically dispersed student population.[9]

Growth. While mission statements generally do not express institutional strategy, DeVry's mission clearly defines its strategy for achieving advantage. Through expansion of physical locations, training programs, and distance education, DeVry intends to reach more learners and to grow. It will do so by moving *more quickly* than rivals to make *market-relevant* programs and courses *conveniently* available to students when, where, and how they want them. Growth alone, however, is not the full measure of strategy at DeVry. It is cautiously opportunistic about growth based on lessons from experience. In the words of CEO Ron Taylor, "We could have grown more quickly, but unadulterated growth has never been a guiding principle. Rather, we have sought to deliver long-term value to both stakeholders and stockholders through controlled growth dictated by quality. . . . Quality for DeVry is embedded in application-oriented studies which lead to accredited degrees and certificates under a national brand."[10]

Relevance. Businesses succeed when the services they render are relevant to the needs of customers. Relevance has different meanings for different organizations, but at DeVry it means congruence between institutional offerings and stakeholder needs through ongoing dialogue with employers. Courses and curricula are evaluated for currency through regularly scheduled meetings with business and industry leaders. In these meetings employers provide industry-specific information about market trends, industry forecasts, workforce skill-requirements, and implications for curricula and support services. Course content is then modified to provide students with state-of-the-art preparation in specific job and career fields. DeVry contracts with skilled business and industry professionals to deliver instruction and support services. All of its instructors are field-based professionals charged with imparting job-specific knowledge and skills to learners. DeVry seeks to foster career skills through a wide variety of student services. Special programs are offered to assist students in developing soft skills and in locating and interviewing for jobs. Finally, DeVry provides currently enrolled students and graduates with access to a nationwide employer database, career-planning sessions, career fairs, and a lifelong career-placement service.

Speed. The time frame in which institutions operate is an important dimension of competition in today's market. Speed—how quickly an organization can move to identify customer needs, adjust courses and curricula, and develop and implement new programs and services—is of the essence. Institutions can move quickly or slowly in converting information into action, a factor that Hamel and Prahalad (1994) refer to as "speed of iteration."[11] Whereas a traditional provider may require three to four years to gather information about customer needs, develop a new program or service, implement it, and make refinements based on market feedback, DeVry is capable of doing this in twelve to eighteen months. All other things being equal, a provider with a twelve-month iteration cycle will be able to capture a market much faster than one with a three-year cycle. Each successful iteration builds capability in program design and development and adds to DeVry's reputation as a responsive provider.

Convenience. The increased demand for convenience in higher education has created a new avenue for building advantage. Convenience is evident in DeVry's commitment to deliver programs to diverse populations in a variety of formats and at a variety of locations. Tactics that support this frame are the expansion of locations, distance-education offerings, and increasingly flexible programmatic offerings at more than sixty locations across the United States. DeVry's online option now includes four program areas (business administration, computer information systems, information technology, and technical management) in which students can earn their degree entirely online. Services for online students include a virtual library, an online bookstore, companion disks that accompany coursework, and training services similar to those offered on campus.

Quest Career College

A common misconception of proprietary institutions is that they are driven primarily by profit and do not have a comprehensive view of students. While it may be convenient to use a few bad examples to diminish an entire category of institutions, Quest Career College provides an example of a for-profit institution at the top of its game with strategy. Quest was established in 1997 in Parma Heights, Ohio, as a company in the business of refurbishing and reselling computers.[12] Shortly after opening its doors, the company discovered an untapped market in the area of career-oriented computer training for veterans and adults who had not been involved with formal education for many years. A course introducing adult learners to the world of computers was created and met with immediate success. Encouraged by the response of adult learners to its offerings, Quest created certificate and diploma programs in technology and eventually offered an associate degree in Applied Business and Computer Technology. Over a span of eight years, it evolved from an organization in the business of refurbishing and reselling computers to a provider of postsecondary education programs and services for adult learners.

Quest's strategy is implicit in its *student-first* mission statement: "Quest Career College is focused on the individual and directs all of its efforts toward providing the training, services and assistance needed to prepare

students for rewarding jobs that provide the basis for a successful life."
Four objectives centered on student success reinforce this mission:[13]

- To provide students with the most useful, up-to-date training possible
  relevant to a career in a technological vocation.
- To ensure that the student receives all that it takes to achieve success.
- To make sure that students failing or falling through the cracks receive
  timely assistance.
- To maintain a state of constant improvement so that our students will
  get the best educational experience possible.

While the goal of most proprietary institutions is growth, Quest works
with a deep sense of purpose that is rooted in three strategy frames: service, relevance, and holistic focus. These frames serve as a bridge between
institutional mission and objectives, operations, and strategy.

Service. With a focus on adult learners long removed from formal education, Quest is committed to providing an array of services to help students achieve success. A study guide is provided to all students upon
enrollment. This guide consists of seven modules designed to acclimate
students to the skills needed for academic success: time-management
techniques, effective-listening practices, classroom principles, note-
taking, guides for effective studying, test-taking principles, and tips on
effective essay writing. Tutoring is included in the cost of tuition and is
routinely used by students and instructors to support classroom learning.
As part of their classroom routine, watchful instructors identify students
experiencing difficulty and make arrangements for tutoring and academic
assistance. Quest's commitment to service in support of learning is not
limited to the traditional classroom. Its Interactive Distance Learning
program uses sophisticated technology to enrich the classroom experience for students in online courses. Students are supplied with a dual-
monitor computer system and software designed for video, sound, and
two-way interaction. On one screen, the student watches a direct feed of
classroom instruction, while on the other screen he or she receives information and feedback directly from the instructor. This system virtually recreates the classroom experience for place-bound learners who do
not have the time or wherewithal to attend classes on campus.

Relevance. Students enroll in Quest to gain access to a career and job
in the information technology industry. They are successful to the extent
that they land in meaningful IT jobs, thus the curricula and courses Quest
offers must be up-to-date and industry-connected. Quest partners with
Microsoft, Hewlett-Packard, AMD, and Novell to ensure the relevancy
of its courses. Additionally, degree program curricula are designed to in-

crease the marketability of learners by incorporating a full range of skills valued by employers. The Applied Business in Computer Technology program, for example, consists of business, communication, mathematics, and computer technology courses, which are routinely part of such a program. This program also contains courses in the social and behavioral sciences and classes designed to improve soft skills including training in developing customized presentations, interviewing, project management, the art of persuasion, workplace ethics, and more.

Strayer University

A subsidiary of Strayer Education, Inc., the mission of Strayer University is to "make high quality postsecondary education achievable and convenient for working adults in today's economy."[14] From its humble roots as the Business College of Baltimore City in 1892, Strayer has morphed into a thirty-campus system serving 23,000 students in eight states and the District of Columbia. It offers bachelor's and master's degrees organized to "fit the life patterns" of adults. Nearly all of its students work full-time. The essence of strategy for Strayer, therefore, is to fit the college into the life patterns and preferences of its students. This strategy has enabled it to focus on offerings and services for a specific group of learners—working adults—and to provide a level of support and opportunity that few institutions can match. Essentially, Strayer University is a *niche player* using strategy frames of convenience, customization, and relevance to build an advantage over competitors.

Convenience. The word *convenience* is generally used to describe something that is "conducive to comfort or ease." Strayer makes education accessible to learners by offering entire programs online through two delivery methods. Through Strayer Online, a student has the option of enrolling in undergraduate certificate, diploma, associate degree, bachelor's, master's, and executive-graduate certificate programs either in a synchronous or asynchronous format. Convenience at Strayer, however, means more than comfort or ease. It also means that adult learners can make seamless transitions between different educational goals through the seemingly incongruous programs offered by the university.

These programs provide students with options that fit a variety of life situations. While some learners require a bachelor's or master's degree to receive a promotion or to pursue an opportunity, others need an associate degree to qualify for a job. Some professionals enter the executive-graduate program to gain knowledge about a specific field, while others have an advanced degree and need an undergraduate certificate to pursue a new interest that could lead to a second career. It is entirely possible that an individual could work his or her way through each degree level and obtain a comprehensive education at Strayer. In essence, Strayer is a one-stop education for the working adult.

Customization. Strayer University is dedicated not only to providing a variety of degrees for working adults, but also to providing the personalized service necessary to help learners succeed and to find opportunities in new professions. Services such as academic advising, career development, and transfer assistance are customized to the learner and delivered by staff cognizant of adult-learner needs. In addition to faculty advisors, learners are able to access traditional and electronic instructional resources and to acquire tutoring as needed both on- and off-campus. They can also obtain career consultation electronically or face-to-face, use MonsterTRAK to review job listings and post résumés, and receive assistance in obtaining internships and acquiring jobs through a career-development center. Strayer actively works with students to link life experience with coursework using standardized tests such as CLEP and DANTES, previous education, and challenge exams.

Relevance. Like most for-profit institutions, a primary aim of Strayer is to offer curricula and courses that develop knowledge and skills in emerging and existing fields. Strayer is dedicated to providing training in high-demand fields through associate-degree programs in acquisition and contract management and computer networking; bachelor's degree programs in international business and Internet technology; and master's degree programs in communications technology, professional accounting, and information systems. Many of the instructors at Strayer also teach at regional public and private colleges and are interested in the opportunity to work with adult learners. Adjunct faculty at Strayer bring extensive experience from current employment in business and industry and state and federal government agencies.

The *niche strategy* used by Strayer University provides unique value to working adult learners through a variety of programs and services that are designed with sufficient flexibility to meet even the busiest of schedules. It is able to facilitate academic and career progress for adult learners by offering programs that correspond to changing life needs and circumstances (convenience); services that are designed to meet the needs of nontraditional learners (customization); and instruction in high-demand career fields (relevance). Strayer has been using this formula for more than a century with working adult learners and developed it to a point where it now reaps economies of scale and scope.

CONCLUSION

The outlook of traditional colleges and universities on the marketplace is changing, but with change comes resistance to new needs and ideas. For-profit institutions operate according to a "change or die" philosophy. They neither resist the market nor attempt to change it by persuading students or employers that they need something other than what they want. If the demand for wireless telecommunications programs is strong, for example, they respond by creating a customized program in wireless telecommunications rather than channeling students into an existing electrical-engineering curriculum. This approach to the market is the essence of strategy used by for-profit institutions. To create a niche for themselves, they must regularly listen to customers and move decisively and quickly to provide exactly what they want.

There are gains and losses implicit in this strategy. Nonprofit colleges and universities distinguish themselves from for-profits by holding inviolable the belief that the key benefits of education are intrinsic and not immediately measurable, economically or otherwise. For-profits assign value to curricular relevance, customer satisfaction, and operational efficiency and distinguish themselves from traditional providers on the basis of their performance in these areas. Which is better? Each one informs and enriches the other, and there is value in both.

NOTES

1. Richard S. Ruch, *Higher Ed, Inc.: The Rise of the For-Profit University* (Baltimore: Johns Hopkins University Press, 2001), 117–118. Segments of the description of for-profit providers in this chapter are derived from Ruch's seminal analysis of their academic and business practices.

2. Ibid., 113.

3. Ibid., 127–128.

4. Ibid., 116.

5. Ibid.

6. Ibid., 85.

7. Ibid., 87.

8. Ibid., 87–88.

9. Information derived from the Web site of DeVry University, www.devry. com.

10. Direct communication with Ron Taylor, CEO of DeVry University, June 2004.

11. Gary Hamel and C. K. Prahalad, *Competing for the Future* (Boston: Harvard Business School Press, 1994), 263.

12. Information derived from the Web site of Quest Career College, www.quest.edu.

13. Ibid.

14. Information derived from the Web site of Strayer University, www.strayer.com, and Strayer Education Inc. www.strayereducation.com.

PART III

How Strategy Works

CHAPTER

Framing and Articulating Strategy

U p to this point, the focus has been on the *concept* of strategy—its definition and distinction from tactics and how it is conceptualized and formulated in organizations. In this chapter, and those that follow, we shift the focus to *execution*—the actions necessary to enact strategy in a college or university. While concept and execution are interdependent, they require entirely different skills from leaders and staff. While the conception of strategy is best pursued through freewheeling thought and give-and-take dialogue, its execution involves managing people and processes to reach a common goal. The conception of strategy involves assembling and using information to determine where advantage can be achieved. The execution of strategy involves taking the actions that need to be carried out to achieve the advantage.

There is a logical integration of concept and execution as part of a process of forging strategy (*formulation*), enunciating it (*framing and articulation*), carrying it out (*implementation*), and assessing its effects (*evaluation*). At the same time, however, concept and execution need to be kept conceptually distinct. It is important to understand that formulation—the process of using information to forge strategy—transcends organizational policies, decisions, resource allocation, and actions large and small. Strategy will fail in the absence of known and specific steps for articulation and implementation. Further, it will fail if there is inconsistency between what an institution says and what it does.[1] The importance of execution, therefore, is in the act of doing. Execution transforms concept into action and thereby makes strategy real for people and institutions.

FRAMING STRATEGY

To *frame* means to shape through *expression*. Shape and form can be given to just about any kind of information, but the process of shaping strategy is different from that of tactics. Imagine an executive team shaping a plan—what we have labeled as a *tactic* earlier in the book. What comes to mind is an image of orderly thinking; a team comprised of senior administrators sitting in a conference room using a limited bank of information—most of it internal—to determine a course of action that others will implement. The key words are "orderly thinking" and "limited information"—concepts that involve rational control, a reliance on internal information, actions influenced by resources, and an emphasis on the short-term and tangible. For the tactician, to *frame* means to identify specific priorities or objectives as well as the action steps that must be taken to achieve them.[2]

Now imagine an executive team framing strategy. An entirely different image comes into view, as different from tactics as strategy is from operations. Strategy evokes big-picture thinking and creative imagination. What comes to mind is not so much rational and short-term as systemic; strategy involves integrating information and ideas from multiple sources into an overarching statement that gives meaning and direction to the institution. Attention is given to the needs of stakeholders and the value delivered by the institution, the systematic analysis of competitors and markets, to institutional capabilities and weaknesses, all of which leads to an explicit statement of advantage through which strategy evolves. Viewed from this perspective, to *frame* means to put complex information—the ingredients of strategy—into an expression of the advantage an institution wants to achieve by making itself unique among rivals. Advantage is important because the essence of strategy is to achieve leverage over competitors. The process of giving form to (or *shaping*) an advantage, then, is that of *framing* strategy, while the act of *stating* the advantage is essentially one of *articulation*. Strategy that is unclear or incapable of being understood will meet with resistance from staff. It is a given in most organizations that people will not commit to something they cannot understand. This simple reality makes framing and articulation among the most important strategy tasks that an institution can undertake. The question is how to go about this task: What are the necessary and important steps in framing and articulating strategy?

To answer this question, we return to the image of the executive team working with strategy. The team would very likely use a process of deductive reasoning to frame strategy as illustrated in Figure 8.1. Following the stepwise progression for strategy formulation described in chapter 3, the team would gather information from inside and outside of the institution to construct the context for strategy. Important in this regard would be data about stakeholder needs, market forces, and institutional capabilities. Value would be assessed and delineated for *stakeholders* as the sum of their wants, needs, and expectations for education; for the *market*, as the value delivered by all providers; and for the *institution*, as the value delivered to its stakeholders. Advantage would be then determined by using this information to answer the following questions:

Stakeholders

- Who are they?
- What do they want, need, and expect from postsecondary education?
- What do they want from a specific provider?

Market

- How do market forces shape the value expectations of stakeholders?
- What value is offered by different providers?
- What value is being delivered by these providers?

Institution

- What value is an institution capable of delivering to its stakeholders?
- What value does it actually deliver to these stakeholders?
- How does the value delivered by the institution compare with that delivered by competitors?

Advantage

- Does a discrepancy exist between the value expected (by stakeholders) and the value actually delivered (by providers)?
- Where can advantage be achieved by the institution?
- How can this advantage be pursued?

The last question, How can this advantage be pursued?, marks the point at which strategy moves from formulation to execution. The steps leading up to this question involve the use of information to determine where advantage can be found, whereas the steps following this question focus on the actions an institution must take to achieve the ad-

Figure 8.1
Framework for Framing and Articulating Strategy

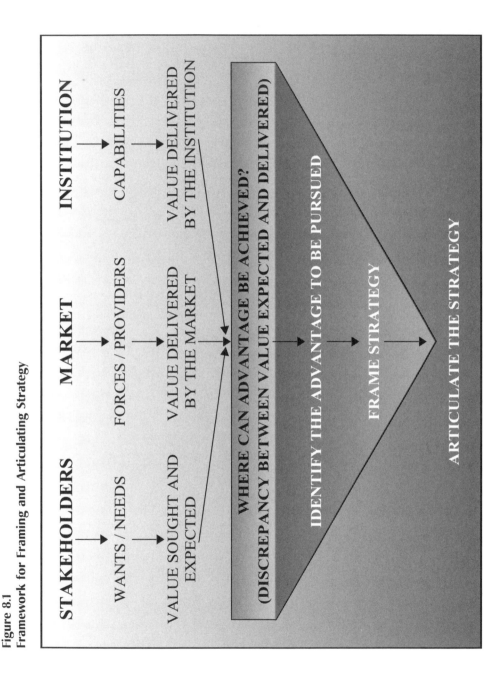

vantage. In the pages that follow, we present two approaches to framing strategy that will help practitioners understand how this process works.[3]

Linear Process for Framing Strategy

One approach to framing strategy involves a graduated process in which decision makers ask and answer questions about different aspects of strategy. These questions help to determine which approach to strategy an institution can most effectively use to establish an advantage and what it must do to implement the strategy.

Formulation

1. What are the institution's mission, purpose, and vision of the future?
2. Who are the primary stakeholders and what value are they seeking from the college?
3. What is the institution's vision of the value it needs to deliver to its stakeholders?
4. What value is the institution actually delivering?
5. What value is being offered and delivered by competitors?
6. What value does the institution need to deliver to establish an advantage over competitors?

Framing

7. Which approach to strategy will afford the best opportunity to achieve this advantage?

Articulation

8. What statement most clearly and concisely expresses this strategy?

A good example of a linear process for framing and articulating strategy is provided by Seminole Community College (SCC), a fast-growing public, comprehensive community college in central Florida.[4] Although Seminole's strategy is not fully articulated, all of the ingredients for successful strategy are in place. Established in 1965, SCC has transitioned from a single-campus institution serving 10,000 students in 1995 to a multicampus system serving more than 32,000 students today. Much of its growth has been accomplished through a strategic-marketing-and-recruitment plan developed under the leadership of a president who came to the college in the late 1990s. This plan focused on reframing the identity of the college by reaffirming its mission, articulating values, and setting goals. Text and examples are used to describe Seminole's progression in strategy formulation from mission to articulation.

SCC MISSION

The mission of Seminole Community College is to serve the community by providing a learning-centered, high-quality educational institution that anticipates and meets the needs of the community by providing a comprehensive range of programs and services.[5]

Seminole Community College promises:

- Exemplary and highly motivated faculty, administrators, and staff who foster a caring and professional relationship with students and the community.
- An excellent academic curriculum that provides the first two years of university studies.
- State-of-the-art career and technical programs that lead directly to employment or career advancement.
- Cutting-edge continuing education that offers opportunities for advancement or recertification.
- Personalized adult education programs that help students learn and strengthen basic academic skills and earn a high school diploma.
- Innovative student development services that support learning and teaching processes and promote student success.
- Dynamic business, industry, and educational partnerships that enhance the region's economic development and vitality.
- Leisure and personal development programs, that contribute to enrichment of the community.
- A distinctive cultural center that provides diverse professional and academic courses, programs, and events.

SCC VISION

Seminole Community College will be renowned, first and foremost, for its enduring commitment and focus on individual student success.[6]

We are *student-centered*, as evidenced by our investment in high-quality, committed faculty and staff; distinctive and diverse programs; and the wide range of innovative services we offer. We are *community-connected*, as evidenced by our commitment to forging mutually beneficial partnerships and alliances that address the specific needs of our diverse community. We are *future-focused* as evidenced by our anticipation of the needs of our community and our proactive development of strategies to meet those needs.

To achieve this vision, we will:

- Create a collaborative learning environment where students are the first priority.
- Champion diversity and inclusiveness.
- Attract and support premier faculty and staff.
- Ensure excellent programs that prepare students for success.
- Achieve leadership in technologically advanced learning.
- Build collaborative corporate, community, academic, and internal partnerships.
- Guarantee institutional effectiveness through ongoing assessment.

Following the eight-question sequence above to guide the formulation, framing, and articulation of strategy, Seminole's mission and vision statements challenge faculty and staff to reach an ideal of excellence in teaching, learning, and service to the community. Students are identified as one of several primary stakeholders along with business and industry, educational partners, and the community. These statements indicate *how* SCC will serve the community, *with whom* it will work, and the *resources* it will use to provide service. They also identify the organizational principles Seminole will embrace and the steps it will take to create value for its stakeholders. Neither statement identifies the value that stakeholders are seeking from postsecondary education or from SCC in particular. This information does appear, however, in Seminole's strategic plan "Making a Difference," which was developed in 2005. Through organized conversations involving 115 leaders from the external community (business and industry, education, government, and prominent citizens) and 285 employees from different work groups on campus, SCC acquired the following information about stakeholder needs and interests:

- Students want access to required courses at convenient times and locations.
- Employers want customized training for current and new employees.

- Local government agencies need help in attracting business and industry.
- K–12 schools want to create a seamless transition from school to college by laddering curricula and dovetailing support services, technology, and basic-skills preparation.
- Business and industry want to improve the soft skills and technological preparation of workers through enhanced programming in colleges and universities.
- Four-year colleges and universities want to absorb more learners and provide better service through collaborative programs with community colleges.
- Disenfranchised populations need and want access to postsecondary education to improve prospects for a job and a reasonable wage.
- Adult learners need customized courses, programs, and services for career mobility and job advancement.

SCC's vision of the *value it will deliver to stakeholders* is expressed through the following words in its vision statement: "We will ensure excellent programs that prepare students for success." This concept of success suggests that Seminole will deliver programs and services to students that, through continuous assessment and upgrading, will enable them to achieve academic, career, and personal goals. Examples of current efforts in this regard are career and technical programs that lead to higher paying jobs in the regional market, general-education transfer programs that enable students to perform the same as, or better than, native students in bachelor's degree institutions at a considerable cost savings, and workforce-development programs that enable current employees to acquire training and certification for higher paying jobs. Seminole annually collects data from students, employers, and transfer institutions on a program-by-program and institutional basis that documents the value it actually delivers to students and stakeholders. This value is delineated in data-reporting outcomes for students such as access to jobs and higher income following enrollment, career mobility, salary enhancement, degree attainment following transfer, cost savings, return on investment, and satisfaction with the college experience. For employers, value is reported as a measure of their satisfaction with the skills and job performance of graduates, and for college and university officials value is reported in the form of an analysis of transfer-student performance compared to native students.

Like most institutions, Seminole has little information about the value offered and delivered by competitors. It knows who its rivals are and what they are trying to do, but is largely unaware of their effect on stakeholders. Conversations with the external community in the strategic-planning process did elicit some information about competitors. SCC learned from employers, for example, that for-profit institutions are effective in preparing students for job and career entry—from preparing a résumé to interviewing skills to workplace ethics. From corporate employers, it learned that college students, in general, are viewed as ill-equipped for success in the corporate world. They lack soft skills, a reasoned and mature work ethic, and savvy related to the workplace. And it learned from educational partners and employers that its quality and "brand" were relatively unknown compared to other providers.

Using this information, Seminole moved to project the value it would need to deliver to establish an advantage over competitors: its basis for strategy. It focused on the performance shortfalls of regional educational providers in three areas: access, workforce preparation, and responsiveness—each a potential source of advantage. Access is a problem for public colleges and universities in Florida because demand for postsecondary education is much greater than capacity. An institution finding ways to support growth through operational efficiency and resource procurement will find favor with communities, voters, and government agencies because of its enhanced capacity to meet demand. A skilled workforce is a requisite for business attraction and retention—a key to economic vitality in a high-growth state like Florida. An institution producing workers with superior soft skills and technical capabilities will become a preferred provider and, in so doing, establish an advantage with employers. Finally, for-profit and nonprofit organizations have yet to realize their full potential for collaboration, a circumstance which has resulted in resource inefficiency and waste. An institution working out-of-the-box to deliver more and better services through creative partnerships will curry favor not only with players in its network but also with the public at large.

The identification and description of regional-provider performance shortfalls in access, workforce preparation, and responsiveness provides Seminole with vital information to frame and articulate strategy. At the time this book was written, the college had not completed the strategy cycle, so what follows is a hypothetical description of the steps it would need to take to frame and articulate strategy.

The next step for Seminole would be to examine the relationship of each source of advantage to its mission and vision, its resources, and its capabilities and decide which advantage it would want to pursue. If it elected to pursue them all, the concept of advantage would be fleshed out and framed into strategy as follows:

We will seek advantage by

- increasing access through lower-cost programs and services offered at convenient times and locations (*convenience*);
- infusing quality into programs through continuous performance assessment (*quality*);
- establishing innovative partnerships with profit and nonprofit organizations (*collaboration*).

Each form of advantage—convenience, quality, and collaboration—is essentially a frame for strategy; that is, a specific approach to strategy organized around a distinct theme and like types of action. To illustrate, convenience can be accomplished through a variety of actions centered on the principle of making the college experience easier and more comfortable for students. Common practices might include designing class schedules to fit student availability, putting services 24/7/365 on the Internet, offering entire degree programs online, controlling out-of-pocket costs, and so forth. Quality is more complex in nuance and makeup, but generally it has something to do with excellence or superiority. In Seminole's parlance, it would refer to the degree of excellence that will be achieved in programs through continuous improvement based on research carried out with students and receiving organizations. Finally, collaboration involves actions carried out by organizations working together for a specific purpose, with each receiving benefit. The objective of collaboration as a strategy frame for Seminole would be threefold: (1) to build relationships with organizations that will lead to revenue enhancement; (2) to acquire advanced information from partners about markets, technology, and competitors; and (3) to reduce expenses by off-loading costly operations to capable partners.

The final step would be to integrate these statements into a clear expression of strategy that would be capable of being understood and supported by staff throughout the institution. This expression would indicate, in a few words, the distinctive position Seminole would strive to occupy in the regional postsecondary education market by distinguishing itself from competitors. It could be developed and stated as follows:

> SCC intends to become central Florida's first choice in education by offering programs unmatched in quality and convenience in partnership with leading-edge organizations.

Unfortunately, few institutions think long and hard about strategy as a systemic expression of their goals. And those that do experience difficulty in condensing their thinking into a few words that capture the attention of staff and guide the institution into the future. As a result, there is usually little more than an assortment of plans, priorities, and lofty statements to guide decision-making and action toward organizational goals.

Framing Strategy Through Reconceptualization

When one conceives of a college or university as a portfolio of competencies, different possibilities for framing strategy open up. The boundaries of an institution's mission and programs represent an enactment of its current market view. But future opportunities are unlikely to correspond perfectly to this view. While an institution is working to establish a secure place in today's market, new markets and new opportunities are unfolding for those that remove their blinders and move beyond existing organizational boundaries. These institutions, in so doing, transform current ways of doing things and establish new competitive space. We call this process *reconceptualization* and it is a different, but equally effective approach to framing strategy.

Albion College in Michigan provides a good example of an institution that has reconceptualized current practice to forge strategy for the future.[7] Chartered in 1835, Albion currently enrolls 1,950 students and has an endowment of $150 million. On the surface it is the very picture of a selective liberal arts college: it is small and expensive, with a core curriculum and comprehensive residential-life program, and its campus buildings have a classic architecture. It is different by design, however, because it has reframed its curriculum to integrate the worlds of living, work, and learning. The Albion College vision "Liberal Arts at Work" marries the best elements of the liberal arts tradition with innovative programs to create a new model for undergraduate education. It is comprised of five dimensions:

- First-Year Experience
- Liberal Arts Core and Academic Major
- Foundation for Undergraduate Research, Scholarship, and Creative Activity
- Institutes
  Institute for the Study of the Environment
  Gerald R. Ford Institute for Public Policy and Service
  Carl A. Gerstacker Liberal Arts Institute for Professional Management
  Prentiss M. Brown Honors Institute
  Liberal Arts Institute for Pre-Medical and Health Care Studies
  Fritz Shurmur Education Institute
- Foundation for Interdisciplinary Study

Entering students at Albion are immediately engaged in their education through specially designed seminars coupled with co-curricular activities to ease the transition from high school to college. The first year seminars—touching on topics such as "Art in the Environment," "Genes and Society," "Innovations in Imaging," "Natural Disasters," and "Vietnam: Then and Now"—are designed to foster open communication, critical thinking, and improvement in writing and speaking skills. Students add breadth and depth to their program of study through a wide-ranging core curriculum and specialization in an academic major. In addition to working on a major, they may join one of the six institutes to obtain real-world experience and prepare for a career. Funded through endowments of $2 million each, the institutes integrate theoretical and practical learning and involve internships, a capstone experience, and a research or applied project. Students may also pursue original research supported by the Foundation for Undergraduate Research, Scholarship, and Creative Activity (FURSCA). Research grants are awarded to students to cover expenses associated with original research carried out under the supervision of a faculty mentor.

The overarching aim of Albion's "Liberal Arts at Work" vision is to prepare students for the next phase of their lives and to do so in a way that provides them with a distinct advantage whether it be admission to a graduate or professional school, beginning a successful career, or involvement in community. By reconceptualizing the tradition of the liberal arts to focus on attributes valued by complex organizations in a changing society, Albion has chosen a strategy of *relevance* to distinguish itself from competitors. The emphasis on communication skills and critical thinking in the First-Year Experience dimension, the integration of theoretical and practical learning in the institutes, and the support for creative scholarship and research through FURSCA are all woven together to give graduates a competitive advantage in a technology-enhanced workplace.

Albion did not engage in a linear, step-by-step process to formulate its strategy. It looked ahead to anticipate the future by developing foresight into trends in lifestyles, technology, health, demographics, and public policy. It then looked back to determine what would need to happen with its curriculum to provide knowledge and skills that would be relevant to societal institutions and complex organizations in the world of the future. Core competencies current to the institution and those needed for the future were identified, the role and objectives of the curriculum were reconfigured, and resources were allocated to bring the "Liberal Arts at Work" vision to life. Albion's vision is the expression of its strategy. It

answers the four questions posed in chapter 1 that are the true test of
strategy:

Who are the primary stakeholders?	Students.
What kind of value is delivered?	Critical thinking, intellectual awareness, and soft skills.
Does the value created lead to advantage?	Yes, it provides an edge for students entering graduate education, a career, and a community.
Is the advantage sustainable?	No, it can be duplicated by other providers.

The questions of advantage and sustainability involve the cumulative
effect of an education that is nurtured before and during college and plays
out over a lifetime in complex organizations and societal institutions.
The dimensions of this effect can best be understood through the story
of Cassandra, which is posted on Albion's Web site:

> Cassandra chooses Albion College because of her interest in sociol-
> ogy and attraction to the Gerald R. Ford Institute for Public Policy
> and Service. In her First-Year Seminar on "Women's Lives: Toward
> a Global Perspective," she becomes interested in the role women
> have played in the world's economy. She pursues this interest
> through classes in economics and women's studies, and through her
> major in sociology. Interdisciplinary workshops and group projects
> supplement her classroom experience.
>
> By her junior year, Cassandra begins to formulate a long-term re-
> search project on the involvement of women of color in traditional
> labor movements in the Detroit area and the benefits they derived
> from such involvement compared with unionized women of color in
> Cape Town, South Africa. The director of the Ford Institute helps
> her make local contacts and arranges an internship with a female
> union organizer in the Detroit area for five hours a week in the spring
> of her junior year. With her growing knowledge and interest in is-
> sues concerning women of color, Cassandra works with the Anna
> Howard Shaw Center for Women's Studies and Programs and the
> Office of Intercultural Affairs to help coordinate a joint co-curricular
> lecture series including a program on the history of access for
> African-American women in the UAW.
>
> In the fall of her senior year, Cassandra spends a semester study-
> ing at the University of Cape Town, where she immerses herself in
> South African culture. With assistance from alumni working in the
> Methodist Church of Southern Africa, she conducts in-depth inter-

views with union organizers and workers. The project becomes a departmental honors thesis. A shorter version of Cassandra's work is published in the College's undergraduate research journal, and, with travel funds from the Foundation for Undergraduate Research, Scholarship, and Creative Activity (FURSCA), she presents a paper with one of her faculty mentors at a national meeting.[8]

ARTICULATING STRATEGY

The purpose of articulation is to transform strategy from its expression of where advantage can be achieved (framing) to a polished statement capable of being understood by all or most personnel in the institution. For the strategy to be understood, it must be expressed in words that have a common meaning for faculty and staff. To garner support, it must link important issues facing the institution with solutions that appear likely to work. Also, it must be expressed in a way that enables staff to forge a connection with it—to personalize it as a guide for one's work in the institution. There must be a coupling, in other words, of issues, solutions, people, and perceptions.

To articulate a strategy that is capable of gaining support, key decision makers must listen carefully to personnel in the institution and be open to the idea of change. The wording of the strategy must be geared to the values, interests, and frames of reference of different individuals and groups since they will choose whether or not to commit to it on the basis of their own judgment. For example, the "Liberal Arts at Work" vision/strategy articulated by Albion College would have little or no meaning in the absence of extensive groundwork laid by college leaders with faculty, staff, and students. Questions would invariably be raised about specific terms: How are the *liberal arts* conceptualized and defined? What do you mean by the word *work*? Why have you chosen to link liberal arts and work? By listening carefully to the modes of thought and expression of individuals and work groups in the college, decision makers were able to acquire a sense of how to word the strategy in a way that would encourage acceptance. Give-and-take dialogues were undoubtedly part of the process, with players seeking to shape specific concepts to fit their outlook, but in the final analysis, consensus was reached by listening to one another.

For the purpose of illustration, we provide several examples of ineffectively articulated strategy, using, once again, the "Liberal Arts at Work" strategy of Albion College.[9]

Albion's strategy is

- To accentuate the importance of creativity and intellectual rigor in envisioning and designing innovative solutions to twenty-first-century problems.

    Problem: The statement is wordy and abstract. It uses many words with multiple meanings. The statement does not differentiate Albion from liberal arts colleges in general.

- To provide a competitive advantage to students through highly developed critical thinking, communication, and problem-solving skills.

    Problem: This expression of strategy does not fit the liberal arts tradition. The action orientation of the statement is more typical of a tactic, and the statement does not adequately represent important facets of the college experience.

- To prepare students for success in work, education, and life through the liberal arts.

    Problem: This statement is indistinct from statements made by other liberal arts colleges. It is abstract and lacks dynamism because the liberal arts are treated passively rather than actively.

Formal articulation of strategy can be decisive and quick or it can move gradually through stages as decision makers mull over different possibilities. Incrementalism guided by a sense of direction can result in a series of small decisions that accumulate into a statement of strategy. Indeed, Quinn (1980) argues that most strategic changes in large corporations are in fact small changes that are guided by a sense of strategic purpose.[10] Incrementally articulated strategy reduces risk, eases implementation, and boosts staff confidence and commitment.[11] On the other hand, rapid movement toward articulation may be necessary when an incremental approach is unnecessary, unworkable, or undesirable for some reason. For example, when an institution is facing difficult conditions or must achieve an important goal, rapid movement toward strategy is essential. This approach can also be used when the time is right; for example, when the need is obvious to a large coalition that the institution must move in a particular direction, the proposed strategy will effectively provide that direction, the tactics are clearly understood, and resources are available to implement the strategy.[12]

PRACTICAL ADVICE

The following guidelines, adopted in part from the work of Bryson (1995), should be kept in mind as decision makers frame and articulate strategy and seek to engage stakeholders in the process:[13]

1. *It is important to subject frames under consideration for strategy to criteria that define strategy at an early point in the articulation process.* For decision makers who have long relied on declarations, plans, and budgets to guide decisions, it is easy to confuse strategy and tactics. To ensure that energy and effort are being appropriately directed, evolving frames should be evaluated in relationship to criteria that are the true test of strategy. These criteria are stated in the form of four questions presented at key intervals in this book: Who are the stakeholders? What value is being created? Does the value created lead to advantage by differentiating the institution from its competitors? Is the advantage sustainable? Frames that cannot readily answer these questions are probably not sufficient for strategy and will need to be rethought.

2. *The "why" underlying strategy is important and should be fully disclosed.* Personnel cannot be expected to support something that lacks meaning or a raison d'être. Therefore, in the process of articulating strategy, decision makers need to indicate why it is important and what it will do for the college. Is it being formulated (1) to respond to contextual conditions inside or outside of the college, (2) to achieve a particular goal, or (3) to realize a vision of the future? Personnel occupy vastly different roles in colleges and universities that impel them to see things differently. A senior administrator, for example, will be likely to comprehend the impact of changing demographics on enrollment and revenue in a different way than will faculty and support staff. The same is true of strategy. Administrators who have had a hand in formulating strategy can be expected to understand its every nuance, but the same will not be true of those encountering it for the first time. Personnel will not get to a place where they can understand and commit to strategy until full information is provided about the value and benefits of strategy to the institution.

3. *Simple is beautiful; to be effective strategy must be framed and articulated in such a way as to be comprehensible to stakeholders inside and outside of the institution.* The way in which a strategy is formulated is less important than how clearly and concisely it is articulated and how easily it is understood by staff. To ensure full understanding among work groups in the institution, the strategy should be stated in simple language using the minimum number of words possible.

4. *Strategy frames should be described in sufficient detail to permit reasonable*

judgments about their efficacy. Strategy is a difficult concept to understand, much less to enact. Personnel new to the concept will have difficulty distinguishing it from tactics and will seek to reduce it to what they have known and practiced. For this reason, important features of frames under consideration for strategy will need to be described in order to provide staff with a basis for determining their efficacy. The following information should be provided in the description of a frame: principal components, intended outcomes, resources required, flexibility and adaptability, implications for personnel, ease of implementation, and procedures for evaluation.[14]

5. *Decision makers should think carefully about how the implementation process will be managed as part of strategy framing and articulation.* The organizations that are most adept at working with strategy seem to combine formulation, articulation, and implementation into a seamless process. Usually top administrators take the lead in developing basic principles for strategy formulation and articulation, while detailed planning for implementation occurs deeper in the institution. The full spectrum of information and action involved in the progression from formulation to implementation can then be viewed at the top for consistency across the institution, and steps can be taken toward implementation.[15]

6. *Strategy is not cast in concrete; to be effective it must be flexible up to the point of articulation.* A proposed strategy is likely to be presented to important decision-making bodies at different times. It is also likely to move through multiple iterations until it reaches a point where key decision makers evaluate it as acceptable. It is important, therefore, to build sufficient flexibility into the framing process to allow different voices to be heard prior to articulation.

7. *A representative and inclusive process should be used to review the articulated strategy before it is finalized.* A draft of articulated strategy should be viewed by governing board members and representatives of key stakeholder groups inside and outside of the institution before a decision is made to go forward with implementation. The review process should be open to encourage maximum participation as a means for improving the strategy. Strategies that are unacceptable to stakeholders will need to go back to the drawing board. Strategies that do not take key stakeholders into account will run the risk of failure.[16]

8. *Build in a period of time for the strategy to settle in among work groups in the institution before proceeding to implementation.* Strong feelings are apt to surface as strategy reaches the point of articulation, particularly if it involves significant changes and challenges the current culture. A groundswell of hostile feelings can turn a promising strategy into a bitter disappointment if not properly managed. The feelings and opinions

of personnel must be recognized, acknowledged, and welcomed into consideration. A settling-in period enabling personnel to vent positive and negative feelings is a necessary step toward building ownership for the strategy and moving on to the next step: implementation.[17]

SUMMARY

The focus in the first seven chapters of this book has been on the concept of strategy; in particular, how it is formulated in colleges and universities as complex organizations. This chapter has shifted the focus to how strategy works, with a particular emphasis on framing and articulation as initial steps in strategy execution. There is a logical integration of concept and execution as part of a process of forging strategy (*formulation*), enunciating it (*framing and articulation*), carrying it out (*implementation*), and assessing its effects (*evaluation*). It is important to remember, however, that while concept and execution are conceptually distinct—one having to do with using information to create strategy, and the other with actions and resources to enact strategy—successful strategy depends on a seamless connection between these components.

Chapter 9 takes up the topic of implementation: What steps can and should an institution take to enact strategy once it has been successfully articulated? This chapter is as important, if not more important, than any in the book because it is the difference between success and failure for strategy. The closing chapter presents a framework for evaluation that institutions can use to determine the effectiveness of strategy. Processes for implementation and evaluation are offered in the hope that they will make the transition from concept to execution as easy as possible for practitioners.

NOTES

1. John M. Bryson, *Strategic Planning for Public and Non-Profit Organizations* (San Francisco: Jossey-Bass, 1995), 130.

2. This analogy is drawn from the approach to thought of Henry Mintzberg, *The Rise and Fall of Strategic Planning* (New York: The Free Press, 1994), 6–33.

3. The approaches to framing strategy described in this chapter were derived from Bryson's *Strategic Planning*. Particularly helpful were Bryson's ideas about alternative approaches to strategy development described on 138–143.

4. The information presented for Seminole Community College was obtained through review of institutional documents and through service to the college in a consulting capacity. From October 2004 to March 2005, Richard Alfred

and Patricia Carter provided assistance to Seminole in the design and development of its strategic plan and the development of organizing principles for an administrative reorganization. In this role, they had access to, and became familiar with, key institutional documents including mission and vision statements, core values, research and planning reports, profile information, and accreditation reports.

5. Ibid.

6. Ibid.

7. The information presented for Albion College, Michigan, was obtained through Web site exploration, www.albion.edu, and project work as part of a graduate seminar on organizational strategy, planning, and budgeting in the Center for the Study of Higher and Postsecondary Education at the University of Michigan.

8. "Scenarios: Liberal Arts at Work in the Lives of Albion Students," www.albion.edu/vision/scenarios.asp, accessed August 3, 2005.

9. Ibid.

10. James B. Quinn, *Strategies for Change: Logical Incrementalism* (Homewood, IL: Richard D. Irwin, 1980).

11. Bryson, *Strategic Planning*, 147.

12. John B. Bryson and B. C. Crosby, *Leadership for the Common Good: Tackling Public Problems in a Shared Power World* (San Francisco: Jossey-Bass, 1992), 235.

13. Bryson's approach to process guidelines for strategy development in *Strategic Planning*, 146–153, served as a framework for developing guidelines that can be followed in the framing and articulation of strategy. Of the eighteen guidelines proposed by Bryson for strategy development, four were adapted and used in the section on "Practical Advice" in this chapter.

14. Ibid., 150.

15. Ibid., 153.

16. Ibid., 152.

17. Ibid.

CHAPTER

Building a Plan of Implementation

Strategy is a commodity. Implementation is an art.

Peter Drucker

When strategy is articulated, it feels as though the major work should be complete. Vast amounts of time, energy, and intellectual resources have been invested. Stakeholders have been identified and their needs studied. Internal and external environments have been scanned, competitors have been scrutinized, and an assessment has been made of value delivered by the institution. A team has worked with this portfolio of information and identified sources of advantage that can be pursued, and strategy options have been framed and considered. As taxing and difficult as it can be, the team has come to consensus and articulated a strategy. The reality, however, is that while a lot of the hard work has been accomplished, it is not over yet. The time has come to *implement* the strategy—to take the words recorded on paper and translate them into action.

Implementation is not a popular topic with administrators. Many, if not most, fumble in their efforts to carry it out, yet it is the glove that fits the hand of strategy. For this reason, senior administrators invest in retreats, peer consultation, and outside consulting services to learn how to develop and execute strategies that will lead their organizations to a prosperous future. More often than not, however, these strategies never come to fruition. At times failure is outside of the organization's control, such as when rapidly declining resources shift attention to the budget. Frequently, however, the cause is a breakdown in implementation. Implementation is an enigma and a source of frustration in many organizations.

When it comes to strategy, implementation cannot be left to chance. Strategy is an episodic event, while execution is constant. If a college wants to realize its vision of the future and strategy is the path to this vision, leaders are going to need to actively direct, coordinate, and manage implementation. There is no alternative. This chapter is about implementation: the steps involved in executing strategy, do's and don'ts, and recommended actions when implementation breaks down.

ESSENTIALS FOR SUCCESSFUL STRATEGY

As colleges and universities become more market-driven, pressure on staff to broaden their view of postsecondary education has become a recurring theme on many campuses. Managers, support staff, and instructors are exhorted to pay more attention to student needs, to learn more about the external environment and competitors, and to put the institution ahead of personal needs. Yet, even the best-intentioned senior administrators find it difficult to translate these aspirations into action. Failed or flawed strategies have many symptoms, most of which are traceable to a lack of commitment to the changes needed to formulate strategy and convert it into action.

If the foundation of successful strategy is, as Porter maintains, the "selection and execution of hundreds of activities," then what are the essentials for successful strategy?[1] First and foremost, strategy must be *championed by leaders* at the top of the organization. Leaders who push strategy, but who belie their commitment through inaction, place the effort in jeopardy. Role congruence (walking the talk) with espoused strategy is a necessity for effective implementation. Incongruence casts suspicion on the entire strategy process thereby increasing the likelihood of resistance. No less important is the need to *focus on conditions supporting the need for strategy*, instead of on the needs and motives of leaders. Leaders who personalize strategy by linking it with their own agenda undercut it by moving it outside the needs-spectrum of the institution. Strategy is not the province of executive leaders. It must be understood and owned by everyone.

Inclusivity is vital. Trust, teamwork, and an open participatory process complicate strategy but increase the likelihood that it will be successful. The entire organization from top to bottom should be involved, but particularly important is the structured involvement of key internal stakeholders including administrators, staff, faculty, and students. Encouraging broad participation has two primary benefits. First, sharing and communication across boundaries permit the meaningful exchange of ideas, thereby enriching strategy. Second, inclusivity promotes commitment and allows for the vocalization of dissent, thereby ameliorating resistance and increasing readiness. There is, however, a downside to inclusivity. Much of the work of colleges and universities is carried out by highly trained professionals whose expertise puts them beyond formal regulatory controls. By necessity, the road to successful strategy will move through the complex structure of academe, but this is a road of twists and turns and passage is often slow. Thus, there is a need to balance inclusiveness with a *sense of urgency* to bring energy to the process and ensure the ability to work efficiently in a rapidly changing environment.

Putting strategy in the hands of everyone implies that strategy can be described in the *language of stakeholders* so that it can be understood and acted upon. A strategy of convenience, for example, requires a specific value-proposition from the stakeholder perspective that describes how an institution will deliver programs and services more conveniently than competitors. Not only must strategy be described clearly, it must also be *reinforced through continuous communication* with stakeholders. Because attention within any organization is a scarce resource, communication about strategy must be precise and repeated relentlessly. A clearly and continuously articulated strategy should serve to motivate and inspire individual commitment and action.

Finally, for strategy to permeate the walls and chimneys of the institution, *cultural change should follow from behavioral change*. Although culture is always a major impediment to execution, there is no evidence to suggest that efforts to change it first will succeed.[2] The pathway to successful execution is through the adjustment of behavioral patterns to fit new performance requirements. *Diagnostics* that measure constancy and change in individual behavior can be helpful in monitoring the extent of strategy execution.

MODELING IMPLEMENTATION

Essentially, strategy execution and implementation has all of the attributes and dynamics of a process of organizational change. It is a continuing process that impacts a lot of people, it has a compelling rationale and an associated degree of urgency, and it gathers enough support to be taken seriously. Borrowing extensively from the work of Noble (1999) and the literature on complex organizations, it is possible to design a model (see Figure 9.1) for strategy implementation consisting of four stages: (1) preimplementation, (2) organizing the process, (3) managing

Figure 9.1
Stepwise Model for Strategy Implementation

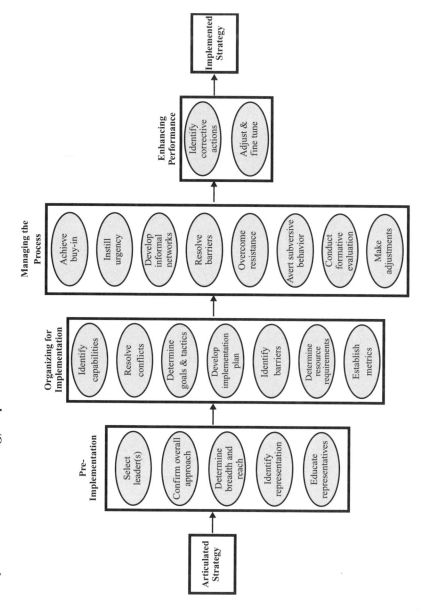

the process, and (4) enhancing performance.[3] By understanding the challenges and actions that are part of each stage, leaders and staff can do much to enhance the prospect of successful strategy implementation.

Preimplementation

The first step in implementing strategy is to select an individual or group within the institution to provide *leadership* for the process. This could be a member of the executive team that developed the strategy, the executive team itself, or a newly created team comprised of members from different parts of the institution. The advantage of a team lies in its reach to different levels and functional areas and, by extension, to staff throughout the institution. Leadership provided through a team can instill a deeper understanding of strategy across the institution and begin to establish cross-functional relationships that will be necessary during implementation.[4] Members can provide mid- to lower-level input into the earliest phases of implementing strategy. They also can bring different perspectives to the myriad of decisions that will be made during implementation.

Another important activity during the preimplementation phase is *determining the overall approach* to the task: will it be centralized, decentralized, or a hybrid? A centralized approach has the advantage of locating control in the hands of a few people thereby enabling the process to move faster because fewer check-offs are needed. The advantage of a decentralized approach is its capacity to engage more people and encourage ownership of the strategy. Careful consideration is advised because the approach chosen has a lot to do with the *breadth and reach* of the implementation effort. It can reach deep into the institution and involve a number of people or it can be restricted to a few. An inclusive process can raise the profile of the strategy and project a high priority for it. Divergent perspectives among staff, however, can sidetrack the strategy and even cause it to fail if interactions become too complex. Inclusiveness is desirable, but so is the need to involve the right people.[5] It is important, therefore, to balance breadth and capability in *identifying representatives* who will work with leaders in the implementation effort.

The areas of responsibility from which representatives are selected is an important consideration. Representatives who are part of a primary function, an area that will be significantly impacted by the strategy, or an area in transition are logical choices for the implementation team. Individuals selected should have the respect of peers and staff and have a capacity to wield influence with operating units. Other important attributes are a flexible communication style, the ability to field criticism, openness, and integrity.

Finally, an important step in preimplementation is *educating internal stakeholders* about the origin, rationale, and desired outcomes of the strategy. The more advance knowledge that is passed on to faculty and staff, the more receptive they will be once the implementation phase begins.[6] Education can be accomplished through formal channels such as memos, video, voice mail, and e-mail messages from senior executives, and regular staff meetings. Less formal channels can also be used such as coffee and lunch breaks, informal office visits, or spontaneous interactions.

Illustrations specific to institutions with different contextual conditions can be used to describe varying approaches to preimplementation. Westhampton College, a fictitious liberal arts college in a mid-Atlantic state, has elected to employ a centralized approach to strategy implementation. Westhampton has an elite reputation built around a core curriculum and a distinguished faculty. Turnover is low because the college's academic reputation is sufficient to attract and hold talented faculty, and its reputation as a stable employer attracts a quality workforce. Personnel who affiliate with Westhampton do not leave; the average tenure for faculty is twenty-two years and for support staff it is twenty-five years. The executive team is no exception; the president has been in office for fifteen years and the team has been intact for twelve years. The management style of the president is top-down. Faculty leaders are consulted on specific issues as appropriate, but strategic decisions are clearly the province of the executive team. Everyone knows where power and authority reside and plays within the limits of prescribed roles.

In a top-down institution such as Westhampton, in which roles and responsibilities are defined by long-standing relationships, the only feasible approach to strategy implementation would be a centralized approach. Overall leadership would likely be provided by the president and the executive team in concert with hand-picked members of the faculty and staff with specialized expertise. The educational function would consist of activities necessary for bringing implementation team members up to speed with important elements of the strategy—most particularly, the role they will play in working with individuals and groups to execute the strategy.

A very different approach to implementation would be used at Northwest Pacific University, a fictitious regional public university in Oregon. Northwest is a dynamically changing institution with a recent history of rapid growth. Over the past three years it has added programs, services, and personnel to meet the educational needs of an influx of new learners. However, like many institutions dependent on the state for operating support, resources cannot keep pace with growth. Northwest has had little choice but to turn to technology to expand its delivery system. It has converted many of its course offerings and a number of degree programs into an online format and made services available to students through the Internet. The upside of growth is enhanced visibility for the university. The downside is growing fragmentation as newcomers and veteran personnel try to find common ground with one another. This condition is exacerbated by a new president and executive team who are seeking ways to energize the institution by aligning people and ideas as part of a strategy for the future.

A decentralized approach to strategy implementation would be necessary and appropriate at Northwest, in contrast to the centralized approach at Westhampton, because of the need to bring fragmented units and staff onto common ground under the umbrella of strategy. Overall leadership would be provided by a team comprised of representatives drawn from different functional areas and work groups within the institution. The educational function would consist of (1) informal activities designed to introduce the implementation team to the concept of strategy, its meaning and importance for Northwest, and the specific roles and responsibilities team members will be expected to carry out, and (2) formal activities to introduce the team and its charge to the college community.

Organizing for Implementation

Activities in the organizing stage center on establishing resources, determining individual and team responsibilities, and identifying barriers to implementation. An early step is *identifying capabilities*—skills and expertise—needed for successful implementation. Depending on the culture of the institution and relationships among faculty and staff, it is possible that communication and interpretive capabilities will be required. Personnel with these skills would logically become part of the implementation team. Expertise in project management and assessment might also be needed, so personnel with skills in these areas would be added to the team. Gauging and acting on the human resource capabilities needed for successful execution is one of the most important decisions an institution will make in the implementation process.

Inevitably, conflicts arise as part of any process involving organizational change. This is particularly true in working with strategy because of the abstract nature of the concept and the effort required to understand, support, and carry it out. Success in implementation depends, therefore, on the capacity of leaders to *anticipate and resolve conflicts* among personnel—particularly among those leading the process. Neutralizing conflict involves identifying the value-perspectives of important players and finding common ground among them.[7] Helpful in this regard is a capacity of team members to view conflict as a natural part of organizational life—a confluence of values, beliefs, and perceptions that, if viewed positively, can serve to guide the implementation effort.

An essential aspect of any successful implementation process is *developing goals and tactics* to guide the process. The same is true of strategy. Higher-order goals are generally established by senior administrators in concert with the implementation team and constituent groups that will be responsible for executing strategy. For example, a goal to increase enrollment as part of a strategy of growth would initially take shape within the executive team through a discussion of assumptions underlying growth. Important questions that would be addressed include: What volume and pace of growth are we talking about? Do we have the resources to accommodate enrollment growth? and What actions do we need to take to generate growth? Once these questions have been answered to the satisfaction of senior administrators, dialogue will begin with personnel in admissions and marketing, financial aid, residence life, academic affairs, and other areas to determine a reasonable enrollment target.

A target is meaningless in and of itself unless it is accompanied by concrete actions to achieve it. If a goal has been set to increase enrollment by 20 percent over five years, an appropriate sequence of actions would involve breaking the goal down by year and determining steps necessary to achieve each year's portion of the larger goal. In this example, the 20 percent enrollment increase could be distributed evenly at 4 percent increments for each of the next five years or split differentially from year-to-year based on varying assumptions. Important steps would include actions designed to increase enrollment by expanding the area from which the institution draws students, enhancing institutional visibility through marketing, augmenting financial aid, streamlining the application process, and a host of other actions depending on the specifics of a given institution. Specificity and clarity of action are very important. For example, a general statement such as "increase financial aid available to students" does not say much to staff in terms of what is expected of them. It should be discarded in favor of a statement that more clearly communicates intent and action such as "increase financial aid dollars available to students by 25 percent over five years." The more specific the stated action, the easier the task of measuring performance toward the goal of successful strategy implementation.

Developing a plan of implementation involves working out the specifics of contributions expected from different individuals and work groups in relationship to each goal and associated action steps. Important elements of this plan are the location of responsibility for specific actions and a time line for execution. Actions and performance targets for each goal should be placed on a time line along with information related to the assignment of responsibility; that is, which individual, group, or unit will initiate and carry out the action. As goals, actions, and performance targets are fleshed out to include accountability for different facets of implementation, involvement will cascade to individuals and units throughout the institution. For example, a goal to make all services available on the Internet 24/7/365 will not be successfully achieved without involvement of faculty and staff from multiple units. Coordination and tracking will be necessary to ensure consistency of effort and a common understanding among personnel of the total implementation effort, not simply their own part.

Implementation plans will have a much greater chance for success if *barriers to implementation* are identified in advance. Identifying barriers involves an interest in, and a capacity for, candid discussion of problems and actions that can be taken to surmount them. A roundtable discussion, in which representatives from different areas identify forms and sources of resistance and craft techniques that can be used to alleviate or remove barriers, is one way to proceed. Another is to create partnerships among internal units as a means for channeling and conflict. Partnerships are only effective if they involve participants as equals and not subordinates; for example, faculty and student services staff on equal footing, senior and midlevel managers having an equivalent voice, and support staff engaged as full participants. This can be accomplished by introducing all partners to the strategy simultaneously rather than using a sequential approach.

Vitally important to the success of the implementation plan is an approximation of the *resources required*—people, money, and technology—to implement the plan. Directives handed down from senior administrators often fail in this regard because they tend to focus on end-goals, such as achieving specific outcomes through strategy, and lack details concerning actions and resources required for successful implementation.[8] Therefore, collaboration involving representatives from different units is generally required to develop a viable estimate of resources. The amount and type of resources available to implement strategy are important to those who will be responsible for implementation. Buy-in and commitment cannot realistically be expected from individuals and groups working with less than adequate resources. Nor can personnel be expected to devote time and energy to a strategy that is handed down to them and resourced by senior administrators. Implementation works best when personnel have the ability to define resource needs at an early stage in the process.

Finally, *metrics* for determining the impact of strategy should be identified in the organizing stage. Did the strategy produce or fall short of its intended effect? What factors need to be examined to determine the impact of strategy? The tendency is to want to measure everything, but simplicity is the key to success in assessment. The smaller the number of indicators and the greater their breadth, the better. For example, if the strategy frame is convenience, an appropriate metric would be constancy or change in the percentage of incoming students who report choosing an institution because of easy access to courses and services. This indicator is easy to measure, it can be generalized to the entire institution, and it has important consequences for institutional performance.

We return to the institutional examples provided earlier—Westhampton College and Northwest Pacific University—to illustrate different approaches to planning and organizing implementation based on context. The small size, liberal arts mission, and centralized administrative structure of Westhampton would impel senior administrators to recruit personnel with particular skills to the implementation team. Recall that long-serving senior administrators comprised the nucleus of the implementation team. Capabilities that would be needed beyond this group are likely to be positional and political in nature; that is, they will reside in the unique configuration of positions in the institution and the distribution of power and influence among staff. Skilled incumbents in key positions would likely be added to the implementation team at Westhampton to broaden administration's reach into the institution. These new players would be expected to push the strategy deep into academic departments and operating units, to assist in identifying barriers and resolving conflicts, and to shape decisions about implementation and resource requirements within the operating realities of departments and units.

By way of contrast, conditions at Northwest Pacific University would encourage a different approach to planning and organizing. The combination of increasing size and complexity, organizational fragmentation, and a new administrative team would impel leaders to seek a broad range of capabilities on the implementation team. Like Westhampton, individuals in key positions would be selected based on the status assigned to them by peers. Unlike Westhampton, however, capabilities outside of position and influence would be viewed as essential for successful implementation. Particularly important would be expertise in marketing and communication, systems and process design, and project management to ensure involvement of staff throughout the institution in strategy. Team members would be responsible for outreach to faculty and staff in academic and administrative units to build understanding of strategy, to minimize resistance, and to develop an implementation plan capable of drawing support from broad segments of the university community.

Managing the Implementation Process

The ongoing management of an implementation process is a significant challenge for several reasons. In addition to obstacles faced in the initial organization phase, new obstacles may surface that hamper the ability of staff to support the strategy. Up to this point, strategy has taken the form of words in print, but these words are not enough to invoke people to action. The team that developed the implementation plan will certainly understand what the words mean, but the same level of understanding will not extend to players throughout the institution. For this reason, *achieving commitment* through communication is the initial and most important step in managing implementation. Without appropriate, adequate, and timely communication, the entire strategy is at risk. An effective communication plan identifies audiences, message, modes, and frequency. The critical audiences include faculty, staff, alumni, donors, the governing board, and other stakeholders. To communicate most effectively with each audience, it might be appropriate to divide them into subgroups based on the types of communication they need to receive. For example, deans and directors may need biweekly status reports on their functional areas while faculty and staff members might need only a monthly update.

Different modes of communication are effective, including e-mail, voice mail, town meetings, top-down dissemination, signage, launch events, and modes uniquely suited to the work groups in the institution. For example, if key personnel in the institution prefer not to use e-mail as a basic communication tool, voice mail or a face-to-face meeting might be a suitable substitute. If the institution tends to have an active and strong rumor mill, town meetings might be the best way to ensure that personnel hear the same message and receive timely answers to their questions. Making use of a variety of modes of communication will help to ensure that the majority of staff is reached.

Although senior administrators would like to think that most, if not all, personnel are committed to maximizing performance in the execution of strategy, the reality is that other goals may come into play. One of these has to do with unit and department activities that are viewed by faculty and staff as more important than institutional strategy. In the absence of a shared sense of urgency about the future, there is no reason to believe that personnel will accord a high level of importance to strategy. A primary task of senior administrators, therefore, is to *instill a sense of urgency* in faculty and staff about the need for strategy and its value to the institution. This task will not be easy. Research has revealed systematic differences between personnel in thought and action. Studies using the Myers-Briggs typology have found that intuitive thinking is pervasive in the executive group, whereas middle managers display more "sensing characteristics."[9] Intuitive thinkers focus on underlying meanings, tend to speculate, and are usually future-oriented. Sensing individuals focus on concrete facts and are pragmatic, present-oriented, and driven by the quest for results. Personality differences such as these can result in inconsistencies in how strategies are understood and acted upon.

Building institution-wide understanding of strategy is a challenge in the fast-changing environment in which colleges and universities operate. A technique that can be used to expedite understanding and facilitate implementation is to encourage the *development of informal networks*. These are personal connections that leaders and staff maintain with functions and work groups throughout the institution. Through such channels, dialogue can occur more easily, decisions made and communicated more rapidly, and barriers addressed and resolved. The *removal of barriers* that stand in the way of implementation is the primary value of informal networks. These barriers exist for many reasons—protection of turf, differences in interpretation, and problems in communication, to name a few. A threat to turf may work against strategy by strengthening the identification of members with a group and reinforcing their resolve to protect their domain.

As described by Noble (1999), interpretive barriers are the differences that arise among functional and work group lines in understanding strategy.[10] Consider the strategy of speed—accelerating the pace at which new programs and services are brought online and made available to students and stakeholders. Senior administrators may interpret this strategy as building a niche in a highly competitive market. Mid-level managers may interpret it as signaling a change in the nature and pace of their work as a premium is placed on timely conversion of information into action. Faculty may view it as an incursion into their role as stewards of the curriculum. Such differences in belief and perception can cause an institution to expend efforts in multiple directions based purely on disparate interpretations of the same information.

Timing and speed are important in strategy implementation. Many strategies are developed in response to an emerging opportunity or competitor action. *Internal resistance* to a newly developed strategy can cause costly delays resulting in lost opportunities. Human nature is at work. Even when personnel do not perceive strategy as a threat to power or position, there is a general tendency to resist change and maintain the status quo.[11] Beyond passive resistance, leaders may at times face *subversive behavior* as individuals or groups try to undermine strategy. An example from personal experience includes "checking and balancing" behavior of opinion leaders as part of a strategic planning initiative at a multicampus community college in the Southeast. Different scenarios for institutional development framed by external consultants involving minimal, moderate, and substantial change were manipulated by opinion leaders to distort the full picture. The "minimal" and "moderate" alternatives were deliberately ignored, leaving the "substantial" alternative as the sole depiction of the institution's future in key areas of development. Needless to say, a view of the future focused exclusively on large-scale change will be perceived as a threat by many and become a basis for resistance to planning.

Identifying the personnel who may harbor subversive feelings toward a given strategy early in implementation is important. To avert such problems, leaders can either create extra incentives to encourage cooperation or minimize the involvement by such personnel in the effort. Leaders can also move to identify and head off problems by undertaking *formative evaluation* to determine how well the implementation process is working. Assessment is useful when it identifies areas that are slowing or impeding implementation and in need of *adjustment* to fully execute the strategy. As a regional university administrator noted:

> In a recent meeting of top personnel in different functional areas, people in finance and academic affairs were sharply divided on a new strategy for growth because they saw it in different ways. The finance people could not understand the importance of an investment of $4 million to update academic programs. They were acting like it was their money and were too focused on their own control issues to support the expenditure of funds for program development. The academic folks had difficulty understanding how finance could think that way—after all, teaching and learning is what the institution is all about and healthy programs are a high priority. That really bothered them. They thought that finance wanted to torpedo the strategy because it involved taking up-front money from "their" budget and allocating it to something that may not yield a dollar-for-dollar return.

This comment touches on the importance of continuous oversight and evaluation of the implementation process to head off misunderstandings and potentially harmful interactions. It also speaks to the need to make mid-course adjustments in the process to accommodate important aspects of institutional culture and climate.

Enhancing Performance

As noted in Drucker's sage words at the beginning of the chapter, implementation is an art. Managing it effectively involves all of the talent and resources that senior administrators and staff can muster, particularly in institutions stretched to the limit of their resources. There are, however, some tactics leaders can use in managing performance that will enhance the likelihood of successful implementation.

First, to avoid inertia, leaders should be encouraged to identify activities that have not worked as planned and to *take corrective action*. Determining adjustments that need to be made in the implementation process through performance assessment is an important but often overlooked step. Too often, leaders lack a sense of perspective in their implementation activities. They stick to a stated course of action based on a belief that it will yield favorable results if carefully followed. Instead of scrutinizing the results of implementation to determine what is and is not working, they ignore early signs of trouble and stay on a chosen path. An essential aspect of implementation is *fine-tuning* of the process based on assessment results. Assessment can be useful in identifying gaps between anticipated and actual results, although leaders may be put on the spot by results that depart from expectations.

Fine-tuning should improve the credibility of the implementation process. The effort made to assess performance, the tone of communication regarding needed changes, and the specific changes made are all influential in this regard. An administrator at a Midwestern liberal arts college described the importance of assessment at his institution in the following way:

> You will not get a successful outcome from a process that works outside of the contextual realities of your college. To the extent that you monitor the performance of key implementation activities and make timely changes, you will be successful. We discovered that staff views of the credibility of our process were determined, in part, by the effort we put into assessment and what we did with the results. When important changes were identified and we moved forthrightly to implement them, the importance of strategy was driven home to a lot of people.

Let's return to Westhampton College and Northwest Pacific University one last time to see how each institution managed the process, progress, and results of implementation. Urgency and buy-in at West-hampton were reinforced by a message from the president, which basi-cally said, "We all need to work together to make this happen." Directives from the top in a small institution get a lot of attention and make things move faster if they are not an everyday occurrence. Through the efforts of the president and the executive team, cooperation was practically mandated at Westhampton and obstacles were removed before they could form. Resistance was limited to sporadic attempts to clarify the purpose and intended outcomes of specific implementation activities. Formative evaluation consisted of steps taken by representatives of functional areas to determine the status of different activities and the extent to which performance met a predetermined standard. Corrective actions were few in number and amounted to obvious changes in resources and account-ability to get things done.

The implementation process at Northwest Pacific University was very different in design and outcome. To encourage buy-in, the implementa-tion team drew on relationships with opinion leaders in informal net-works. These personal connections enabled them to cut through bureaucracy and defuse resistance at the point of origin among faculty and staff in academic and administrative units. Potential obstacles were navigated in the early stages of implementation, and subversive behav-ior was neutralized through grassroots support deep within the institu-tion. Formative evaluation consisted of oversight activities conducted by implementation team members and opinion leaders in work groups and informal networks throughout the university. Information was gathered through informal conversation to determine the status of implementa-tion activities, problems and resource needs, and progress toward com-pletion. Adjustments needed to keep the strategy on track were passed on to the implementation team and acted upon without delay. Changes in the implementation process were made in ways that were visible to personnel throughout the institution to reaffirm their connection with strategy and their role in execution.

SILENT KILLERS OF IMPLEMENTATION

Strategy is of limited value unless it is acted upon. Yet, as important as it is to the development of organizations, strategy has a poor track record when it comes to implementation. Why is this so? What can be done to more effectively turn strategy into action? As often as not, it is the result of an institution being unaware of, or failing to address, "silent killers" of implementation. These can be grouped into three categories corresponding to the chronology of implementation activities: challenges of initiating implementation, challenges of building and sustaining momentum, and challenges of determining success.

Challenges of Initiating Implementation

The institution has a history of failed strategy or strategic planning efforts that constrain interest and discourage involvement. Staff beyond the executive team have difficulty making a commitment to an initiative that resembles, or is perceived as resembling, an initiative that failed in the past. Even if acknowledged by the executive team, feelings of doubt or insecurity associated with previous failures are difficult to ameliorate. To get strategy up and running in an institution with a poor track record, college leaders need to acknowledge and address previous problems and demonstrate through word and deed how the current effort is different and how it will avoid pitfalls of the past.

The strategy is not worth implementing. In many cases, what is referred to as strategy is (1) nothing more than a series of vague statements or a collection of priorities and action plans and/or (2) deficient in analytical vigor, creative insight, ambition, or practicality. The strategy represents simply more of what has happened previously, with no sense of vision or challenge for the institution. A strategy worth implementing should give the institution something to strive for and become a source of inspiration for staff.[12]

The strategy does not correspond to the realities of organizational context, either because it has been developed in isolation from information about the external environment or because it fails to address important attributes of the institution's culture and climate. If the strategy is going to command attention and get the active support of staff, it needs to address important features of the organization's context. Failure to do so will limit its potential in the eyes of staff and seriously impair prospects for successful initiation.

The leadership style of senior administrators is top-down or laissez-faire, thereby limiting involvement in strategy or undercutting the attention that should be directed to it. Successful initiation requires more than the presence of a leader; it requires teamwork from a leadership group that through dialogue and collaboration stays connected to the staff in units and departments throughout the institution.[13]

The strategy does not enjoy support and commitment because personnel do not feel that they were involved in its development. There is always a strong desire to get started with strategy and make it happen. This is most readily accomplished by a small group working independently that is not at the beck and call of institutional operations. While there is an inherent efficiency in the small-group approach, there is also a cost. Failure to systematically engage staff from different parts of the institution in strategy creation will almost inevitably lead to resistance. Questions about the origin of strategy and its relevance to different functional areas are not easily answered in the absence of staff involvement.

Faculty and staff do not think that the strategy is the right one or do not feel that they have the requisite skills to implement it, so they resist its initiation. A feeling of connectedness among staff to a strategy that reflects their perceptions of institutional context and circumstances puts the institution on a sound footing with strategy initiation. This footing is further improved by a strategy that is crafted within the limits of staff capabilities and capable of being implemented with current resources.[14]

Challenges of Building and Sustaining Momentum

Top management spends insufficient time communicating about the strategy and managing the organizational changes involved in implementation. Too often, communication is seen as a one-time activity to announce and describe a strategy to staff and stakeholders. Effective communication, on the contrary, is an ongoing activity throughout the implementation process. The implementation plan should include a communication plan identifying who needs to be told what about the strategy. The communication plan should include a provision for continuing restatement of the expectations and objectives of strategy to ensure that all personnel understand its importance and that it will not go away.

Staff do not fully understand how the strategy will be implemented. As strategy moves through the early stages of implementation, there is often impatience to make it move further and faster. The time and energy spent on planning and organizing for implementation are seen as wasteful, as delaying tactics, or as indecisiveness. Corboy and O'Corbui (1999) have identified a number of implementation issues that need to be addressed to help staff achieve a better understanding of the implementation process. These issues include determining and reaching consensus on the following:[15]

- *Priorities*: What are your priorities? Which parts of the strategy do you want to implement first? Have these priorities been made clear?
- *Timescale*: How quickly do you want to implement the strategy? Is it feasible to do it in that timeframe?
- *Lessons Learned*: What have you learned from your previous experiences with organizational change?

- *Impact*: What impact or implications will the strategy have on your staff and stakeholders and how you do things now?
- *Participation*: Who needs to be involved and when? Have they got what it takes to make it work?
- *Risks*: What are the risks that might prevent you from implementing the strategy? Can you manage or reduce those risks?

Individual and unit responsibilities for implementing the strategy are unclear. Senior administrators often have a tendency to communicate about strategy on a need to know basis. If those responsible for implementing the strategy feel that they do not understand it and cannot tell senior administrators about problems they are having with it, an institution has no early warning system. It is not sufficient to develop a relevant and insightful strategy and hope that the logic behind it will be enough to inform personnel of what to do. Communication regarding actions needed to execute the strategy must be continuous and clear; responsibilities need to be explicit and reinforced through word and deed; and performance targets need to be incorporated to serve as a helpful guide for action.

Senior administrators step out of the picture once implementation begins. Frequently the interest and involvement of the chief executive or senior administrators will diminish once strategy implementation begins.[16] However, it is very important to provide strong leadership during implementation. Faculty and staff must believe that implementing strategy is one of the institution's highest priorities. They will be looking for clues to confirm their judgment. If they feel that senior administrators are not fully committed to the strategy, their commitment and enthusiasm for it will wane.

No provision is made for (1) developing new skills and competencies required by staff to successfully carry out their responsibilities in implementation; (2) instituting appropriate institutional systems for selecting, motivating, and rewarding staff in accord with the new strategy; and (3) creating a fit between the overall strategy and the operations of academic departments and administrative units. There is always a risk that developing strategy will become the all-consuming concern of the CEO or senior administrative team and that they will minimize the task of connecting the strategy to operations. It is important to remember that strategy is directly linked with, and cannot function independently of, people and operations. Academic and administrative units do not stand still while strategy is being implemented, and strategy will need to be adapted to internal operating realities even as it is being rolled out. Check to ensure that the strategy parallels, or at least approximates, the objectives and activities of operating units. Make sure that operating units have the resources and training mechanisms needed to implement the strategy. Identify incentives and rewards that will keep staff on task.

No attempt is made to analyze the culture of the institution and identify attributes that could become barriers to and facilitators of implementation. Colleges and universities operate in an ever-changing and dynamic environment. Obstacles and unforeseen difficulties can arise quickly during implementation. It is important that these and other barriers that inevitably will be encountered along the way are acknowledged and addressed early in the implementation process.

Challenges of Determining Success

The commitment of leaders to success of the strategy is unclear, or too much time passes between implementation and evaluation to determine the success of the strategy. Without a doubt, implementation is a continuing process that requires a commitment to evaluation to determine modifications needed for improvement and enhancement. If leaders appear hesitant about or disinterested in evaluation, the commitment of faculty and staff will erode in a conclave of doubt about how important the strategy really is to leaders.

Criteria used to evaluate the success of implementation are undeveloped, unclear, or imprecise. The lack of clear and precise indicators to determine the success, or lack thereof, of implementation deprives the institution of a rallying cry for continuing effort. Effective implementation is about making choices and determining the effect of those choices. Information about performance guides and improves choice and serves as an inducement for staff to further their efforts in implementation.

CONCLUSION

Implementation is perhaps the most difficult part of strategy. It is challenging for organizations in general, but perhaps even more for colleges and universities where leaders have not had to manage change at the higher frequency and pace familiar to executives in for-profit organizations. Insight and values must coalesce for leaders to organize successfully for implementation. The president and the executive team must believe that implementation is as important, if not more important, than strategy formulation. They must maintain a high level of interest and engagement in the strategy from beginning to end. They must be willing to learn and do so in partnership with faculty and staff. And they must be able to recognize and confront the silent killers of implementation.

Strategy execution is fraught with the danger of being abandoned through inertia or resistance at multiple points in the implementation process. Change is never easy, but the task of putting strategy to work will be made much easier and have a much greater chance of success by recognizing and avoiding the silent killers of implementation. Particularly important in this regard are efforts to assess the progress and outcomes of strategy in different stages of implementation—our topic in the next and final chapter.

NOTES

1. Michael E. Porter, "What Is Strategy?" *Harvard Business Review* (November/December 1996): 61–78.

2. George S. Day, "Creating a Market-Driven Organization," *Sloan Management Review* (Fall 1999): 11–22.

3. Charles H. Noble's "Building the Strategy Implementation Network," *Business Horizons* (November/December 1999): 19–28, contributed significantly to the development of the implementation model presented in Table 8.1. The stages in this model—preimplementation, organizing for implementation, managing the process, and enhancing performance—are adapted from Noble's work as are a number of the steps in implementation described within each stage.

4. Ibid., 20.

5. Ibid., 21.

6. Ibid.

7. Ibid.

8. Ibid., 22.

9. Ibid., 23.

10. Ibid.

11. Warren Boeker, "Strategic Change: The Effects of Founding and History," *Academy of Management Journal* (September 1989): 489–515.

12. Martin Corboy and Diarmuid O'Corrbui, "The Seven Deadly Sins of Strategy," *Management Accounting* (November 1999): 29–30.

13. Michael Beer and Russell Eisenstat, "The Silent Killers of Strategy Implementation and Learning," *Sloan Management Review* (Summer 2000): 29–40.

14. Ibid.

15. Corboy and O'Corbui, "Seven Deadly," 29–30.

16. Beer and Eisenstat, "Silent Killers," 29–40.

CHAPTER 10

Evaluating for Impact

Strategy is a vital ingredient in determining an institution's future. An effective strategy will yield growth, visibility, or whatever end-goals an institution is trying to achieve. An ineffective strategy will not only fail to yield benefits, but also will tie up resources that could be more effectively used elsewhere. A corporate executive would not deploy resources on a large scale without a clear notion of the company's strategy and its plan for measuring results. An experienced politician would not run for office without a way of measuring returns on a campaign strategy. A high-tech firm would not choose to invest millions into a new product without information about customer satisfaction. The same is true for colleges and universities: the results of strategy need to be measured.

Working with the definition provided in the first part of the book, the success of strategy would be linked to the value created by an institution for its stakeholders. In a tangible sense, this would include growth in numbers (students, programs, facilities, and resources), evidence of stakeholder satisfaction, enhancement of quality, and improvement in tangible assets of just about any kind. We live in a world, however, in which intangible assets are becoming ever more important. The writings of futurists and strategy architects point to the growing importance of intangibles as key parts of the playing field on which organizations will compete for the future. Intangibles such as ideas, competencies, quality, and image have a lot to do with success and are so closely intertwined with value that it is almost impossible to separate aspects that are tangible and intangible. Both tangible and intangible contributors to success are important and must be taken into account in efforts to evaluate strategy.

The central question and theme of this closing chapter is one of the impact and effect of strategy: Did the strategy make a difference? Did it achieve the intended impact? Or, using the definition of strategy in the first chapter: Was the institution able to differentiate itself from competitors and achieve a sustainable advantage? To answer these questions, assessment will need to be pursued that examines strategy from two perspectives: (1) its "fit" with important dimensions of institutional context, and (2) its impact on stakeholders inside and outside of the institution. Beyond this lie considerations related to indicators or "markers" that can be used to determine the impact of strategy and methods for stating the results of strategy.

IS THE STRATEGY RIGHT FOR THE INSTITUTION?

In a classic article in a 1963 issue of the *Harvard Business Review*, Tilles asks and answers fundamental questions about the fit between strategy and organizations. Six criteria were used to frame the determination of fit:[1]

- internal consistency
- consistency with context
- appropriateness with respect to available resources
- degree of risk
- time horizon
- workability

There is no such thing as a right or wrong strategy in an absolute or objective sense, but there are strategies that are better or worse. In Tilles' scheme the strategy is probably a good fit for the institution if most or all of these criteria are met.

1. *Is the strategy internally consistent?* Internal consistency refers to the cumulative impact of tactics embedded in the strategy on the goals and operations of the institution.[2] Internal consistency is especially important in evaluating strategy because it identifies the areas where choices will eventually have to be made. Effective strategy uses tactics that fit comfortably with goals and established ways of doing things. It is important to note, however, that consistency can never be taken for granted. For example,

Many fast-growing institutions pursue tactics which eventually become inconsistent with context. Consider, for example, rapid expansion and superior service. If an institution is successful in growing enrollment, the need for additional resources to provide more services for more learners will eventually create major problems concerning service availability and quality, if additional funding is not available.

The criterion of internal consistency is especially important for evaluating strategy because it identifies areas where difficult choices may need to be made. Strategy that is inconsistent with institutional goals and operations is not necessarily bad, but it will demand time and resources for successful implementation. Leaders and staff will need to pay careful attention to how it is implemented or they may find themselves forced to make choices without suitable alternatives.

2. *Is the strategy consistent with the context?* A college or university that creates a strategy around price, quality, or convenience is saying that it has chosen to relate itself to students and stakeholders in a certain way. By extension, its tactics with resource acquisition, lobbying, alumni relations, salary determination, and government contracts are expressions of its relationship with other groups and forces. Hence, an important test of strategy is whether the strategy and its associated tactics are consistent with the environment, or what is going on inside and outside of the institution.[3]

Consistency with context has both static and dynamic dimensions. In a static sense, it implies examining the efficacy of strategy with respect to the context as it exists today. In a dynamic sense, it means examining the efficacy of strategy with respect to the context as it appears to be changing. Since the context of any college or university is constantly changing, ensuring success of the strategy over the long term means that leaders must assess the degree to which strategy is consistent with the institution's present position, the speed and direction of change, and the institution's desired position. Failure to do so can be costly, as would happen in a situation where an institution aggressively pursues enrollment growth or uses restricted resources to pursue a strategy of growth in a period of resource decline. Strategies that are inconsistent with context are increasingly common in higher education because of the velocity of change and the fact that, even today, few institutions intensively engage in analyzing environmental trends and assess their internal culture and climate.

3. *Is the strategy appropriate in view of available resources?* Resources include tangible and intangible assets that an institution uses to

achieve its objectives and respond to an opportunity or threat. One of the most difficult issues in strategy is achieving a balance between goals of the strategy and available resources—money, personnel, competencies, facilities, technology, and more. This requires a set of practical estimates of the total resources required to achieve particular objectives, the rate at which they will need to be committed, and the likelihood that they will be available.[4] The most common errors are a failure to employ a full bank of information that results in incorrect estimates, and excessive optimism.

An urban community college in a declining economy provides a good example of the outcome of erroneous forecasting of resource requirements and excessive optimism.

> In 1995, a multicampus community college in the Southeast passed a successful bond issue to support construction of three new campuses. The sale of bonds for new campus construction was a logical move in a metropolitan region experiencing dynamic growth. Everything was "up" as evidenced in the optimism of public officials who envisioned a boom of historic proportion. Workers and families were flocking to the region to find work in a bustling economy, the construction industry was running full bore, schools were bursting at the seams with enrollment, and demand for postsecondary education was high. The overarching strategy of the college was growth and the frame through which it would be accomplished was convenient access through new facilities.
>
> Construction was soon under way and, as facilities were completed, students enrolled in numbers that quickly grew to capacity. However, the very success of the new campuses in enrolling students caused the institution some serious problems. The crush of incoming students required the institution to put money and people into operations that it did not have. This would not have been a problem in a healthy state economy where operating resources for new facilities would have routinely been allocated in the state budget. However, the state was experiencing a rapid economic downturn— a downturn the institution had not anticipated or factored into its resource projections. Furthermore, state policy makers viewed the growth of the region as an "aberration" that was out of kilter with the rest of the state, a dilemma that the local legislative delegation could not resolve. This left the institution with a severe shortfall in operating resources for the new campuses. In order to staff the new facilities, personnel had to be reassigned from other campuses, resulting in staff shortages throughout the entire institution. Similarly, operating dollars had to be drawn from existing budgets resulting in

budget cuts for all departments and services. As a result, while the strategy was initially successful—growth through convenient access was realized—quality of service declined and internal tensions emerged that threatened the long-term success of the strategy.

Apparent from this example are two questions that must be considered in strategy deliberations: (1) How much of its resources can and should an institution commit to current opportunities? and (2) How much should it keep uncommitted as a reserve against unanticipated demands?

4. *Does the strategy involve an acceptable degree of risk?* Strategy and resources, taken together, determine the degree of risk which the institution is undertaking.[5] This is a critical managerial decision. For example, when a regional teaching university in the Southwest hired a score of new faculty on the basis of enrollment and revenue projections developed during a period of economic growth, it was making the right decision. However, the fact that its budget was unexpectedly cut when the state economy went into a sharp decline after 9/11 and the faculty were already on board, turned its anticipation of growth into an exercise in reduction. Each institution must decide how much risk it can tolerate. Of particular concern are a series of qualitative factors that warrant consideration when evaluating the degree of risk inherent in a strategy. To what extent can the institution be assured that the amount and type of resources required will be continuously available? What is the time frame over which resources will need to be committed? What proportion of its resources is the institution able to commit to a specific strategy?

Tilles cautions that the best strategy may not be the one with the least risk; in fact, advantage is frequently associated with high-risk strategies.[6] Failure to exploit resources may well be the riskiest position of all, as demonstrated by institutions that have fallen on hard times. Making an intentional and careful assessment of the risks involved in any strategy does, however, provide the institution with the opportunity to determine its readiness for the strategy and to establish back up plans should it encounter unforeseen circumstances.

5. *Does the strategy have an appropriate time horizon?* Viable strategy reveals not only what goals will be achieved, but establishes the expected completion time frame as well. Strategy, like resources, has a time-based utility. A new program, a new delivery system, or a new marketing plan, often yield advantage only if accomplished within a certain time frame as delays may neutralize their strategic significance.[7] A good example of this in colleges and universities is the amount of time required to obtain approval for a new course or curriculum. If a strategic objective is to provide course offerings that create opportunities in the market and, in so doing, attract new students, fast-moving for-profit institutions, unhampered by lengthy approval mechanisms, are likely to reach this market more quickly and render the strategy useless to the slower institution.

In choosing an appropriate time horizon, internal stakeholders, as well as competitors, should be given careful attention. Goals that are established far enough in advance to allow staff time to adjust to them are more likely to attract support. This is especially true in large institutions that cannot turn on a dime. It is not by coincidence that large universities do not undertake the development of institution-wide strategic plans. They break the planning unit down to colleges, schools, and institutes within the university to better manage the effort through compression of staff. It is important to ensure that the timing of the strategy does not under- or overshoot stakeholders' need for time to adjust to it. Poorly timed strategy is destined to failure even if fully resourced and supported by the executive team and key stakeholders.

6. Is the strategy workable? For many institutions the simplest way to evaluate strategy is to ask the pragmatic question: Does it work? Less simple, however, is the process of determining what criteria can be used to determine whether a strategy is working. For example, quantitative indices such as enrollment, revenue, stakeholder satisfaction, and external ratings are a good place to start, but they only provide a portion of the full picture. Questions about fit with the institution, the extent to which personnel identify with the strategy and the skill with which it is being executed also need to be explored. Serious thought needs to be given to indicators that can be used to determine how workable the strategy actually is. Are quantitative indicators—discrete gains in performance measured by numbers—enough? Or, is the strategy's fit with internal operations, culture, and the flow of work also important in determining whether it is workable for personnel in the institution? The logical answer is undoubtedly "some of each," but the best answer must be determined by the institution and its leaders.

IMPACT ON STAKEHOLDERS

Strategy is ultimately designed to position the institution in a favorable way with stakeholders in a chosen market. If it is effective, the institution's position will elevate. If it is ineffective, it will remain unchanged or diminish. While position is important, it is not the sole

Table 10.1
Key Stakeholder Groups in Colleges and Universities

Stakeholder	Defining Attribute
Internal	
Faculty	Commitment to teaching, learning, and scholarship
Students	Self-advancement and goal achievement
Administrators	Contribution to institutional goals and success
Support Staff	Service to the institution
Governing Board	Oversight and stewardship
External	
Alumni	Affiliation and institutional advancement
Government Agencies	Goal achievement and accountability
Coordinating Boards	Oversight and accountability
Business and Industry	Workforce preparation/research and development
Schools and Colleges	Access and achievement in further education
General Public	Enhancement of quality of life

determinant of a strategy's effectiveness. A strategy that effectively positions, or repositions, an institution with external stakeholders but neglects the well-being and vitality of staff, overlooks the institution's most valuable resource: its human capital. In most institutions the president and executive team play the primary role in the development of strategy, however, the mainstays of institutional culture are the *internal* stakeholders: faculty, staff, and students. If a strategy does not resonate with their values, beliefs, and needs, it is destined to fail, just as a strategy that does not correspond to the needs and expectations of external stakeholders will fail. These stakeholder groups are identified in Table 10.1 along with key attributes that define their relationship to a college or university.

Since a fundamental premise of strategy is that it strengthens the relationship of an institution with stakeholders in its environment, it is important to evaluate how relationships with internal and external stakeholders might be impacted. Stakeholders include parties that render or receive service from an institution, provide resources, or influence behavior and performance. They are individuals or entities that have a vested interest in the success of an institution. Those holding the most influence over the institution are generally considered first. For example, if the institution depends heavily on alumni dollars, a focused evaluation of strategy in relation to its effect on alumni giving will be a high priority. If tuition dollars are a college's primary source of revenue, the effect of strategy on recruitment and retention of students will need to be addressed through evaluation.

Internal Stakeholders

Students. Whether an institution's mission involves liberal arts, transfer, career and professional, workforce training, or graduate education, strategy must take into account the needs and expectations of students. Successful strategy will always involve a favorable impact on students—measurable improvements in convenience, satisfaction, cost benefit, and other indicators. If *cost* is the frame for strategy, the institution will need to determine the impact of different tactics for controlling cost, including increased efficiency and acquisition of alternative sources of revenue. If the thrust of strategy is to attract more and better students by holding tuition constant, the cost strategy would be evaluated as successful if higher-quality students enroll in greater number and the institution does not have to spend much to get them. If relevance is the strategy frame, the need to assess student perceptions of the salience of courses and curricula in preparing for a career or further education will need to be given careful attention.

Faculty. Instructors have a vested interest in the overall health of the institution as well as that of their department and discipline. Whether at a research university where the primary focus is on scholarship, a community college where the focus is on teaching and learning, or a proprietary institution where job training is the principal goal, faculty are at the heart of operations through their interaction with students and involvement with academic policy and decisions. Their collective position has a significant influence on the culture of the institution and the probability of success of any kind of change initiative including strategy.

Using cost as the frame for strategy, the impact on faculty is likely to be different from that determined through assessment for students. A residual effect of holding the line on tuition is almost always diminished resources available for salary enhancement, hiring and retention of support staff, and acquisition of equipment and supplies. Since this will be perceived by faculty as having a direct effect on their productivity and quality of life, an effort will need to be made to determine the relationship between the cost strategy, resources, and morale. Specifically, at what point in implementation does faculty morale begin to decline as part of a cost strategy? Are there certain forms of benefit (e.g., a regular salary-enhancement program) that ameliorate the effects of lost benefits elsewhere (e.g., resources for equipment, supplies, and travel)? This illustration reveals that strategy creation and implementation can be a differential experience for stakeholders—favorable for some, but a negative experience for others. Assessment is essential for uncovering the reality of the "strategy experience" for different groups.

Administrators and Support Staff. Outside of senior administrators, personnel in these work groups are often the forgotten soldiers of academe. They hold operations together by working directly with students and staff to solve problems, by attending to detail that is beyond administrative interest and comprehension, and by staying on task with routine operations that are taken for granted but keep the institution afloat. Evaluation of the impact of strategy for this group will need to center on factors of inclusiveness, insight and understanding, adjustment time, and commitment. Returning to the cost strategy once more, the following series of questions can be asked to assess strategy's impact and potential for success: Were you included in discussions that led to adoption of this strategy? Do you understand the cost strategy? Are you aware of the implications and effects of this strategy on operations in different parts of the institution? Do you understand your role in implementing the strategy? Do you feel you have had sufficient time to learn about and adjust to this strategy? Are you committed to the success of this strategy?

Governing Boards. Since governing boards are charged with stewardship for the overall health and viability of the institution, strategy is apt to be perceived as successful when it improves the visibility, reputation, or financial condition of the institution. A strategy frame of *collaboration* would compel a college to pursue new forms of relationship with K–12 schools, other higher education institutions, or business and industry in order to share costs, best practices, or resources. These partnerships would allow the college to maintain and strengthen program and service offerings while containing cost. Similarly, a strategy focused on reputation or prestige would be favorably received if it reflected the board's role in development of the institution. Boards are generally most interested in indicators of public perception of college performance in meeting educational needs, providing access, operating efficiently, embracing quality, and other local priorities. Therefore, the focus of assessment will need to be on relevance (or perceptions of relevance) of the strategy individually and collectively to members of the governing board.

External Stakeholders

Alumni. Alumni are valued stakeholders who, when organized, can be of great benefit, especially in periods of resource decline. Many have fond memories of their college experience—sometimes to the point of viewing this as comprising the best years of their lives—and seek to rekindle this experience through continuing ties with the institution. A strategy focused on reputation would be attractive to this stakeholder group. Assessment would focus on indicators of performance related to community perceptions of institutional and student quality, business and industry perceptions of the extent to which students are prepared for work, the rate of admission of students into graduate and professional schools, advanced degrees attained by students, career mobility and advancement of graduates, and outstanding achievement. Alumni are an increasingly important source of support for institutions. Keeping them involved through inclusion in strategy is a wise investment.

Government Agencies. Several levels of government influence colleges or universities, depending on the type of institution. Four-year institutions are influenced by federal and state government while two-year colleges must also be concerned with local governments. It is doubtful that an institution's strategy would directly affect its relationship with the federal government, but a successful strategy should improve its relationship with state and local governments. In an age of accountability, strategy should provide empirical evidence of value added to students and taxpayers in the form of earnings reports, economic outlook, quality-of-life enhancement, business attraction and retention, and various other forms of information coming from institutions, for-profit organizations, and governmental agencies.

Coordinating Boards. These entities hold significant influence over public colleges and universities in most states. Their purview typically involves financial appropriations, the coordination of services, budgetary issues, legislative needs, and the approval of degrees and curricula. Like government agencies, this stakeholder group is focused on improving the efficiency and effectiveness of college operations. A strategic frame, therefore, that would interest coordinating boards is efficiency. A college can demonstrate its efficiency through budget comparisons, articulation agreements, or measures related to streamlining programs and services. Successful strategy should demonstrate that a college has carried out initiatives to operate more efficiently, created additional resources, and provided more value.

Business and Industry. Business and industry is playing an increasingly significant role in college operations. Colleges are looked to for preparation of tomorrow's workforce. They also are relied upon for the integration of traditional and adult learners into an increasingly complex and diversified workplace. Many institutions have embarked on a strategy of collaboration—the creation of partnerships to provide services and benefits that are mutually valued—in their relationship with business and industry. Strategy indicators that would be of interest to business and industry partners would include the number and financial value of contracts with business and industry, the number of employees enrolled in college programs, courses and training activities, ratings of employee and employer satisfaction, and enhancement in productivity based on improved worker skills and performance.

Schools and Colleges. A primary interest of schools and colleges in strategy is access to, and preparation for, further education. K–12 schools will want to know the effect of strategy on access and success for their students. Has college entry been made easier through the strategy? Do students experience fewer problems in the transition between high school and college? Do they perform better in courses and curricula? Do they achieve better outcomes and experience greater satisfaction as a result of the strategy? Similarly, four-year colleges and graduate and professional schools will want to know the impact of the strategy on student preparation for advanced study. How, specifically, does the strategy contribute to their preparation for advanced study, their adjustment to changing expectations and norms, and their overall experience?

General Public. Most public institutions receive a major portion of their operating revenue from state funds. Legislators allocate these funds based, in part, upon priorities established by taxpayers and other constituents if they hope to be reelected. For public institutions, this means selection of strategies that will resonate with voters and the general public. The general public is most likely to be interested in strategy that involves reputation, value added, and service to the community. Criteria that can be used to measure strategy performance in these frames include elevation or decline in public perception of the institution, a greater presence within the community, and increased revenue through grants and bonds.

Although there are different methods and measures for assessing how strategy might strengthen and modify relationships between stakeholder groups and the institution, the overall message remains the same. Each stakeholder group has a vested interest in the institution, to which strategy must appeal and demonstrate how value is added by responding to its interest.

STRATEGY MARKERS

In chapter 1, successful strategy was defined as resulting in the *creation of value that differentiates an institution from its competitors and leads to a sustainable advantage.* The key concepts in this definition—creation of value, differentiation from competitors, and sustainable advantage—provide an organizing framework for establishing indicators or markers for evaluating the overall success or bottom line of strategy. These concepts and the markers that can be used to determine the impact of strategy are presented in this section.

Creation of Value

Stakeholders are the ultimate judge of value, an expression of an institution's capacity to deliver an equivalent or better return on investment than competitors. In its most simple form, value is achieved through unique competencies, higher quality, greater efficiency, lower cost, or some combination of these elements. Unique competencies might include a capacity for innovation, systems and technology, operational efficiency, and the like. In attempting to identify value delivered, an institution must continually ask itself if a particular competency, service, or activity makes a significant contribution to value as perceived by an individual or group. Questions that need to be asked include: What elements of value are implicit in this strategy? What value do stakeholders expect to receive? What value are they actually receiving? Why are they more (or less) interested in receiving value from one institution than others? What elements of value are most important to stakeholders and thus make the largest contribution to success of the strategy? Answers to these questions will help an institution assess the impact of strategy in creating value that makes a difference to stakeholders.

Differentiation from Competitors

To differentiate itself from competitors, an institution must be aware of its own internal capabilities as well as those of its competition. Uniqueness lies at the heart of differentiation. With competitors offering similar services in convenient locations at comparable value, the challenge is to set the institution apart by (1) identifying qualities that distinguish it from competitors, and (2) determining the extent of differentiation on a specific quality. This can be accomplished by identifying what the institution is best known for. A college committed to convenience, for example, would choose to measure itself against competitors on indicators such as ease of access to programs, courses, and services; student satisfaction with systems and services; and, in the case of community colleges, time required for travel to educational facilities. Similarly, a college committed to speed would want to measure its performance against competitors on factors such as the frequency with which assessment is carried out with stakeholders to identify needs and expectations; the length of time required to modify programs, courses, and services based on assessment information; and speed to market with new programs and services. Finally, an institution committed to a strategy of providing unparalleled value to students would determine the extent of differentiation between itself and competitors through examination of several indices related to the cost of tuition and fees, short- and long-term student outcomes, student satisfaction, and the quality appraisals and satisfaction of receiving organizations.

If the discrepancy in value measured by these indicators is significantly in favor of the institution, then the value-added strategy may fit the institution at this point in time. The caveat is that what is different today is often commonplace tomorrow; therefore, differentiation is an area that requires regular and systematic assessment.

Sustainable Advantage

The creation of advantage is perhaps the most important outcome of strategy. For most institutions, management's agenda is dominated by tactics to achieve growth through marketing, resource procurement, and enhancement of visibility. Such tactics are a prerequisite for survival, but they limit an institution's horizon to short-term gains achieved through routine tactics in contrast to long-term advantage created through strategy. The behavior of institutions in financial crisis provides some insight into sustainable advantage. Some institutions cut class sections, programs, and staff without regard to future opportunities. An institution using strategy is more likely to view crisis as an opportunity for long-term development. Mission and vision might be reexamined, strategic choices may be made regarding programs to expand or retire, and the organizational architecture might be altered to better position the institution for the future.

A view of advantage as sustained, rather than temporary, and as strategic, rather than tactical, means that *stretch* is important as a means of differentiating institutions. Defined as the difference between an institution's ambition and its resources, stretch involves vigilance over the behavior and intentions of competitors.[8] A college that has an abundance of ambition and a dearth of resources will quickly discover that it cannot achieve a lasting advantage by mimicking the behavior of more affluent competitors. It cannot match their spending, tolerate their inefficiency and slack, or risk playing by their rules. Sustainable advantage is achieved by figuring out ways to exceed the existing advantages of competitors.

This can be accomplished by creating entirely new forms of value, stretching the institution beyond its capacity, or creating experience for stakeholders that is impossible to replicate. A number of measures can be used to determine the success of strategy in achieving a sustainable advantage. All of them involve the determination of the discrepancy in value delivered by an institution in relationship to competitors and the ease or difficulty with which competitors can duplicate an existing advantage.

CLOSING THOUGHTS

Colleagues and clients often ask, "There is so much to learn about strategy, where and how do I get started?" This question typically comes up when the realization hits that the declarations used over time to guide institutional direction are tactics, not strategy. Our answer is simple: "Get into motion with activities that encourage you to use big picture thinking." Sit down with a newspaper or magazine and cut out the articles that seem to have a bearing on the future. Read them carefully and try to identify themes that have implications for your institution, your department or administrative unit, or your job. Free yourself from the constraints of time, place, and the past, and let your imagination run loose. Record these implications on paper or electronically as statements and interpret their meaning. What changes would or could they portend for your institution, department, or position? What steps would be necessary to encourage a positive development or to ward off a potential threat? Look at what you have written and ask yourself one more question: Will I read a newspaper or magazine in the future in the same way as I have in the past? If your answer is no, you are using strategic thinking and you have entered the world of strategy.

We started this book by raising a series of questions. We asked you to rate your institution on a series of dimensions including awareness, distinctiveness, focus, and urgency. If these questions piqued your interest, we asked you to read further and enter the world of strategy. Now that you have read the book we want to pose another set of questions concerning your readiness to engage in strategy. Little or nothing will have changed in the time that it took to read this book, but your answers to these questions may give you a sense of where to start and how to tap the unrealized potential of strategy in your institution, your division, or your department.

Six Questions About Strategic Capability

- Are faculty and staff familiar and conversant with trends, forces, and opportunities in the external environment—*do they see the big picture?*
- How much do they know about competitors and what they are doing or apt to do—*are they focused on competitors?*
- Are they interested in innovative practices in institutions and organizations outside of this college—*do they have a curiosity about other organizations?*
- Are they familiar with the concept of "value"—*do they look at their work in terms of the benefit it creates for stakeholders?*
- Are they interested in being different, distinct from, or better than other institutions—*are they conscious of, and committed to, advantage?*
- *Do they possess a sense of urgency about the future?*

These questions capture our point of view about the readiness of institutions, leaders, and staff for strategy. Our point of view is one that emphasizes a big-picture approach to management, a keen awareness of stakeholders and competitors, an appreciation of the importance of value, a commitment to differentiation, a continuing quest for advantage, and a sense of urgency about the future. Implicit in all of this is a deep and abiding desire to make a difference in the lives of students and stakeholders.

The journey to strategy is not easy or short, and it requires commitment and perseverance across institutional boundaries and roles. Leaders who can sustain the effort and put strategy at the center of the enterprise will develop a new understanding of how institutions work and what they can become for those that they serve.

NOTES

1. Seymour Tilles' "How to Evaluate Corporate Strategy," *Harvard Business Review,* July/August 1963, 111–121, provides a sage and carefully considered overview of principles and techniques for evaluation of strategy. Tilles' ideas about evaluation are as important today as they were in 1963 because of their fundamental nature and capacity for use in any type of organization. For this reason, the ideas related to "fit" between strategy and organizational context in this chapter are adapted exclusively from the work of Tilles.

2. Ibid., 114.

3. Ibid., 115.

    4. Ibid., 115–116.
    5. Ibid., 118–119.
    6. Ibid., 120.
    7. Ibid.
    8. Gary Hamel and C. K. Prahalad, *Competing for the Future* (Boston: Harvard Business School Press, 1994), 151.

INDEX

ABOUT THE AUTHOR
AND ASSOCIATES

RICHARD L. ALFRED is professor of higher education at the University of Michigan and resides in Milan, Michigan. During a 38-year career in higher education, he has held mid-level and executive administrative positions in community colleges in Cleveland, Kansas City, and New York City; created and served as a principal in the Center for Community College Development; and has been a consultant to more than 500 colleges and universities in the United States and Canada. Alfred is the author of more than 100 articles, books, and monographs on issues related to management and leadership, organizational strategy, and institutional stature and effectiveness. A recipient of numerous honors and awards, he earned master's and doctoral degrees in higher education and sociology from Pennsylvania State University and a baccalaureate from Allegheny College.

ERIC CHAMBERS is a candidate for the doctoral degree in Organizational Behavior and Management in the Center for the Study of Higher and Postsecondary Education at the University of Michigan. Concurrently he holds administrative responsibility for planning and budgeting at Concordia University in Ann Arbor. Eric began his collegiate career as a dual-enrollment student attending Johnson County Community College while attending high school in Kansas City. He received a bachelor's degree from Grove City College and a master's degree in Higher and Postsecondary Education from the University of Michigan. His scholarship and budding career focus on organizational strategy and leadership in liberal arts colleges. Eric developed material related to liberal arts colleges in the book.

DANIELLE KNABJIAN-MOLINA has held administrative positions in student development at Vassar College and Heidelberg College. She received a bachelor's degree from Northwestern University, a master's degree from Bowling Green State University (Counseling and Student Personnel), and is currently enrolled in the doctoral program in Organizational Behavior and Management in the Center for the Study of Higher and Postsecondary Education at the University of Michigan. Dani's scholarly and professional interests center on the impact of technology on organizational behavior and architecture in colleges and universities. She was involved in developing the sections of the book devoted to liberal arts colleges and framing and articulating strategy.

MARY RAMIREZ took on the yeomanly task of editing and proofing the entire book. A baccalaureate graduate of Michigan State, with masters' degrees from Central Michigan University (Business Management) and Michigan State (Multidisciplinary Social Science), Mary is currently enrolled in the doctoral program in Organizational Behavior and Management in the Center for the Study of Higher and Postsecondary Education at the University of Michigan. She has held administrative positions in Student Affairs/Residential Life at the University of Michigan and Indiana University. Her current work focuses on generational differences among employee groups in colleges and universities. In addition to her role as proofreader, Mary developed material related to regional teaching universities in the book.

CHRISTOPHER SHULTS holds a master's degree from the University of Michigan, a bachelor's degree from Morgan State University, and is enrolled in the doctoral program in Organizational Behavior and Management in the Center for the Study of Higher and Postsecondary Education at the University of Michigan. Before coming to Michigan, he served as research associate at the American Association of Community Colleges. He has authored numerous articles and research briefs and is becoming increasingly visible on the national scene through his work on institutional strategy, effectiveness, and leadership. Chris was the point person among the associates who worked closely with me in the preparation of all phases of the book. He was directly involved in developing material related to community colleges, for-profit institutions, and strategy evaluation.

TARA SULLIVAN is director of campus life at the Chicago Institute of Art and a candidate for the doctoral degree in Academic Affairs and Student Development in the Center for the Study of Higher and Postsecondary Education at the University of Michigan. She has extensive experience in change design and management through administrative posts at Northwestern University, the University of Michigan, DePaul University, and Keane Consulting Group. Tara holds a bachelor's degree from Indiana University (Business and Finance) and a master's degree from the University of Michigan (Higher and Postsecondary Education). She was involved in developing the sections of the book devoted to research universities and implementation of change.